THE JEWISH WOMAN

THE JEWISH WOMAN

New Perspectives

Edited by
ELIZABETH KOLTUN

SCHOCKEN BOOKS · NEW YORK

First Published by SCHOCKEN BOOKS 1976
Third Printing, 1978

Copyright © 1976 by Schocken Books Inc.

Library of Congress Cataloging in Publication Data

Main entry under title:
The Jewish woman.

   Bibliography: p. 283
   1.   Women, Jewish—Addresses, essays, lectures.
   2.   Women in Judaism—Addresses, essays, lectures.
   I.   Koltun, Elizabeth.
HQ1172.J48   301.41'2   75–35445

Manufactured in the United States of America

ACKNOWLEDGMENTS

We are indebted to the following authors and publishers for permission to reprint:

"The Jewish Feminist: Conflict in Identities." by Judith Plaskow. Reprinted from *Response* Magazine, no. 18, Summer 1973 with the permission of the author.

"On the Birth of a Daughter," By Daniel I. Leifer and Myra Leifer. Reprinted from *Response*, no. 18, Summer 1973, with the permission of the authors.

"*Tumah* and *Taharah*: Ends and Beginnings," by Rachel Adler. Reprinted and slightly abridged from *The Jewish Catalog; A Do-it-Yourself Kit*, Edited and compiled by Richard Siegel, Michael Strassfeld and Sharon Strassfeld. © 1973 by the Jewish Publication Society of America.

Quotation from "East Coker," lines 1, 101–2 and from "Little Gidding," lines 214–15: 225–31. Both selections by T.S. Eliot. Reprinted from *Four Quartets*. © 1943 Harcourt Brace Jovanovich, Inc.

Quotation from "And Death Shall Have No Dominion," by Dylan Thomas. Reprinted from *The Poems of Dylan Thomas*. © 1943 by New Directions Publishing Corporation. Reprinted by permission of New Directions Publishing Corporation.

"Portnoy's Mother's Complaint: Depression in Middle-Aged Women," by Pauline Bart. Reprinted from *Transaction*, VIII (1–2), Nov-Dec. 1970 by permission of Transaction, Inc. © 1970 by Transaction, Inc.

"Jewish Women's Haggadah," by Aviva Cantor Zuckoff. Reprinted and abridged from *Sistercelebrations*, edited by Arlene Swidler. ©1974 by Fortress Press.

CONTENTS

THE JEWISH WOMAN

PREFACE
Elizabeth Koltun

The idea for an anthology of writings from the new Jewish women's
movement was conceived by William Novak, then editor of *Response*
magazine, who approached several women who had been instrumental in organizing the first National Conference of Jewish Women in
1973 to compile and edit a special issue of *Response,* dedicated to the
concerns of Jewish feminists. An editorial board representing Jewish
women of differing cultural, religious, and political views, was assem-
bled. As editor of that issue, I found the task exciting and fulfilling,
thanks to the cooperation and creativity of the board and the contributors, and the guidance and sensitivity of William Novak. In addition, the generosity of the Max and Anna Leventhal Foundation during
a financial crisis of *Response,* ensured its publication.

The issue contributed both financially and educationally to the
growing women's movement, reaching individual women and diverse
groups all over the United States and Israel. It helped raise the question
of women's role in Jewish life to a place of high priority and interest for
the Jewish community.

When, two years later, I was given the opportunity to expand and
update the issue for publication as a book, I discovered how much the
movement had grown in the interim. Today there are many women
and men thinking of new solutions to old problems, investigating
Jewish women's history, Jewish law in relation to women, new rituals,
new roles for women in the community, and new approaches to Jewish
texts and education. Clearly, it is impossible to include in one book all
the examples of new thinking and writing that are currently available. I

hope that this volume will be a significant contribution to a new, growing literature on Jewish women which which will continue to be published in coming years, and that the selections presented here will generate more ideas, study, experimentation, research and, most important, participation by women in all areas of Jewish life, especially in the movement for their own fulfillment and equality.

This book would not have been possible without the dedication and support of Steven M. Cohen (the current editor of *Response*), the editorial board of the *Response* anthology, particularly Arlene Agus, Paula Hyman, Vivian Silver Salowitz, and Aviva Cantor Zuckoff, and the encouragement of my women's group, Ezrat Nashim.

In recognition of the community from which this volume emerged, the royalties will go, in part, to *Response,* which continues its efforts to publish the views of young Jewish writers and, in part, to a special fund to be distributed by the contributors to this book to projects supportive of Jewish women's concerns.

INTRODUCTION
Martha Ackelsberg

When the *Response* issue on *The Jewish Woman* was first published in 1973, the Jewish women's movement was young and unorganized. Now, three years later, the movement is larger, broader, and more structured. Nevertheless, it is engaged in continuing debate about its direction and questioning of its relevance.

Much has happened during these three years. From its beginnings in such groups as Ezrat Nashim and Kol Ishah, the Jewish women's movement has grown remarkably. The First National Conference on Jewish Women, sponsored by the North American Jewish Students' Network in February 1973, was followed by the 1974 National Conference on Jewish Women and Men. Each attracted over three hundred participants. Out of that second assembly, the national Jewish Feminist Organization was born. The roster of Jewish organizations now includes one which proclaims:

> We are committed to the development of our full human potential and to the survival and enhancement of Jewish life. We seek nothing else than the full, direct and equal participation of women at all levels of Jewish life—communal, religious, educational and political. We shall be a force for such creative change in the Jewish community. ("Statement of Purpose," Jewish Feminist Organization, April 28, 1974)

The impact of the movement has been varied and widespread. Courses on Jewish women are being offered in increasing numbers in educational institutions at every level. New educational materials which treat women as active participants in Jewish life—past and present—are being discussed and prepared. Groups of Jewish women are organizing on local and regional bases, sponsoring conferences and workshops, and pressuring for change in all areas of Jewish life. In the area of liturgy and ritual, the Committee on Law and Standards of the (Conservative movement's) Rabbinical Assembly has ruled that women may be counted in a *minyan* (the quorum of ten required for communal prayer); and in increasing numbers of Conservative congregations throughout the country, the near-equal participation of women in ritual is becoming a reality. Reform and Reconstructionist rabbinical schools have ordained their first women rabbis. Within the Orthodox community as well, pressures are being felt: interpreters of *halakhah* (Jewish law) are more and more addressing themselves to issues of particular concern to women. Although many important issues remain unresolved, the Jewish women's movement seems to have arrived.

Yet, at the same time, a recent symposium on "The Congregational Rabbi and Conservative Judaism," (*Conservative Judaism*, Winter 1975), indicated that many rabbis found "no widespread support" for increasing women's roles within the synagogue—particularly on the level of ritual. Responses to an open-ended question on this point were varied, but a substantial proportion replied that women do not seem to show an "overwhelming desire to participate," or that they detected "no groundswell of support" on these issues.[1] It is true, of course, that this evaluation is, itself, subjective; that many rabbis did find considerable interest in these issues; and that support might be more common, in fact, than might appear. Nonetheless, while there have been some substantial gains on the level of organization, and even, perhaps, of rights formally won, the Jewish women's movement faces an uncertain future. What, in fact are its goals? How can they best be achieved? Has the movement already accomplished as much as it can?

The contributors to this volume all speak out of, or to, these questions. While some focus on progress already made, most attempt reexaminations of Jewish history, culture, law, ritual, and communal organization in an attempt to understand more clearly both how the community has been structured in the past, and what changes might be possible for the future. All question traditional sex-role differentiation within Judaism while maintaining strong commitment to Jewish tradition and survival. The tension between these two perspectives provides the framework for this anthology.[2]

Within Judaism, social, political, and religious roles have been distributed according to sex, with the most prestigious roles and duties falling to men—as is characteristic of all patriarchal cultures. Such a differentiation may have had its origins in biological differences between men and women—women gave birth to children and, in the years before birth control became readily available, were often confined to the home and its immediate environs for much of their lives. While they could be—and were, even in early times—important contributors to the *family* economy, their biology, and responsibilities for the family, were used to justify their virtual exclusion from communal responsibilities beyond the family. Indeed, the very "commonplace" quality of women's daily lives, as defined by their domestic setting, very likely contributed to their exclusion from the sacred and more elevated spheres of social-communal life.[3] Judaism, moreover, has formalized that exclusion with an overlay of legal, ritual, and communal restrictions which, while reflecting such a social response to biology, now, ever more clearly, serve simply to limit unnecessarily the range of activites open to women (and to men.)

As Rabbi Saul Berman has noted ("The Status of Women in Halakhic Judaism" pp 114-128), Jewish law created an "independent juristic status" for women, which shaped *every* relationship in which women engage. *Halakhah* did not specifically legislate that a woman must define herself primarily (or even solely) as wife and mother; it merely favored that role and "adjusted" her responsibilities to protect it. The point is clear. The family is—and always has been—a crucial institution in Judaism. Woman was identified with, and given primary responsibility for the family. Thus, maintenance of sex-role differentiation has been linked (through the family) to the survival of the Jewish people and tradition.

But, as the women's movement, both secular and Jewish, has long argued, that differentiation both stunts the lives of women and is unnecessary—even harmful—to the continued existence of a vital Jewish life. Even in earlier times, there was no necessary reason why a woman's biology had to determine and limit her life choices as much as it did. But even more is this the case today. The growth of knowledge, particularly of technology, has freed both women and men from the limitations previously imposed by their biology, rendering the social overlay even more inappropriate. Women are not tied to the home from the age of thirteen to death, and few people need depend merely on their physical strength in order to support themselves. Even if one recognizes and accepts the centrality of the family—or, to be more accurate, the importance of raising and educating children to full Jewish adulthood—within Jewish tradition, there is no reason why such responsibility need or ought be the exclusive preserve of women. The "Jewish home" need not be synonymous with the continuation of the traditional woman's role; to allow women to move out of the home need not mean its disappearance. Such a move simply demands greater creativity on our part, with the goal of achieving the same ends by different means.

If, then, women and men together share responsibility for the home, they can also share equally in religious, educational, cultural, and communal responsibility. This sharing of responsibility necessitates, at the very least, restructuring both religious and communal roles, and questioning the nature and goals of participation in both sorts of activities. In particular, since the structures themselves (both ritual and communal) reflect differentiation of roles on the basis of sex, it may not be sufficient simply to demand "equal access" (i.e., counting women in minyanim, ordaining women rabbis, etc.). Our analysis suggests, in fact, that the existing roles may well incorporate into their structure attitudes and values which are unacceptable. If such is the case (whether in liturgy, ritual practice, underlying theology, or communal decision-making structures), then the goals of the Jewish women's movement must shift away from simple equal access to existing roles; rather, we may need to challenge the foundations and definitions of the roles themselves.

The liberation of women from the confining roles of wife and mother, then, could free their energy for both personal growth and deeper and more fulfilling involvement in a revitalized Jewish community. As Paula Hyman writes:

> In an age when the alienation of young Jews from Judaism is a major concern for the Jewish community, we can hardly afford to ignore fully one-half of young Jews. Thus, the challenge of feminism, if answered, can only strengthen Judaism. ("The Other Half: Women in the Jewish Tradition"—pp 105–113.)

All this seems clear: secular feminists have been making similar arguments for generations. Nevertheless, some recent surveys have claimed to demonstrate a lack of widespread concern on the part of Jewish women for full and equal participation. How are we to assess such an assertion?

We might note, at the outset, that we are dealing here with the relationship between those in positions of power and prestige and those excluded from such positions. As suggested above, there is a tendency in such situations for those in established power positions to ignore or underestimate the extent of discontent on the part of the excluded group. Such a perception might explain part of the alleged lack of concern on the part of women.

Beyond that, however, there are barriers to equal participation which affect more directly the members of an excluded group. Jewish women, for example, confront all the ambivalences and complexities which present themselves to any potential participant in a movement for social change. The primary question any person in such a situation tends to ask is, Why bother? What difference will my participation make, either to me or to the community? And, within the Jewish community, such questions must be asked (and answered) on at least two levels: that of religious/ritual participation, and that of more general participation in the institutions and structures of the community as a whole. In the area of ritual, for example, one must ask, What might more equal participation mean? Would equal participation of women in religious ritual mean spiritual fulfillment? Are the rituals themselves so infused with masculine values that women would feel uncomfortable participating? Do we need to develop rituals to express women's dialog with God? Do we need rituals which would introduce and reinforce new ways of looking at relationships between women and men, and—since the male-female relationship is often used as a model for God-human relationships—new ways of understanding or conceptualizing the relationship between the human and the Divine? In the area of participation in communal institutions, will more widespread participation simply result in ratification of the same types of decisions, but with more votes on each side? Or can the institutions and processes be restructured sufficiently so that the process of participation, in itself, becomes personally valuable and rewarding?

Finally—perhaps most important—there are known gratifications and rewards built into the existing roles. (The "woman of valor," although her role is limited, nevertheless receives considerable praise and admiration.) Any Jewish woman, in making her decision about whether to participate in—or lend her support to—a movement for social change, must weigh the risk of loss of such rewards against the uncertain benefits to be gained by large-scale restructuring of institutions and roles.

In any case, it is important to note that individual choices of this sort are made in the context of social and communal structures and institutions. And it is these same structures and institutions which tend to shape modes of thought and feeling to make it difficult for individuals to strike out in new directions. If such barriers to initial commitment and participation can be overcome, then those committed to change must strive for access to institutions not only to change the sex characteristics of the incumbents of power, but to question the very structures and modes of decision making and of ritual participation.

It is an unfortunate fact that, in most advanced societies, many—if not most—individuals do not take an active part in determining the conditions of their lives. Many have been excluded from such participation on grounds of class, sex, race, age, or education. But it is important to understand that many others have been excluded by the setting of the agenda itself: if what is being discussed is (or seems to be) of no interest or concern to my life, why should I bother trying to have a voice in the decision? And if those things which *are* important to me are not included on the agenda, my participation becomes even more problematic. Any community which calls itself democratic has a responsibility to confront these issues, and to try to structure itself in such a way that the primary concerns of *all* individuals reach that agenda. The Jewish community—because of its history of exclusion from power and control over the centuries—ought to be even more sensitive to such issues. And that is one important element of what Jewish feminism is ultimately about.

Furthermore, such questioning of both the form and the content of participation applies to participation in the religious-ritual as well as in the communal-political sphere. Thus, if important aspects of my life experience find no expression in religious ritual, I am unlikely to find ritual participation of crucial concern. And, since public rituals have been designed essentially for *male* Jews, it would not be surprising if women—whose needs, experiences, and concerns have often been ignored (at least on the level of public ritual)—expressed little desire to take part in such practices. Once again, the community as a whole has a responsibility to recognize such needs, and to encourage—and incorporate—rituals and practices which reflect the concerns and experiences of "the other half" of the Jewish community.

One might argue, then, that the alleged lack of widespread concern for full and equal participation on the part of women can be attributed to the nature and structures of the Jewish community. It is certainly true that concern for fuller participation—especially in ritual and education—has come primarily from younger women. But these women are the ones who have benefited from the wider and more equalized education recently afforded to Jewish women, and who are feeling much more strongly than older women the denial of opportunity to act on the knowledge they have gained. We might predict, then, that with the spread of full Jewish education to women—especially with curricula which do not eliminate women entirely from the history and culture of the Jewish people—such discontent will increase. Too, women who have begun to participate actively in communal organizations are already sensitive to the limitations of those structures, and are advocating not only fuller roles for women, but the restructuring of their organizations as well (c.f. Jacqueline K. Levine, "The Changing Role of Women in the Jewish Community," in *Response*, 18 [Summer 1973], pp. 59–65). As increasing numbers of women begin to participate equally in ritual and liturgy, they, too, are likely to find these areas lacking: Jewish prayer was, after all, written by and for men.

This is not to suggest that the Jewish women's movement advocates the total abolition of existing religious, educational, and communal structures. It most certainly does not. Rather, as the contributions to this volume demonstrate clearly, growing numbers of women (and men), committed to the maintenance of Jewish tradition, have come to believe that its continued vitality depends, as it has in the past, on openness to change and willingness to see, and incorporate as legitimate, alternatives to rigid patterns and roles. We have tried to present here, then, examples of the kinds of reevaluation and creativity which need to be encouraged. The reader will find attempts at Midrash (reinterpretations of Biblical stories), examinations of women's roles as seen by rabbinic tradition, investigation of the history of women, suggestions for new liturgy, and, perhaps most exciting, a new look at the life cycle of women, in an attempt to discover new roles for women and men, and to develop rituals to sanctify both the old and the new.

We hope that this collection of writings will help to encourage the development of more rituals, myths, *halakhot*, historical research, text study, new educational materials and a general reexamination of communal structures and practices—in the interests not only of Jewish women, but of the vitality of Judaism itself.

Notes

1. See also similar findings reported in Zelda Dick, "Light from Our Poll on Women's Role," *Women's League Outlook,* Vol. 45, No. 4 (Summer 1975): 15.

2. On this tension, see especially Judith Plaskow, "The Jewish Feminist: Conflict in Identities," pp. 3-10.

3. This argument was derived from the more general perspective offered by Michelle Zimbalist Rosaldo. "Women, Culture, and Society: A Theoretical Overview," in M.Z. Rosaldo and Louise Lamphere, eds., *Women, Culture and Society* (Palo Alto: Stanford University Press, 1974), pp. 17–42.

The parallels with traditional Jewish culture are obvious: the male was identified with *ruhniut,* or spirituality; to the female was left the realm of *gashmiut,* or practicality.

SPIRITUAL QUEST

Since the beginning of the Jewish women's movement, we have tried to confront the question of women's spiritual nature. Are women spiritually different from men? Do women have unique feelings, experiences, and thoughts which are not expressed in our liturgy, rituals, and literature? How would prayers, ceremonies, religious language, and theology be different if created by women? How would women express their relationship to a God who is not described in male imagery? We present here (to borrow a term from one of our contributors), a modest beginning.

THE JEWISH FEMINIST: CONFLICT IN IDENTITIES

Judith Plaskow

This is the text of an address to the National Jewish Women's Conference in New York, February 1973.

What I would like to discuss is our identity as Jewish women. It seems to me that the identity of the Jewish woman—or rather of some of the Jewish women I know including, first of all, myself—lies somewhere in the conflict between being a woman and being a Jew and in the necessity of combining the two in as yet unknown ways. So I want to speak about this conflict in three of its aspects.

I can best begin to explain what I mean by a conflict between being a woman and being a Jew by saying that it is not a coincidence that we are discussing the questions we are now discussing. We are not doing so due to some unfolding of the Jewish tradition, due to the fact that this is a Jewishly appropriate moment. We are here because a secular movement for the liberation of women has made it imperative that we raise certain Jewish issues now, because we will not let ourselves be defined as Jewish women in ways in which we cannot allow ourselves to be defined as women. This creates a conflict not just and not primarily because the women's movement is a secular movement whose principles we are attempting to apply to an ancient religious tradition, but because the women's movement is a different community around which we might center our lives. The conflict between communities is the first level on which I experience the conflict between being a woman and being a Jew.

Now of course we can belong to many different communities, and in fact we do. We identify as Jews, as women, as Americans, as students, as human beings. But it seems to me that though we can belong to many communities, only one can be our organizing center.

3

Only one community can be the "Rosetta Stone"[1] through which we view and interpret and give room to others.

Since we are raising questions about the Jewish community because of it, it is clear that the women's movement makes some claim on us to be that organizing center. But it makes that claim not only because it forces us to raise new questions. For some of us—certainly for me —being involved in the women's movement has been one of the most important and exciting experiences of our lives. It has indeed changed the eyes through which we see the world. And through it we have experienced sisterhood—a community far more vital than anything most of us have experienced through the traditional institutions of the Jewish "community."

Despite this, our relationship with our Jewishness would not need to be one of conflict were it not for a second problem—that the Jewish community will not let us, as feminists, feel at home in it. Every time I let myself be lulled into thinking that I as a whole person am a member of this community, some event lets me know in no uncertain terms that I am wrong.

This sense of exclusion arises partly from the fact that everything in our written tradition comes from the hands of men. The *halakhah*, most obviously, is the product of many generations of men. The same is true of the *aggadah*. The bible was written by men. The myths from which the Bible borrowed and which it used and transformed were written by men. The liturgy was written by men. Jewish philosophy is the work of men. Modern Jewish theology is the work of men. It was men who wrote even the special books for women, and it was men who designated women's three *mitzvot* and wrote the blessings.

Now my point is not that therefore all these things are irrelevant to us. That is simply not true, of course. The Bible is very much our Bible. There are male-written Jewish stories that we love. There are prayers that express our feelings as well as the feelings of the men who wrote them.

My point is rather that all these things have a *question mark* over them. As Mary Daly has said, women have had our power of *naming* stolen from us. From the day that God brought the animals to Adam in the garden of Eden to see what *he* would call them, it has been through the words of men that we have known and addressed the world.[2] Although we do not know in advance that their words are not our words, neither do we know that they are. At a time when we are newly discovering and naming ourselves, we need to name anew the world around us.

If there are certain things which we will just call by their old names again, there are other words we will most definitely need to speak for the first time, for there are many times when the male power of naming has oppressed and excluded us. I needn't discuss this fact in relation to *halakhah* since it has been and will be a central topic of discussion here. I do want to say though that the exclusion of women intrudes itself into other, very different areas of Jewish life. I was recently reading Franz Rosenzweig's beautiful essay "The Builders," in which he talks about how the assimilated Jew can return to and reappropriate the tradition. One point he makes is that the demarcation line between what is forbidden by Jewish law and what is outside the realm of law and therefore permitted must be broken down in order both that the law take on a positive character and that the realm of what is permitted become a Jewish realm. There I was, reading this essay, moved by it, trying to understand it as it was addressed to me, when all of a sudden, I came to an example of what he means by endowing the law with positive meaning. "In this united sphere of the doable lies, for instance," he says, "the legal exclusion of the woman from the religious congregation; but also in it lies with equal force her ruling rank in the home. . . ." Thus what was one moment my essay the next moment was not. What I wanted to use as a gate back into the whole tradition became a door shut against me.

Let me give an example of another very different way in which our tradition excludes women. There is the fact that we address God as *he*. And it is not just that we use the masculine pronoun in the absence of a neuter one, we image *him* in male terms. Thus he is King, Lord, Shepherd, Father, etc. Now there are times when this imagery would seem to work in our favor, to make it easier for us to relate to God. In the central part of *The Star of Redemption,* Rosenzweig has a long discussion of revelation in which the relation of the beloved and lover in "Song of Songs" becomes the model for the relation between God and humankind. In this case, it is the woman who symbolizes humanity while God is the lover. This is a conception of the human/God relation which is by no means limited to Rosenzweig. And this image, while a limited one, since we relate to God in many ways, is fine. But aside from the fact that the exclusive use of male imagery is inaccurate—we know that God is not male—we are just beginning to explore the effects that this use has on the self-image and understanding of men and women. I recently read an article which quoted several church commission reports on the admission of women to the ministry.[3] Many of the arguments they came up with against the ordination of women were just incredible. One not atypical clergyman argued that the minister, whether he likes it or not, is a God figure, and that since in the Bible God is imaged in exclusively male terms, it is inappropriate for women to take this role. Just think what a statement like that says about its author's attitude toward women—and toward men! The Jewish community has not yet needed to resort to arguments like this to exclude women from the rabbinate,[4] but there is no reason to suppose that the psychological dynamic they evidence is foreign to Jews, or that we do not draw equally horrendous—if unexpressed—conclusions after calling God "he" all our lives.

The problems we as women face in relation to our tradition are deep and complex, involving almost every aspect of tradition. Where then are we going to find the new words, our words, which need to be spoken? How can we find the words which are our words and yet are Jewish words? Can we—how can we—assure ourselves in advance that if we are true to our own experiences we can remain in continuity with tradition?

This brings me to the third aspect of the conflict I want to discuss. It is this. The difficulties in my speaking both from my own experiences and from tradition are aggravated by the fact that I have no way to Jewishly express my experiences in the women's movement. Let me explain what I mean by this.

This past summer, I participated in a week-long conference of about sixty women who had gathered to discuss what women as women have to contribute to theology.[5] Each morning, we broke into small groups to deal with different aspects of the question. One of the things the group I joined tried to examine was the issue of in what way our experiences in the women's movement could be considered religious experiences. Not until I got home did I realize that the "religious" language we were using to describe our experiences was in fact Christian language. The words that kept cropping up again and again in our conversation were "conversion," "self-transformation," "grace." We were using Protestant language, a vocabulary of personal change, to express the fact that within the community of women something very important happens to each of us individually.

There are two things to be said about this. One is that, looking back on our meetings, I don't think we used these words just because they are only common vocabulary and familiar to us. I think we used them because they are accurate. In any event, they accurately described my experiences. And the other thing is that there are no—or, I should say, I do not know any—Jewish words that express the same things. This may well be a reflection of my own ignorance. It could be that there are aspects of the Jewish tradition—mysticism, for example—that would be sources of a language of personal experience. But so far as I know, whereas the Protestant woman might claim that she is in contact with the true working of the Holy Spirit and understands grace in its full reality for the first time, I cannot, as a Jew, say any of these things. As a Jew, I must remain silent.

So again we come back to the problem of finding new words. Where will they come from? How can we speak who we are?

I don't have a solution to this problem. The questions are really much clearer to me than the answers, but I would like to conclude by saying something about the direction in which I think we need to look for answers.

I know that when I pose the question to myself, "How can I find new words to express my experiences as a woman?" I have a tendency to mythologize the expression "women's experience." What I mean by this is that I unconsciously assume that there is something called "women's experience" which is separate from the lives and histories of real women and which we can discover only now that we have begun to question our traditional roles. In a way, this makes the lives of women who lived before us irrelevant. Only now are we going to find out who we really are, who we really have been. When I think about this objectively, however, I realize that this mythologizing process is also a falsifying one. There is no such thing as "women's experience" apart from what have been the experiences of real women, and that means experiences always in relation to what men have said being a woman means. This is the first factor in where our answers might be found.

The second is that in belonging to many different communities that shape and feed our lives, and despite the conflicts between them and the division of our loyalties, there are points in time in which our histories as Jews and our histories as women intersect—in Sarah's laughter at the idea of bearing a child in her old age, for example, in Miriam's song at the Red Sea, in Hannah's prayer at the dedication of Samuel, in Deborah's battle hymn, in Beruriah's learning. I think that if we want to speak words as women that will also be Jewish words, we need to try to recover and reappropriate the histories of Jewish women who managed to be persons within the boundaries alloted to them. If "women's experience" and the experience of women are the same thing, we have to begin looking for "women's experience" in their experiences. Can we know how they viewed their experiences? What in them do we want to appropriate? Are there things in their experiences that implicitly or explicitly judge the boundaries assigned to those experiences? What in them do we want to reject or to modify and why? It is not that through them we can say everything we want to say. But without them we might not even be able to begin.

With apologies to those of you who have heard it already, I would like to read the result of one attempt to reappropriate, with modifications, two of the women in our tradition.[6]

Applesource

In the beginning, the Lord God formed Adam and Lilith from the dust of the ground and breathed into their nostrils the breath of life. Created from the same source, they were equal in all ways. Adam, being a man, didn't like this situation, and he looked for ways to change it. He said, "I'll have my figs now, Lilith," ordering her to wait on him, and he tried to leave to her the daily tasks of life in the garden. But Lilith wasn't one to take any nonsense; she picked herself up, uttered God's holy name, and flew away. "Well now, Lord," complained Adam, "that uppity woman you sent me has gone and deserted me." The Lord, inclined to be sympathetic, sent his messengers after Lilith, telling her to shape up and return to Adam or face dire punishment. She, however, preferring anything to living with Adam, decided to stay right where she was. And so God, after more careful consideration this time, caused a deep sleep to fall upon Adam and out of one of his ribs created for him a second companion, Eve.

For a time, Eve and Adam had quite a good thing going. Adam was happy now, and Eve, though she occasionally sensed capacities within herself which remained undeveloped, was basically satisfied with the role of Adam's wife and helper. The only thing that really disturbed her was the excluding closeness of the relationship between Adam and God. Adam and God just seemed to have more in common, both being men, and Adam came to identify with God more and more. After a while, that made God a bit uncomfortable too, and he started going over in his mind whether he may not have made a mistake letting Adam talk him into banishing Lilith and creating Eve, seeing the power that gave Adam.

Meanwhile Lilith, all alone, attempted from time to time to rejoin the human community in the garden. After her first fruitless attempt to breach its walls, Adam worked hard to build them stronger, even getting Eve to help him. He told her fearsome stories of the demon Lilith who threatens women in childbirth and steals children from their cradles in the middle of the night. The second time Lilith came, she stormed the garden's main gate, and a great battle between her and Adam ensued in which she was finally defeated. This time, however, before Lilith got away, Eve got a glimpse of her and saw she was a woman like herself.

After this encounter, seeds of curiosity and doubt began to grow in Eve's mind. Was Lilith indeed just another woman? Adam had said she was a demon. Another woman! The very idea attracted Eve. She had never seen another creature like herself before. And how beautiful and strong Lilith had looked! How bravely she had fought! Slowly, slowly, Eve began to think about the limits of her own life within the garden.

One day, after many months of strange and disturbing thoughts, Eve, wandering around the edge of the garden, noticed a young apple tree she and Adam had planted and saw that one of its branches stretched over the garden wall. Spontaneously, she tried to climb it, and, struggling to the top, swung herself over the wall.

She did not wander long on the other side before she met the one she had come to find, for Lilith was waiting. At first sight of her, Eve remembered the tales of Adam and was frightened—but Lilith understood and greeted her kindly. "Who are you?" they asked each other. "What is your story?" And they sat and spoke together, of the past and then of the future. They talked for many hours, not once, but many times. They taught each other many things, and told each other stories, and laughed together, and cried, over and over, till the bond of sisterhood grew between them.

Meanwhile, back in the garden, Adam was puzzled by Eve's comings and goings and disturbed by what he sensed to be her new attitude toward him. He talked to God about it, and God, having his own problems with Adam and a somewhat broader perspective, was able to help him out a little—but he was confused too. Something had failed to go according to plan. As in the days of Abraham, he needed counsel from his children. "I am who I am," thought God, "but I must become who I will become."

And God and Adam were expectant and afraid the day Eve and Lilith returned to the garden, bursting with possibilities, ready to rebuild it together.

Notes

1. H. Richard Niebuhr. *The Meaning of Revelation* (New York: Macmillan, 1941), p. 113.

2. Mary Daly, "After the Demise of God the Father: A Call for the Castration of Sexist Religion," *Women and Religion: 1972* (Missoula, Mont.: American Academy of Religion, 1973), pp. 7–23.

3. Elizabeth Farians, "Phallic Worship: The Ultimate Idolatry," *Women and Religion: 1972* (Missoula, Mont.: American Academy of Religion, 1973), pp. 63–74.

4. Interestingly, since this speech was delivered, some Jewish leaders have resorted to exactly this argument against ordaining women as rabbis. See Mortimer Ostow's comments in "Women and Change in Jewish Law," *Conservative Judaism* XXIX(1) (Fall 1974): pp. 5–12.

5. At Grailville, Loveland, Ohio, June 18–25, 1972.

6. The ideas for the myth emerged from a Biblical/Theological subgroup at the Grailville conference: Karen Bloomquist, Margaret Early, Elizabeth Farians, and myself.

WOMEN'S LIBERATION AND THE LIBERATION OF GOD: AN ESSAY IN STORY THEOLOGY

Carol Christ

In a story which concludes *The Town beyond the Wall,* Elie Wiesel suggests that the liberation of God and the liberation of humans depend on the renewal of an ancient dialogue between them which is charged with hatred, with remorse, and most of all, with infinite yearning. Wiesel's story gives form to the feelings[1] of resentment and betrayal many Jews direct toward God after the Holocaust. His story also gives shape to the feelings of many women as they become conscious of their exclusion from the stories of God's relation to man.

Wiesel's story tells of a time in the distant past when God and man changed places. As I retell it, the story is of a time in the present when God and woman change places. I told the story to express hatred and resentment of God, but the logic of the story led me to an insight about God's relation to woman which I had not guessed when I began the telling.

Wiesel tells the story in this way:

> Legend tells us that one day man spoke to God in this wise:
> "Let us change about. You be man, and I will be God.
> For only one second."
> God spoke gently and asked him, "Aren't you afraid?"
> "No. And You?"
> "Yes, I am," God said.
> Nevertheless he granted man's desire. He became a man, and the man took his place and immediately availed himself of his omnipotence; he refused to revert to his previous state. So neither God nor man was ever again what he seemed to be.

Years passed, centuries, perhaps eternities. And suddenly the drama
quickened. The past for one, and the present for the other, were too
heavy to be borne.

As the liberation of the one was bound to the liberation of the other,
they renewed the ancient dialogue whose echoes come to us in the
night, charged with hatred, with remorse, and most of all, with infinite
yearning.[2]

I tell it like this:

One day woman spoke to God in this way:

"Let us change places. You be woman, and I will be God. For only
one second."

God smiled and asked her, "Are you afraid?"

"No, and you?"

"Yes, I am," God said.

But woman thought to herself bitterly, No matter. I want you to know
how it feels to be me. I want you to know how much I have suffered
because you let yourself be named in man's image as the God of the
fathers, as the man of war, as king of the universe. I don't believe you'll
know how I feel until you become woman. No, I am not afraid.

So woman becomes God and God becomes woman. But as woman
takes the place of God she finds herself led to an insight she has not
expected. . . . As woman takes the place of God, she hears what she
can only describe as a still, small voice saying, "God is a woman like
yourself. She shares your suffering. She, too, has had her power of
naming stolen from her. First she was called an idol of the Canaanites,
and then she ceased to exist as God." As woman becomes God, the God
who had existed for her only as an alien ceases to be a stranger to her. In
this moment, woman realizes the meaning of the concluding words of
the story, which say: The liberation of the one is bound to the liberation
of the other, so they renew the ancient dialogue, whose echoes come to
us in the night, charged with hatred, with remorse, and most of all, with
infinite yearning.

According to the story, both women's liberation and God's depend
on their understanding what it means to stand in each other's place.
Moreover, the liberation of both depends on their renewing an ancient
dialogue. What does it mean to speak of God's liberation, and how is
God's liberation related to the liberation of women?

In the story, woman wants to change places with God in order to
force God to experience being a woman in a world shaped by God's
covenant with man. She wants God to experience the suffering of
women in a world where the mothers, the daughters, and the sisters do

not exist—even for God. She hopes that after experiencing her suffering God will change the world he has created.

However, as she changes places with God, woman comes to recognize an essential kinship with God which had been hidden from her in the patriarchal stories of the God of the fathers. She learns that patriarchal history has led to a primordial alienation within God. There once was a goddess and stories of a goddess, but she was called the idol of the pagans, her stories were forgotten, and she herself ceased to exist. In patriarchal culture, not only the human image of God, but the true God in her/his[3] primordial nature as both female and male, neither female nor male, is alienated from her/himself. The power of women to liberate themselves from a patriarchal history in which God is still chained makes women in some sense more powerful than God, as is suggested in the image of God and woman changing places.

According to the story, this new power of women over God is a power which may assist the very liberation of God. The concept of God's liberation is alien to theological traditions in which God is conceived as all-powerful, in which God is conceived as the initiator of all significant action, and in which the divine nature itself is sometimes conceived as totally unaffected by all human action. However, the notion of divine bondage and powerlessness is rooted in the Jewish mystical tradition with its symbol of the Messiah in chains. Kabbalistic and hasidic stories say that God needs humans to free him from bondage. The divine self-estrangement and the concomitant need for divine liberation[4] are familiar themes in Jewish mystical theology. They are expressed in the symbol of God's alienation from his female counterpart, the Shekhinah, who wanders the earth weeping over the suffering of the Jewish people. According to Jewish custom, the act of intercourse on the Sabbath reunites God with his Shekhinah, or female counterpart. Women can perhaps reinterpret these symbols to counter the view that God is to be totally identified with the patriarchal image of God.[5]

The stories and the symbols insist that the alienation of God is not limited to the poverty of human symbolic expression, but affects the very life of God. God, like humans, has been in bondage to patriarchal history. Thus, the story speaks of a divine liberation which is not simply a matter of human symbolic expression, but has immense consequences for the divine life itself, that is, the liberation of God spoken of here is not simply a matter of changing the way we talk about God. God himself and not just human language must be liberated. Divine bondage and potential liberation is also suggested in the Lilith story as told by Judith Plaskow. In the words of the story, God, so to speak, admits his bondage, saying, "I am who I am," and acknowledges that he must change, saying, "I must become who I will become."[6] In both the Lilith story and the stories told here, God is held accountable for the patriarchal history in which he was enchained, *and let himself be enchained.* Yet in both stories, God, like women, may achieve liberation from that history. The notion that God be held accountable for the patriarchal history in which he has been known is essential if the Biblical notion of a significant divine-human encounter in history is to be maintained. If God is totally unaffected by the history in which he has been known, or if our words about God are entirely a human projection, then the notion of God's accountability for patriarchal history is absurd. But if God really is involved in history, then God must be held at least partially responsible for that history and for the image of himself he allowed to be projected in it. Thus, renewal of a dialogue with the God of the patriarchal tradition will not only bring him out of his alienation from women, but also out of a primordial self-alienation.

The story says that this renewed dialogue with God will be charged with hatred and with remorse. Women's hatred and remorse stem from exclusion from the stories of God's covenant with man. Hearing the Biblical stories, women must refuse to sit silent, they must charge God with his failures to them. Imagine the following scene. The Bible is read:

> And the people of Israel groaned under their bondage . . .
> And God heard their groaning, and God remembered his covenant
> with Abraham, with Isaac, and with Jacob. (Exodus 2:23ff)

> This is my God and I will praise him,
> My father's God and I will exalt him,
> The LORD is a man of war . . . (Exodus 15:2–3)

> And I will abolish the bow, the sword,
> and war from the land. (Hosea 2:18)

Hearing that God had compassion on the Hebrews in their time of slavery, a woman feels hopeful that her bondage, too, will be ended. But as she listens further, she hears that the covenantal promises were addressed to Abraham, Isaac, and Jacob. She feels her stomach tighten, her neck tense, her mind resist, as she experiences her exclusion from the tradition which shaped her deepest longings for redemption. Instead of swallowing her anger, choking back the words forming in her throat, she rises and cries out, "What happened to the mothers, the daughters, and the sisters? How can we give allegiance to a tradition of fathers and sons? Where is the woman of God who could aid our quest? Where are the goddesses? You, God, with the aid of your patriarchs and prophets, destroyed the powerful earth-mother goddesses of the ancient Near East as you continue to destroy us. By your very existence as male, you legitimatize the patriarchal order in which I cannot fully exist. How could you, God? You promise to abolish the bow, the sword, and war from the land, but you yourself are called a man of war. How can you ever fulfill the promises you have made to us?"

The expression of such anger and bitterness may be offensive to some, but it is essential to the achievement of both women's liberation and God's. Only through the expression of hatred and remorse will women bring to consciousness—their own, men's, and perhaps God's—the extent of God's alienation from them *and* the extent of God's alienation from her/his true selfhood. Just as in the women's movement expression of anger and resentment toward men precedes a reconciliation which can come only after anger has clarified the extent of mutual alienation, so, too, women's relation with God must proceed through anger to a possible reconciliation on the other side.

It should be noted that the indictment of God projected in the words of an imagined woman has Biblical and traditional precedent. It is a woman's adaption of the covenant lawsuit form. The prophets made great use of this form; they presented God as indicting Israel for failing to live up to its side of the covenant, and threatening to give up his promise to protect the people from their enemies. At times, representatives of the people have reversed this form and called God to account for failing to fulfill his side of the covenantal agreement. Rabbi Levi-Yitzhak of Berditchev, tradition says, called God to account on Yom Kippur for ignoring the sufferings of his people. He was following Abraham, who questioned God's righteousness in destroying Sodom and Gomorrah, and Moses, who asked to be blotted out of the Lord's book if God utterly destroyed the people for worshiping the Golden Calf.

The story also suggests that the renewed dialogue with God will be charged with infinite yearning. Many women today reject the notion that they require the God of the patriarchal tradition for their liberation.

That God is, they rightly say, part of the problem, and therefore, they conclude, could have nothing to do with its solution.[7] And yet, perhaps precisely because he is part of the problem, he must also be involved in its solution. Many women find that their feelings toward the God of the tradition are not those of indifference, but are indeed, as the story says, hatred and remorse. To pretend indifference to the God of the tradition when anger and bitterness are one's true feelings is to deaden a part of oneself. This may be too high a price for women to pay. Furthermore, the God to whom those feelings of anger are directed is also the source, for many women, of their own hopes for liberation. It was, after all, from the Exodus story that many women learned that those who had been in bondage could achieve liberation. Thus women whose deepest identities were formed in religious traditions may find that to cut themselves off from the God of the tradition separates them from the root of the longing for liberation which has nourished their hopes in the women's movement. Even women who do not think themselves related to a religious tradition may find that their betrayal by all the liberation movements of patriarchal culture calls for metaphysical and ultimately religious expression.

Women, then, will perhaps move through expression of anger at God to a new relation with God. They will never again submit themselves to an all-powerful father figure. They will never forget—nor will they let God forget—that such a God is the symbol and source of their oppression. In renewing dialogue with a God who has betrayed them, women may follow the protagonist of Wiesel's *The Gates of the Forest* who hears a voice telling him, "He doesn't need your love, he can do without it; but you can't. It's not a question of him but of yourself. Your love, rather than his, could make the difference."[8] The love of women, who long for God, likewise will be from a position of mutuality and power as they recognize that not God's love, but their own can make the difference. They will love the God who is the source of their yearning for redemption and whose loss diminishes them. Like Jacob with the angel, these women will struggle with God, and perhaps at the end of the night, both women and God will emerge with new names and the power of new being. At dawn women may hear a still, small voice speaking to them saying, "In God is a woman like yourself; she, too, has suffered and ceased to exist through the long years of patriarchal history." With that sister God, and the sister earth she once represented, women will perhaps make a new covenant: promising to liberate her and the earth as they liberate themselves.[9]

Notes

1. See Suzanne Langer, *Feeling and Form* (New York: Charles Scribner's Sons, 1953).

2. *The Town beyond the Wall* translated by Stephen Becker, (New York: Avon Books, 1969), p. 190.

3. The use of pronouns is consistent in this essay. Masculine pronouns used of God refer to the God revealed in and known in patriarchal history. "She/He" did not lead us out of Egypt, for the God who led out of Egypt is a male God, a "man of war." Dual pronouns used of God refer to the God who "somehow" lies beyond patriarchal religion.

4. These symbols are discussed in Gershom Scholem's *Major Trends in Jewish Mysticism* (New York: Schocken Books, 1969), esp. pp. 244–86 and in his *On the Kabbala and Its Symbolism,* translated by Ralph Manheim (New York: Schocken Books, 1970), esp. pp. 109–17.

5. The idea that the doctrine of the Shekhinah might be reinterpreted as a resource for a feminist theology was suggested to me by Rita Gross. I recognize that to reinterpret these symbols from the perspective of women's alienation in patriarchal culture goes beyond the probable intent of their kabbalistic formulators, and that such an interpretation does not exhaust their significance.

6. Printed in Rosemary Ruether, ed., *Religion and Sexism* (New York: Simon and Schuster, 1974).

7. This case is powerfully presented in Mary Daly's *Beyond God the Father* (Boston: Beacon Press, 1973). I endorse her indictment of God the Father and the patriarchal tradition. However, as I suggest below, I read her indictment as a case against *God,* and I do not think the interchange between women and God is completed (at least for some women) with the presentation of the indictment. I realize that this position involves me in anthropomorphic theology (story theology cannot be any other kind), but so be it.

8. Translated by Frances Frenaye (New York: Avon Books, 1967), p. 222.

9. I do not endorse traditional identifications of women and nature which have served to exclude women from many scholarly and spiritual dimensions of religious life. However, I do believe that rethinking traditional views of women ought to lead to rethinking traditional views of nature as well.

THE LIFE CYCLE
AND NEW RITUALS

Jews have always expressed their relationship to God, and their membership in the community of Israel through ritual—concrete, formalized acts, symbols and words. Women, however, have traditionally been barred from leadership of public ritual, relegated to observer status in the synagogue, and assigned but a few private rituals which, moreover, were formulated by men. In the last few years, Jewish women and men have begun to explore and create new Jewish rituals—to include women equally in public worship and to celebrate female experience and spirituality.

Ceremonies marking and celebrating the life stages of women are an appropriate starting-point, for such moments are conspicuously neglected by the tradition, which did not regard women as communally important or spiritually equal to men.

In addition to life-cycle moments—birth, bat mitzvah, marriage—women and men who believe in the equality of the sexes before God have sought other ways to include women in Jewish ritual life. Women are experimenting with their own forms of prayer, sacred symbols, such as *tallit* and *tefillin,* and uniquely feminine aspects of such communal moments as Shabbat and holidays.

A beginning has been made. Birth and naming ceremonies for girls are becoming popular. New marriage ceremonies make women equal participants. New attention is being paid to bat mitzvah, childbirth, menstruation and menopause as uniquely feminine experiences appropriate for ritual commemoration. Women are participating more fully in public worship than ever before in Jewish history. Many questions remain to be explored. Should women's rituals and symbols imitate men's or should they be unique? How do we create new ceremonies? How far can we go in departing from traditional forms and language? How should we deal with halakhic restrictions on women's participation in ritual?

This section presents some examples of new ceremonies which have been created, in the hope that other individuals, families and communities will develop innovative ritual forms to express their own understanding of women's spirituality.

In addition, we examine here some of the life stages of women —adolescence, singleness, aging—which have profound implications for Jewish communal and religious life. These areas call for new approaches. How will we deal with these life-stages and with issues of childrearing, family planning, changing sexual mores, as Jews committed to the Jewish past, a Jewish future, and Jewish feminism?

ON THE BIRTH
OF A DAUGHTER

Daniel I. Leifer and Myra Leifer

We wish to share with others our recent efforts to develop and create Jewish ritual expressions. As is so often the case, an immediate and concrete reality forced us to grapple with a problem and to meet the challenge of putting our principles into practice. Early in the morning of February 22/20 Adar I 1973, we were graced with the birth at home of our first child, a daughter—Ariel Hanna.

We had planned to have our baby at home and had participated in classes in the LaMaze method of childbirth. Though we believe that the claims sometimes made for a painless childbirth through this technique are false, the exercises, breathing and pushing techniques, teamwork of man and woman and the knowledge of what to expect all contribute to making childbirth a positive, natural experience. This was our attitude and because we dislike the ambience of maternity wards, because of our negative experience at the best of local hospitals when Myra had a miscarriage, because of the danger of infection in hospitals and because childbirth is not a disease, we wished not only to have our baby at home but to be together as a family in our own home from the very first moments of a new existence for all three of us. We understood that that would be possible only if medical examinations in the last month of pregnancy revealed that everything—especially the position of the baby in the womb—was normal. If not, we were prepared to go to a hospital. We worked with the Chicago Maternity Center whose doctors and midwife nurses deliver babies at home in emergencies, for poor families, and for an increasing small number of middle-class families such as ourselves. We were very pleased with the medical care we received and felt at ease because the obstetrician and midwife came to our home with emergency equipment (oxygen, incubator) and were prepared to take us, in case of emergency, to the major hospital with which the Center is connected.

Ariel Hanna was not born without Myra's pain and struggle (the description of childbirth in the prophets and psalms are all true and now have personal meaning to us). But for both of us, though in very different ways, it was a "peak experience" in which we were working together, awake and aware of what we were doing. The most meaningful part of the experience for Daniel was being part of the actual delivery team, holding one of Myra's legs while the midwife held the other and the physician helped Ariel into the world. To see our child gradually "opening the womb" of her mother and bursting into life with a cry before our very eyes is indeed, as everyone knows and says, a profound and religious experience.

There is no special *berakhah* in Jewish tradition to celebrate that moment.[1] So two hours after Ariel's birth, when the physician and midwife had left and all three of us were together in our bed and Ariel had nursed for the first time, we said together the following seven *berakhot* in Hebrew and English (our own translations) with a cup of wine from which we all drank. These blessings were chosen from the Blessings for Various Occasons, and the seven Wedding Blessings. We chose those blessings that had general and particular personal meaning for us. We deliberately paralleled these blessings in number and content with the wedding blessings, seeing in the birth of our child one of the fulfillments of our marriage, and because of the fullness and sacral quality of the number *seven* in Jewish tradition. As will be described below, we said these seven blessings together at the Kiddush following the naming of our daughter in *shul*.

בָּרוּךְ אַתָּה ה' אֱלֹהֵינוּ מֶלֶךְ הָעוֹלָם עֹשֶׂה מַעֲשֵׂה בְרֵאשִׁית.

Praised are you, Adonai, our God, Lord of the Cosmos, Creator of the Mystery of Creation.

בָּרוּךְ אַתָּה ה' אֱלֹהֵינוּ מֶלֶךְ הָעוֹלָם שֶׁהַכֹּל בָּרָא לִכְבוֹדוֹ.

Praised are you, Adonai, our God, Lord of the Cosmos, Creator of Everything for your Glory.

בָּרוּךְ אַתָּה ה׳ אֱלֹהֵינוּ מֶלֶךְ הָעוֹלָם יוֹצֵר הָאָדָם.

Praised are you, Adonai, our God, Lord of the Cosmos, Creator of Humanity.

בָּרוּךְ אַתָּה ה׳ אֱלֹהֵינוּ מֶלֶךְ הָעוֹלָם, אֲשֶׁר יָצַר אֶת הָאָדָם בְּצַלְמוֹ, בְּצֶלֶם דְּמוּת תַּבְנִיתוֹ, וְהִתְקִין לוֹ מִמֶּנּוּ בִּנְיַן עֲדֵי עַד.   בָּרוּךְ אַתָּה ה׳ יוֹצֵר הָאָדָם.

Praised are you, Adonai, our God, Lord of the Cosmos, who created human beings in your image after your likeness, and out of their very selves you prepared for them a perpetual spiritual being. Praised are you, Lord, Creator of Humanity.

בָּרוּךְ אַתָּה ה׳ אֱלֹהֵינוּ מֶלֶךְ הָעוֹלָם שֶׁכָּכָה לוֹ בְּעוֹלָמוֹ.

Praised are you, Adonai, our God, Lord of the Cosmos, who has such as these creatures in your world.

בָּרוּךְ אַתָּה ה׳ אֱלֹהֵינוּ מֶלֶךְ הָעוֹלָם זוֹכֵר הַבְּרִית וְנֶאֱמָן בִּבְרִיתוֹ וְקַיָּם בְּמַאֲמָרוֹ.

Praised are you, Adonai, our God, Lord of the Cosmos, Rememberer of the Covenant and steadfastly faithful in your Covenant, keeping your promise.

בָּרוּךְ אַתָּה ה׳ אֱלֹהֵינוּ מֶלֶךְ הָעוֹלָם שֶׁהֶחֱיָנוּ וְקִיְּמָנוּ וְהִגִּיעָנוּ לַזְּמַן הַזֶּה.

Praised are you, Adonai, our God, Lord of the Cosmos, who has sustained us in life and being and brought us to this very moment.

Followed by:

בָּרוּךְ אַתָּה ה׳ אֱלֹהֵינוּ מֶלֶךְ הָעוֹלָם בּוֹרֵא פְּרִי הַגָּפֶן.

Praised are You, Adonai, our God, Lord of the Cosmos, Creator of the fruit of the vine.

The giving or taking on of a Hebrew name connotes the acquisition of being and identity within Jewish language-culture. When done amidst a quorum of ten Jews, a congregation, it connotes the introduction and acceptance of the new member and the celebration of the community in its enhanced strength and vitality. Our daughter was given the name Ariel Hanna at a Shabbat morning service of our "Upstairs Minyan" at the University of Chicago Hillel Foundation. The "Upstairs Minyan" is a conservative-liberal-experimental group which has been in existence for eight years. One of its central features is the equality of status and participation of women. It was in character but particularly appropriate that the service was led by a woman *hazzanit* and women readers and that our discussion (a regular part of the Shabbat service) was about the role of women in Jewish religious life, including a report on the recent Network Jewish Women's Conference.

The traditional practice of naming a daughter calls for the father to be called to the Torah *(aliyah)* on the Shabbat (or Monday or Thursday when the Torah is read) immediately following her birth and for her name to be announced within the text of a special prayer *(mi sheberakh)* asking for health and blessings. We chose, as do many today, to wait until Myra was well enough and Ariel old enough (until her immunity system had developed)—two weeks—to come to *shul* so that all three of us would be together with our family and friends for the ritual entrance of Ariel into the community of Israel and humanity. Daniel and Myra together with Ariel had an *aliyah* and said the *berakhot* together. Following this, Ariel's paternal grandfather read the naming prayer. The text we used is that on pages 48–9 in the Reconstructionist Sabbath prayerbook. As indicated there, we followed this with the *sheheyanu* blessing.

Immediately following and to mark the occasion, members of the *minyan* were asked to read in Hebrew, in accompaniment with the English response of the congregation, the verses of a specially selected Psalm. We comprised a Hebrew letter acrostic spelling Ariel Hanna from Psalm 119, which itself is an eightfold acrostic. (We chose verses 1, 156, 73, 8, 90, 58, 109, 37.) This was not an original idea but its origin is unknown to us, except that we had heard of its use by Prof. Petuchowski of Hebrew Union College. Thus the entire community was included in the celebration of Ariel's birth and entrance into its fold and in the expression of hope and prayer for her rearing within Jewish life, for the verses selected expressed values in our tradition which we wished to affirm at this moment.

As mentioned above, a kiddush followed the service and discussion. It was begun by Myra and Daniel reciting Kiddush. This Kiddush was the above seven blessings added to the traditional Shabbat Kiddush.

Perhaps most important of all, in our efforts to celebrate the birth of our daughter with the same equality and dignity with which the birth of a son is traditionally celebrated, was our decision to have a *pidyon habat*, a redemption of our firstborn daughter. Biblical command and rabbinic *halakhah* call for the redemption of a firstborn son at a brief and simple ceremony on the thirty-first day of the child's existence. The passage of a month's unit of time assures the greater chance of viability of the child, thus making its redemption possible and necessary. The Torah (Ex. 13:1–16; Num. 18:8–19; Lev. 19:23–25, 23:19–22; Deut.15:19–23) compares the first fruits of human fertility with that of animals, fruit trees, grapevines and cereal grains. The divine powers of fructification and life-giving are as equally necessary for vegetable, animal and human life as the biological activity of these species which generates that life. Thus all life, but most especially the first fulfillment of the potential of fertility, belongs to God. As leige lord of creation, it is right and just that first fruits be given to God. Thus the human *peter rehem*—the child that first opens, frees and redeems the womb of its mother—belongs to God. While the first fruits of grains, trees and animals are in truth given back to God—sacrificed—the human child is redeemed, i.e., substitution is made via the payment of a fixed sum (5 *shekalim*) to God's emissary on earth—the priest. Many have objected to the ceremony of *pidyon haben* because they no longer wish to maintain the distinctions between and the privileges of office of Priests, Levites and Israelites. While we subscribe to this point of view, to rest one's opposition to the concept of *pidyon*—redemption—upon the role of the priest in the ceremony is sorely to misunderstand the nature of this religious ritual.[2] The holiness acquired by the firstborn males "at the time that I (God) smote every firstborn in the land of Egypt" (Num. 8:17) is the *kedushah* of life, a supplemental and extraordinary gift of *hesed* and redemption, bestowed by God when all other firstborn human life was annihilated. The "twice-born" sanctity of the firstborn is a result of the joining of the *kedushah* from Nature with the *kedushah* from History so characteristic of our tradition.

We wished to retain the awe and gratitude for a *peter rehem* child which is reflected in the traditional ceremony. We also wished to emphasize, as does the traditional ceremony, the dedication of the parents to rear their child for a Jewish life of "Torah, *hupah* and good deeds." However, we wished to shift the latter emphasis to include the broad range of values, traditional Jewish and nontraditional Jewish and humanitarian values, with which we hoped to imbue our daughter. Thus we eliminated the role of the priest, and the five *shekalim;* the former, for the reason mentioned above, and the latter, because the monetary scale of value of persons of different ages (Numbers 27:1–8) rests upon a consistently lower evaluation of women, e.g. "If the age is from one month to five years, the equivalent for a male is five shekels of silver, and the equivalent for a female is three shekels of silver" (v.6). Instead, we chose to donate a sum of eighteen dollars (the numerical value of the Hebrew letters of the word *hai,* life, is eighteen) in Ariel's name to three Jewish and three non-Jewish organizations which are engaged in Arab-Jewish cooperation and antiwar activity such as military counseling and Vietnam reconstruction—values we affirm and hope to convey to her. In each case, we sent a letter explaining the meaning and occasion of our contribution. (In almost all cases, we received warm letters in response—we are saving these for Ariel.) We followed the traditional text and format of the ceremony; changing, adopting, adding so as to create what we hoped would be a ritual that took our tradition forward, unabused but invigorated. The ceremony itself took place within the community of the regular members of our Hillel "Upstairs Minyan." The text of our ceremony follows. The English translations are our own.

Ceremony of Redemption and Hallowing of a Daughter

1) Myra read a poem—*Natasha* by Barbara Friend (*Ms.,* December 1972, p. 87)

2) Daniel explained the origin and meaning of the ritual.

3) A woman friend read some of the relevant Biblical passages: Numbers 3:11–13, 18:13–16.

4) Ariel's godmother read Deut 29:9–14 (all the generations even those unborn, were at Sinai and participated in the covenant making) and two rabbinic passages about children: *Canticles Rabba* 1, 24 and *Pesikta* de R. Kahana 121a. Both can be found in Nahum N. Glatzer's *The Rest Is Commentary* (Boston: Beacon, 1961) pp. 218 and 229.

5) Ritual—a cup of wine and a loaf of *hallah* is present.
   a) Statement of parents—Daniel and Myra

זֹאת בִּתֵּנוּ בְּכוֹרָתֵנוּ הִיא פֶּטֶר רֶחֶם לְאִמָּה
קֹדֶשׁ הִיא לַה׳ כַּכָּתוּב, "קַדֶּשׁ לִי כָל בְּכוֹר פֶּטֶר כָּל
רֶחֶם בִּבְנֵי יִשְׂרָאֵל בָּאָדָם וּבַבְּהֵמָה לִי הוּא"
וְטוֹב בְּעֵינֵינוּ לִפְדּוֹתָהּ וְהִנֵּה כֶּסֶף פִּדְיוֹנָהּ וְקִדּוּשָׁהּ.

This is our firstborn daughter.
She opened, freed and liberated the womb of her mother.
Holy is she to Adonai, as it is written, "Consecrate to Me every
firstborn; man and beast, the first issue of every womb among the
Israelites is Mine." (Ex. 13:1).

Now it is good in our eyes and our desire to redeem her.
And here is the money of her redemption and hallowing.

   b) Setting aside of the money for *tzedakah* contributed in Ariel's
name.
   c) Blessings said by parents—Daniel and Myra

בָּרוּךְ אַתָּה ה׳ אֱלֹהֵינוּ מֶלֶךְ הָעוֹלָם אֲשֶׁר קִדְּשָׁנוּ בְּמִצְוֹתָיו וְצִוָּנוּ לְהַכְנִיסָהּ
בִּבְרִיתוֹ שֶׁל עַם יִשְׂרָאֵל.

Praised are you, Adonai, our God, Lord of the Cosmos, who has made
us holy through your Commandments and commanded us to bring our
daughter into the covenant of the People of Israel.[3]

בָּרוּךְ אַתָּה ה׳ אֱלֹהֵינוּ מֶלֶךְ הָעוֹלָם אֲשֶׁר קִדְּשָׁנוּ בְּמִצְוֹתָיו וְצִוָּנוּ עַל פִּדְיוֹן
כָּל בְּכוֹר פֶּטֶר רֶחֶם בִּבְנֵי יִשְׂרָאֵל.

Praised are you, Adonai, our God, Lord of the Cosmos, who has made
us holy through your Commandments and commanded us to redeem
every first born, the first issue of every womb among the Israelites.

בָּרוּךְ אַתָּה ה׳ מְשַׂמֵּחַ הוֹרִים עִם הַיְלָדִים.

Praised are you, Adonai, who makes parents rejoice with their
children.[4]

בָּרוּךְ אַתָּה ה' אֱלֹהֵינוּ מֶלֶךְ הָעוֹלָם, שֶׁהֶחֱיָנוּ וְקִיְּמָנוּ וְהִגִּיעָנוּ לַזְּמַן הַזֶּה.

Praised are You, Adonai, our God, Lord of the Cosmos who has sustained us in Life and Being and brought us to this very moment.

d) Statement and Blessing of the representative of the community—read by Ariel's godfather.

זֶה תַּחַת זֹאת

זֶה חִלּוּף זֹאת

זֶה מָחוּל עַל זֹאת

וְתִכָּנֵס זֹאת הַבַּת אֲרִיאֵל חַנָּה בַּת מִיכַל וְדָנִיאֵל יִצְחָק לְחַיִּים, לְתוֹרָה וּלְיִרְאַת שָׁמַיִם.

This tzedakah instead of this child, this in exchange of that, this money redeems this first born. May this daughter, Ariel Hanna, daughter of Michal and Daniel Isaac, enter into Life, Torah and the awe of the Divine. May it be God's will that just as she has entered into Redemption and the Covenant, so may she enter into the study of Torah, under the marriage canopy and into the doing of good deeds. Amen.

אֲחוֹתֵנוּ אַתְּ הֲיִי לְאַלְפֵי רְבָבָה.

יְשִׂימֵךְ אֱלֹהִים כְּשָׂרָה, רִבְקָה, רָחֵל וְלֵאָה

יְבָרֶךְ ה' וְיִשְׁמְרֶךָ

יָאֵר ה' פָּנָיו אֵלַיִךְ וִיחֻנֶּךָּ

יִשָּׂא ה' פָּנָיו אֵלַיִךְ וְיָשֵׂם לָךְ שָׁלוֹם.

O sister! May you grow into thousands of myriads (Gen. 24:60). May God make you as our Mothers Sarah, Rivka, Rachel and Leah. Adonai bless you and keep you. Adonai make his face to shine upon you and be gracious to you. Adonai lift up his face to you and grant you peace.

בָּרוּךְ אַתָּה ה' אֱלֹהֵינוּ מֶלֶךְ הָעוֹלָם בּוֹרֵא פְּרִי הַגָּפֶן.

Praised are You, Adonai, our God, Lord of the Cosmos, Creator of the fruit of the vine.

בָּרוּךְ אַתָּה ה' אֱלֹהֵינוּ מֶלֶךְ הָעוֹלָם הַמּוֹצִיא לֶחֶם מִן הָאָרֶץ.

Praised are You, Adonai, our God, Lord of the Cosmos, who brings bread out of the earth.

Selections from Psalm 119
in Honor of Ariel Hanna Leifer

(1)   א : אַשְׁרֵי תְמִימֵי דָרֶךְ הַהֹלְכִים בְּתוֹרַת ה'

How happy are those whose way is blameless, who walk in the Torah of the Lord.

(156)   ר : רַחֲמֶיךָ רַבִּים ה' כְּמִשְׁפָּטֶיךָ חַיֵּנִי

Great are your mercies, Lord; give me life in resonance with your justice.

(73)   י : יָדֶיךָ עָשׂוּנִי וַיְכוֹנְנוּנִי הֲבִינֵנִי וְאֶלְמְדָה מִצְוֹתֶיךָ

Your hands made me and fashioned me; give me insight that I may learn your commandments.

(8)   א : אֶת חֻקֶּיךָ אֶשְׁמֹר אַל תַּעַזְבֵנִי עַד מְאֹד

I will keep your statutes; O forsake me not utterly.

(90)   ל : לְדֹר וָדֹר אֱמוּנָתֶךָ כּוֹנַנְתָּ אֶרֶץ וַתַּעֲמֹד

Your faithfulness endures for all generations; you established the earth and it stands fast.

(58)   ח : חִלִּיתִי פָנֶיךָ בְכָל לֵב חָנֵּנִי כְּאִמְרָתֶךָ

I long for the favor of your face with all my heart; be gracious to me according to your promise.

(109)   נ : נַפְשִׁי בְכַפִּי תָמִיד וְתוֹרָתְךָ לֹא שָׁכָחְתִּי

I hold my life in my hand continually, yet I do not forget your Torah.

(37)   ה : הַעֲבֵר עֵינַי מֵרְאוֹת שָׁוְא בִּדְרָכֶךָ חַיֵּנִי

Keep my eyes from seeing falsehood, and give me life along your paths.

Notes

1. The Talmud (Berakhot 59b, *Shulhan Arukh, Orah Hayyim* 223) specifies the saying of a *berakhah*, "Blessed art thou, O Lord our God, King of the universe, who art good and dispensest good" when a *male* child is born. There is no blessing for a female child. This is a general blessing to be said upon hearing good tidings, and is not specific to the occasion of childbirth. The Talmudic discussion *ad loc.* makes clear that this blessing is said when one is a partner to the cause of good tidings. Here the man is partner with his wife in the birth of a son. Obviously, it is the man who says the blessing. And this accounts for the choice of a blessing marking good news in a partnership as the most fitting mode of expression for the new father of a male child. This blessing may be said at the successive birth of sons.

2. We refer to a recent and commendable alternative ceremony of the Sanctification of the Firstborn, developed by Rabbis Mark S. Golub and Norman Cohen (*CCAR Journal*, Winter 1973, pp. 71–78). While we found ourselves much in sympathy with their values and emphases, we found we could not use their ceremony for the following reasons: 1) It totally failed to recognize and come to grips with the central religious fact that life, in some sense and to some degree, comes from and belongs to God. This aspect of the traditional ceremony they excised and never reworked. 2) They slighted the aspect of the opening of the womb, a most profound experience for us, perhaps because we had our child at home. 3) Their ceremony is too rabbi-centered, paradoxically, objecting to the traditional role of priest but then giving the rabbi a priestly role. 4) Their rhetoric is the unfortunate public priestly speech of many rabbis.

3. This was the most important statement for us in the entire ceremony. It is a new *berakhah,* a variation on that said by the father at the circumcision of his son. The last phrase of that *berakhah* is: to bring him into the covenant of Abraham our Father. Obviously, this *berakhah,* can not be said for a girl. However, it was absolutely intolerable for us that we should not have the privilege and joy of affirming that we were bringing our child into the Covenant. Because the ceremonies of naming and redemption are rites of passage into the Community of the Covenant, we decided that it was right and proper to construct this new *berakhah.*

4. This *berakhah* was borrowed from the *pidyon* ceremony of Golub and Cohen, op. cit. We liked it because of its resonance with the concluding blessing of the seven wedding blessings.

WOMEN AND JEWISH EDUCATION: A NEW LOOK AT BAT MITZVAH

Cherie Koller-Fox

A few years ago, I was asked to offer the first Jewish Women's Conference the same sort of analysis of Jewish education that had been done in general education, i.e., to identify and expose sexism in textbooks and in the classrooms, As Susan Rosenblum Shevitz points out in "Sexism in Jewish Education,"[1] there are many examples of blatant sexism in the textbooks used in Jewish schools.

Yet, despite the truth of her observations, it is important that books for children mirror the realities of the community. The secular feminist movement urged publishers to depict American society without traditional sex-role differentiation; as a result, many textbooks today show women doctors, policewomen, etc. This is more than proper, since women can and do occupy such diverse roles in American society. This is not the case, however, in traditional Jewish life. For example, Orthodox and Conservative Jews do not have female cantors and rabbis, and the Orthodox consider it wrong for women to say Kiddush if a man is present. Liberal Jews do not consider such things illegal, but prejudices are strong and such behavior is still thought "strange." Strong cultural patterns cannot be changed by revising illustrations or accounts in textbooks. If children saw such pictures in books without any confirmative action in the home and synagogue, they would either ignore or ridicule them.

Then, too, Jewish textbooks would not be much improved by changing the sexist references in them. Most textbooks currently in use present an intellectually unstimulating, joyless, and superficial picture of Jewish life to children. I would prefer to see such textbooks removed from our classrooms entirely and would not feel any differently about them were every trace of sexism removed.

Consequently, when I spoke at the Women's Conference, I explained that the problems of Jewish education go far beyond the question of textbooks. Jewish schools convey a negative image of Jews to boys no less than girls. I honestly believe that in the average supplemental Hebrew school, boys and girls are treated equally—they receive an equally bad education.

And yet, one must strive to maximize the classroom experience for all the students. Certainly all efforts should be made to make sure that, at least within the classroom, a climate of nonsexism prevails.[2] In addition, any sexism in the community at large or in textbooks should be pointed out.

Just as the textbooks cannot bring about communal change but must reflect it, so too the classroom, however innovative, cannot replace the community as the setting for change. Further, what adults practice influences children much more than what they profess to believe.

For example, even though Reform Judaism recognizes the equality of women in theory, practice has been slow to follow. In the Belmont, Mass. congregation (in which I worked from 1970 to 1975 in the supplemental Hebrew School), only in the last few years did the ritual committee vote to allow women full ritual equality. Since this ruling, I have noticed a significant change in the behavior of the girls, as illustrated in the following story:

Some years ago, I attended a "marathon" weekend with Jewish feminists. That Sunday, I told my ten-year-old students that a group of Jewish women had been talking about whether women should be included in the *minyan* and given *aliyot*. A heated discussion ensued, but I suddenly noticed that the usually talkative girls had been silent. When asked why, they said that they were unfamiliar with the terms I was using. The boys, who had had the same classroom experience as the girls, apparently knew the terminology because they had been to the Temple and had seen their grandfathers, fathers, and brothers participating in ritual. They understood that, as adults, they too would be expected to participate. The girls were not curious about those aspects of the service which they did not see as a concern of theirs. Now that women have been counted in the *minyan* and routinely have *aliyot* in their synagogue, girls of ten in Belmont are as likely to know these terms as the boys.

One cannot create a world in the classroom and expect the child to find it viable when it is contradicted by the practice of the community. Therefore, if we want to move toward equality of women in the community, we must find occasions within the real life of the community to use as vehicles for education and growth. To educate a young woman to take her place in such a society, we must find moments in which questions of Jewishness and womanhood intersect, so that she can make a synthesis of these two essential elements of her being. If we can learn to maximize such moments through education, we will go beyond the limits of the classroom and find a significant new perspective on the question of educating Jewish women.

The life-cycle rituals are the obvious place to look for such peak moments. Here, women go through significant personal changes, while at the same time participate in rituals which are of high import to the community as a whole: birth and the ritual of naming, puberty and ritual of bat mitzvah, marriage and the wedding ritual. Recently there have been significant attempts to make the celebrations of birth and marriage religiously important to women.[3] However, these are both moments in which women stand in relation to others—parents, children, husbands. In this way, bat mitzvah is unique. Although the bat mitzvah girl is seen as a daughter on this occasion, part of the significance of the day is a separation from childhood and the family. This is the one occasion in Jewish life in which the girl is asked to confirm her personal membership in the Jewish people and to link her fate with theirs. Coming as it does in the throes of puberty and the beginnings of adolescence, this is the occasion of the maximal intersection of the issues of identity as a woman and as a Jew.

The ritual of bat mitzvah, then, has tremendous potential for both education and personal growth.

Bar/bat mitzvah is a ceremony quite unusual in the Western world, for at an age when children are usually the most unbearable, often deviant, and most often dealt with in groups, Judaism sets aside a special moment for them in which they are the center of attention and familial adoration. The presents and parties (important to this age group because of their concern with appearance and self-image) are connected to a religious ritual. Indeed, this appeals to the frivolous side of the adolescent, while at the same time, the precise and demanding nature of the religious task appeals to his or her need to accomplish adult tasks. The demand here exceeds anything that they have done as Jews in the past and, for many of the girls, is more than they will ever be allowed to do in the future.

In looking at bar/bat mitzvah, it is helpful to examine the puberty rites and initiation rites of other cultures. S.N. Eisenstadt, in his "Archetypal Patterns of Youth," lists five characteristics of the transformation from child to adult:

> 1. A series of rites in which the children are symbolically divested of the characteristics of youth and invested with those of adulthood, from a sexual and social point of view, e.g. body mutilation, circumcision, taking on a new name.
> 2. The complete symbolic separation of the males from the world of their youth, especially from their mothers.
> 3. The dramatization of the encounter between the several generations . . . may take the form of a fight or encounter.
> 4. The transmission of the tribal lore and rules of behavior through formalized teaching and ritual acts.
> 5. Relaxation of the control of adults over the adolescents, substituted by self-control and adult responsibility.[4]

At first glance, one might assume that bar mitzvah is not an initiation rite according to these categories. Circumcision is not performed at puberty, and Jews begin teaching their children the "tribal lore" as soon as they walk and talk. Jews, so long divested of a homeland and the right to bear arms, substituted intellectual achievement and religious piety as their standards for both masculinity and adulthood, and it is these accomplishments that bar mitzvah has come to symbolize. The major changes for boys at bar mitzvah are personal legal responsibility and religious responsibility. If circumcision is symbolic of the covenant, the Torah is its confirmation, and it is to this awesome scroll that the youth is called for the first time at his bar mitzvah. The boy is not given a new name, but is called by his own name in the synagogue.

This *aliyah*, the putting on of *tefillin* (phylacteries), and other religious rights and obligations symbolically separate the boy from his mother and sisters, for they are forbidden to participate in these areas of Jewish life; furthermore, at this age, in Orthodox synagogues, girls are banished forever from the main section and sent to sit with their mothers in the women's section.

While there is no physical competition between the generations, the bar mitzvah boy does give a *derashah* (Talmudic discourse) from the pulpit or at a banquet following the service, in which he flexes his intellectual muscle, and thus enters the realm of status competition determined by scholarship.

Putting on *tefillin* is an example of the transmission of "tribal lore" through a ritual act. The *tefillin,* a combination of straps and boxes containing sections of the Shema, are worn every weekday morning at prayer. Placing the boxes on the forehead and opposite the heart, and winding the straps around the hand—in a form which spells the divine name—can be a powerful mystical experience.

Thus we see that, despite surface differences, bar mitzvah, occurring at age thirteen, does belong in the category of puberty-initiation rites. But we must note that, as an initiation rite, bar mitzvah is a much stronger experience than bat mitzvah, even in a liberal synagogue. Girls are more relegated to their "place" at puberty than separated from childhood. There is no generational confrontation, and any "tribal lore" (for women, mainly *mikveh, kashrut, hallah,* and candle lighting) is more applicable at the time of marriage. As far as religious responsibility is concerned, although a girl becomes so obligated at puberty, she never has the wide range of personal obligation that a male assumes. In addition, there are no central symbols, representing new roles, similar to the male's *tallit* and *tefillin.*

The bat mitzvah ceremony in the synagogue customarily takes place on a Friday night, when the Ark is not opened and the Torah is not read. These will be done the next morning, and so, when the girl recites the *haftarah* (section from the Prophets), there is an air of make-believe, since it will be repeated the next day by a "qualified" (male) reader. On the other hand, now that the Conservative Rabbinical Assembly and the Reform movement are allowing women to be called to the Torah, it is only a matter of time before the bat mitzvah will take place on Saturday morning and, tied directly to the reading of the Torah, will take on some of the awesomeness of the bar mitzvah. This gain in importance for the bat mitzvah is reflected even among the Orthodox, who are beginning to develop a home ceremony for girls of this age known as bat Torah. Bat mitzvah will continue to grow in importance as an initiation rite since it is about to enter a new era of possibilities for its celebration, and since it is a meaningful moment both for the community, which thus brings a new member into its midst, and for the girl herself. For it is at this age, when girls are first experiencing themselves as women, that they are asked by the community to participate in a ritual of Jewish womanhood.

Here, the developmental literature can help us understand some of the special needs of adolescent girls, so that we can examine bat mitzvah as a potentially powerful experience both religiously and psychologically in order to maximize its impact.

One of the major problems with bat mitzvah as it stands today is that it is often the last time that girls are allowed to participate in the synagogue service. They are taught all the skills necessary for the occasion and then are never called upon to use them again. In "The Problem of the Generations,"[5] Bruno Bettelheim states that a girl is raised in contradictions. On one hand, she is taught to be a wife and mother and thus to define herself in relationship to other people. On the other hand, in school she is taught to compete and search for self-fulfillment, and thus to define herself in relation to her work. What is she to do with all her success motivation upon reaching the child-bearing years, when she is expected to be completely selfless in nurturing her family? This contradiction is found also in the religious life of the Jewish girl. In school she is told that she can and should learn everything that boys learn (except in some Orthodox schools), and she is even asked to demonstrate that knowledge at her bat mitzvah. Sometimes in high school she is allowed to participate in services on special occasions. However, as she grows up, she is asked less frequently to participate in the service, and the ethnic memory that men's dominion is the synagogue and women's, the home, takes over. Without concomitant changes in the roles of adult women in the Jewish community, merely expanding the bat mitzvah ceremony in the direction of imitation of the bar mitzvah will only compound the adolescent girls' confusion and frustration. Elizabeth Douvan, in *Feminine Personality and Conflict*,[6] explains that adolescent girls have a great need for validation from others; they need constant reassurance from both peers and adults that they are all right despite the internal physical changes and emotional turmoil of puberty. At this time, it is important for girls to have confidantes their own age and older to whom they can look for support.

It is the goal of adolescence to leave childhood behind and to find a place in the adult world. Correspondingly, the task of preparation for a bat mitzvah is to learn a difficult adult skill, i.e., reading a section from the Bible in Hebrew, using the traditional musical chant. Further, the girl may be required to lead part of the service and deliver a short speech. All of this is magnified by the ceremony's occurring in the presence of almost everyone important to her. This task is certainly difficult enough so that the girl can experience a real feeling of success and accomplishment.

Matina Horner's studies of success in women[7] teach that it is precisely at this stage (seventh and eighth grade) that girls begin to question the relationship between their femininity and their ability to succeed. Usually girls play down their intellectual achievements, in contrast to boys. In the rite of bat mitzvah, the girl is shown that her femininity is being *affirmed* by her successful completion of a difficult intellectual task. Thus, in the bat mitzvah, the concerns of the girl as adolescent and as Jew are united in positive and mutually beneficial ways.

Therefore, girls at this age need a number of crucial things which the bat mitzvah offers them in a Jewish context—a chance for large-scale communal validation and a chance to have an extended period of personal attention and validation from an adult as part of the preparation for the event.

Role Model

Unlike previous generations, adolescents today do not have a very clear image of what it means to be an adult. If bat mitzvah is to be seen as a rite of passage, we must understand what it is a passage from and to. Many parents whose Judaism is a marginal aspect of their lives cannot serve as role models of Jewish adulthood.

In order to test my hypothesis that girls do not have a clear understanding of the role of the Jewish woman, I asked all the eleven and twelve-year-old girls in the Belmont School to respond to the question, "What does a Jewish woman do that makes her a *Jewish* woman?"[8] The results were quite instructive. Some of the girls mentioned general nurturing, like "take care of kids," which showed that *Jewish woman*, for them, was synonymous with *woman*. Some of them translated the nurturing into Jewish terms, such as "going out to buy *hallah*" or "cooking for the Sabbath." Other girls associated the Jewishness of a woman with her performance of home rituals such as "keeping a kosher home," or "lighting the candles." A few mentioned very peripheral roles in the synagogue, such as "going to Temple on the important holidays."

Some of the answers had to do with the coercion of children, such as "going to the trouble of sending kids to Hebrew school," or "convincing them to have a bar/bat mitzvah." Relatively few girls mentioned teaching children about their heritage and learning about it themselves. Two or three girls with more active mothers said things like, "being in the *minyan*," or "anything men can do."

This experiment should be useful in pointing to possible future research. As a group, the girls *did* express a Jewish role model, albeit not a very liberated one; yet most of the images were very thin indeed. Even when pressed, they could think of only one or two things that made a Jewish woman Jewish. One girl, for example, felt that Jewish women "clean out the Sabbath candle holders." If that is your picture of growing up Jewish, why bother?

All this points to the importance of a positive role model. Some may feel that it is presumptuous to suggest that any woman can be a model for another because of the changing nature of our society and because women themselves are questioning their roles. Further, we would not want to limit the individual's freedom to develop in her own way. What, then, can a role model mean today?

The answers lie in seeing bat mitzvah as an initiation rite. I feel that we have a responsibility to give girls a picture of the world that we hope to initiate them into, including the possibility of living a richer Jewish life as a woman than any of the girls in my study had experienced. The bat mitzvah tutor could be such a role model.

A thirteen-year old girl, as we have seen, needs much outside validation which can be provided by her tutor. Since they are involved in a task together, the tutor has many opportunities to build up the student's ego. Obviously, questions of success and performance come to bear in the tutor/student relationship, but in addition, as the relationship develops, the student often comes to ask for validation about many other things: how she should deal with her parents, how she should look, etc. This level of conversation can occur most often if the tutor is of the same sex as the student. Moreover, a woman tutor could provide a relationship in which questions of adult Jewish womanhood could be broached and explored.

Larry Kohlberg states that people tend to "model or imitate persons who are valued because of prestige and competence and who are perceived as like the self."[9] Thus, having a tutor of the same sex is crucial for role identification. Of course, the woman must be sensitive enough to establish a close personal dialogue with her student in addition to instructing her. Such a system of tutoring could have important ramifications, not only for the girl, but for Jewish society as a whole. Kohlberg discusses the importance of extrafamilial roles in determining sex-role differences.[10] If a thirteen-year-old girl sees that her teacher for this important synagogue event is a woman actively involved in study and ritual, she might perceive for herself the possibility of participating in Jewish life as an adult in a richer way than before.

Therefore, if only to share the complexity and struggle which characterize the Jewish women's movement, or to show young girls how committed Jewish women carry out their role in society, there is reason enough for women to take on the responsibility of tutoring girls for bat mitzvah. Although we may not have the answers to questions of Jewish womanhood ourselves, these girls are growing up hardly aware of the questions.

Having identified the salience of bat mitzvah to girls, and understanding that it is an event centered in the community itself, we can again ask how we can maximize this crucial period in the classroom. Here is a case in point.

The Ideal Bat Mitzvah

Men and women live in different bodies, and therefore have different life experiences. From reading Virginia Woolf's A Room of One's Own, and from my own experiences, I have come to believe that women should not merely copy men, but should discover their own modes of expression. I therefore think that bat mitzvah should not be an exact imitation of bar mitzvah, but should come to make a statement of its own.

The "ideal bat mitzvah" grew out of a class in my school for twelve-year-olds called The Bar/Bat Mitzvah Club. Designed to review basic religious beliefs, the curriculum was quickly changed due to a request by the students that the bar and bat mitzvah ceremonies themselves be addressed in class, since that was the experience they were all facing in the coming year. I responded to their request by ordering Thirteen, a film distributed by the Jewish Media Project, in which a group of children satirically portray their parents' concept of the bar mitzvah by juxtaposing the receiving lines, chopped liver hearts and fountain pens to their own ideas of an authentic religious experience. This touched my students deeply and they decided to make their own film.

First, the boys and girls, finding that their concerns were quite different, split into two working groups. The boys produced a clever and well-thought-out satire of bar mitzvah and felt satisfied with their work. The girls, however, were not content merely to satirize. Rather, they became involved in a process of self-discovery in which they faced the inadequacies of the present bat mitzvah ceremony and the need for change.

The girls dealt with a number of difficult issues, including the extent to which their Jewish education was a preparation for bat mitzvah, the way in which that event could play a more meaningful role in their lives, in what respects it could be different from a bar mitzvah, which traditional forms should be included, questions of ritual dress for women, and the roles of the congregation and families in the ceremony.

In the end they came up with a script that started with a flashback. The girls preparing for bat mitzvah would be thinking about their families, their Jewish education, their preparation for the day, and the commitments they would make. The ceremony itself would be different from usual. It would take place on Saturday morning because they wanted to be a part of the Torah service and wanted the Torah itself to be an integral part of their ceremony.

The Torah would be read in the midst of the congregation, not on a platform. Instead of only uncles having *aliyot,* uncles and aunts would say the blessings together. And before the Torah was blessed, each couple would say a blessing for the bat mitzvah girl which would be taken from tradition, such as, "May you grow to be as beautiful as Sarah, as wise as Beruriah, and as courageous as Deborah." Then the bat mitzvah's family would bring her up to the Torah, and the whole family would recite the traditional blessing as well as personal blessings for her. Finally, she herself would recite the blessings and read from the Torah and *haftarah.*

Since this was to be a film, the question arose of what the girls would wear. They decided not to wear the traditional male prayer shawl and skullcap. After weeks of discussion, they agreed upon the idea of designing a blue satin headband, with a meaningful verse from the Bible or prayerbook embroidered on it. They envisioned their prayer shawl as a jacket designed and decorated by each girl. The girls were quite pleased with their innovations. Since time was so short before the next week's bat mitzvah, I volunteered to make the first headband if the girl would choose the sentence for it. She looked through the Bible and chose a verse about the creation of light from Genesis.

On the day of her bat mitzvah, Devorah wore her headband proudly. At first the rabbi failed to mention it; later he told her it was pretty and that her face looked like the light mentioned in the verse. Although she had explained the significance of the headband to the rabbi in advance, he hadn't really understood. Devorah considered her act revolutionary; the rabbi thought it cute.

Despite this, every girl wore her headband in the following weeks, not only at her bat mitzvah, but every time she went into the synagogue. The girls felt that they were doing something important that was at best being ignored and at worst being discouraged. Eventually they lost confidence in the idea and dropped it.

Nevertheless, the following year, one of these girls decided to try the idea of the woman's prayer shawl. Karen picked out the material and her grandmother sewed the jacket. Another teacher and I helped her with the lettering and the design, and Karen wore her *tallit* at her bat mitzvah instead of the usual white robe. Her wearing of the *tallit* met with much controversy in the community. Given the vulnerabilities of this age group, the other girls were understandably unwilling to put themselves on the line as Karen had. Had the community supported them, other families might have had the moving experience that Karen, her mother, and I shared on the day of her bat mitzvah when we taught Karen how to tie the ritual knots on the *tallit* she had created.

All of this points out the potential power of the bat mitzvah experience for young women, provided it is not thwarted either by the experience itself or by the actions of the community. The bat mitzvah can be an incredibly strong ritual which could help frame the goals of adolescence in Jewish terms and perhaps help teen-agers feel more connected to Jewishness at this critical time in the formation of their identity.

Notes

1. Susan Rosenblum Shevitz, "Sexism in Jewish Education," *Response* 18 (Summer 1973): 107–13.

2. Cherie Koller, "Joy in the Classroom: the Open Classroom and the Jewish School," *Response* 12 (Winter 1971–72): 43–50.

3. See, for example, Daniel and Myra Leifer, "On the Birth of a Daughter," pp 21–30; Daniel Leifer, "On Writing New Ketubot," pp. 50–61; Mary Gendler, "Sarah's Seed—A New Ritual for Women," *Response* 24 (Winter 1974–75): 65–75.

4. S.N. Eisenstadt, "Archetypal Patterns of Youth," in Erik Erikson, ed. *The Challenge of Youth* (New York: Doubleday, 1965), pp. 33–34.

5. Bruno Bettelheim, "The Problem of the Generations," in Erik Erikson, ed. *The Challenge of Youth* (New York: Doubleday, 1965), pp. 76–110.

6. Elizabeth Douvan, "New Sources of Conflict in Females at Adolescence and Early Adulthood," in J.M. Barwick, ed. *Feminine Personality and Conflict* (Belmont, Calif.: Brooks and Cole Publishing Co.), pp. 31–43.

7. Matina Horner, "Toward an Understanding of Achievement-related Conflicts in Women," *Journal of Social Issues* XXVIII (2) (1972): 157–75.

8. Cherie Koller, "Sex Role Stereotyping in Adolescent Jewish Girls." Unpublished research.

9. Larry Kohlberg, "A Cognitive-Developmental Analysis of Children's Sex-role Concepts and Attitudes," in Eleanor Maccoby, ed., *The Development of Sex Differences* (Palo Alto, Calif.: Stanford University Press, 1974), p. 133.

10. Ibid.

SINGLE AND JEWISH: TOWARD A NEW DEFINITION OF COMPLETENESS

Laura Geller and Elizabeth Koltun

We have all grown up as daughters and sons in Jewish families expecting that some day we would have our own daughters and sons in our own families. We learned that Judaism was a family-centered tradition which was perpetuated through the family model. As daughters and sons we knew how to be Jewish; we had generations of role models. When we left our parents' home to go to university, there were still models because we were part of the university Jewish community where everyone else was like ourselves. When we left the protection of the university, the next step, of course, was to get married and start our own families. But those people who did not take the next step—or who chose to defer it for a while—have suddenly found themselves in limbo. To the extent that Judaism is a family-centered tradition, people who do not see themselves as part of a family have no models to express their Judaism. Since single people are no longer primarily defined as their parents' children, and are not—or at least not yet—defined as part of a couple and a new family, they do not fit into the Jewish community. As more people are choosing to marry later or to remain single, and as more people become single again after a period of marriage (either through divorce or the death of their spouse), the problem of single people and the Jewish community can be expected to grow dramatically in coming years.

Is there a place within Jewish life for a single person? To explore this question, we first need to examine the Jewish image of marriage. Tradition states very clearly that marriage is necessary for the good life. The primary statement of this value is found in the second chapter of

Genesis: "It is not good for man to be alone. I will make a helper for him. . . . Therefore a man leaves his father and his mother and cleaves to his wife, and they shall become one flesh." From this we learn that marriage is valued in that it provides companionship and support. It is also valued in that it creates a proper environment for the fulfillment of the *mitzvah* of *peru urevu,* procreation. The rabbis add a third value to marriage: it minimizes the possibility for illicit sexual activity. For example, a passage from Kiddushin 29b states: "He who reaches the age of twenty and has not married spends all his days in sin. 'Sin' actually? Say better, all his days in the thought of sin." The implication of this statement is that not being married leads one to temptation. Temptation exposes a man or a woman to suspicion and is considered an obstacle to holiness.

Marriage is viewed by Judaism as the paradigm of completeness. In Yevamot 63a it is stated: "A man without a wife is not called a man, as it is written: male and female created He them and He called *their* name Adam." We learn from Sanhedrin 22b that "A woman is a *golem,* a shapeless lump, and concludes a covenant of marriage only with him who transforms her into a finished vessel." Or again, from the Zohar (Zohar Hadash 4, 506), "The Divine Presence rests only upon a married man because an unmarried man is but half a man. The Divine Presence does not rest upon that which is imperfect."

We also find a very significant identification of "wife" with "home." For example, "Rabbi Yosei said, 'Never have I called my wife 'my wife,' but rather 'my home.' '" (Shabbat 118b). Additional evidence for this identification comes from Aramaic, the language of the Talmud, where the word for wife is *d'baita* (of the home). It seems, then, that to the extent that Judaism is a family- or home-centered tradition, a woman must become a wife to participate in it.

Is there any support within Judaism for an alternative view? There appears to be one famous exception to the model of marriage as the only acceptable life-style—that of the Talmudic sage Ben Azzai. When he was confronted by his colleagues about his nonmarried state, he excused himself by saying "What can I do? I am in love with the study of Torah! The world will be perpetuated by others." (Yevamot 63b). While the weight of tradition argues that Ben Azzai is not to be emulated, his example does offer the insight that not all people can be fulfilled by marriage. His example encourages us to redefine the traditional concept of completeness. Since marriage is the traditional paradigm for completeness, perhaps by isolating the purposes of marriage we can discover alternative models for completeness.

What are the elements of a complete Jewish life? Traditionally, marriage was seen as the way to ensure the essential elements of procreation, companionship, and avoidance of illicit sex. These three components of completeness can be redefined as commitment to Jewish survival, fulfilling human relationships, moral sexual activity (or avoidance of immoral sexual activity). We believe that these three values inherent in the traditional Jewish marriage can be maintained in a variety of life patterns and choices. Marriage is not and should not be seen as the only possible vehicle for attaining completeness, but rather one model among many. Other models and options may ensure Jewish completeness in a more satisfying and productive way for many people. We do not mean in any way to denigrate marriage, but to open the options more than they have been up till now.

We must emphasize that other models of the good life which incorporate the above elements are to be taken seriously because they are valid options for completeness today, and not merely because the refusal to accept them would cause pain to the excluded.

Let us now examine these components with a view toward other possible life choices and alternate life-styles which would incorporate them in a nontraditional way.

Commitment to Jewish Survival

Surely the centrality of procreation as a goal of marriage reflects the tradition's concern with the future of the Jewish people. Considering today's low Jewish birthrate and high rate of assimilation and intermarriage in America, there is just cause for concern about guaranteeing a Jewish future. However, it is a grave mistake to concentrate our concern on the rate of childbirth alone, as so many Jewish leaders have recently done, for surely we need great efforts to enrich the quality of Jewish life today so that there will be a meaningful Jewish life in coming years. People who choose not to have children, but to contribute to Jewish life in other ways, such as Jewish education, scholarship, service to the community, rescue of Soviet Jews, contributions to Jewish culture, philanthropy or building Eretz Yisrael, are performing vital tasks in building a Jewish future; tasks they might not be able to accomplish were they raising their own children. We would therefore expect a complete Jewish life to include some active commitment to the survival of Jewish traditions, values, and people, but we would affirm and value all of the myriad ways of expressing that commitment. The stress placed on having children as the essential way of expressing concern for Jewish survival is not only narrow and restrictive, but may be detrimental as well; for this attitude may contribute to a future in which Jewish children have no compelling reason to remain Jewish, and thus increase the assimilation, intermarriage, and apathy which the insistence on raising the birthrate is intended to combat. In addition, the Jewish birthrate might well be increased by more creative means as yet untried in our community, such as providing incentives, including Jewish day-care facilities, subsidies for Jewish education, and reduced medical costs for bearing children.

Companionship

The second element of the traditional ideal of marriage is companionship or relationship. Although in the past the state of marriage may have been the most effective way to attain committed and fulfilling relationships, this is certainly not true today for a large number of people. There are other models which are as satisfying and meaningful to the individuals involved as a monogamous institutionalized heterosexual union. Options in this area are so varied and changing that thorough examination of all possibilities is impossible here. What is most important is that each person have the freedom and encouragement to discover his or her own most fulfilling patterns. Among the alternate models which are being chosen today are (1) a close committed relationship with one central person, of the same or opposite sex. This relationship may or may not involve sexual intimacy, economic sharing, and living together. (2) the relationship of an individual to a group of people, be they a family, a commune, a friendship group, a havurah, or a Jewish communal group. (3) a variety of significant relationships with a variety of people, experienced either serially or simultaneously, possibly involving sexual relations as well.

We believe that relating on a meaningful level is essential to a complete Jewish life. But the style of that relating should be determined by the individual, sincerely striving to incorporate Jewish values and ethics in his or her life. The important questions to ask of relationships, we think, are not whether they are marital, but whether they are moral; whether they fulfill the needs and aspirations of all people involved, and whether they are Jewishly valid.

What is a Jewishly moral and valid relationship? This question is central to our lives and deserves careful and serious exploration. We can outline only a few elements here: respect for the other and for oneself as embodiments of the image of God, concern, responsibility, sensitivity, loving the other as yourself, caring for the lives of all people involved. These elements are essential in all Jewish relationships, and any relationship embodying them would have to be seen as sacred, valuable, and valid. Using these criteria, many nonmarital relationships are Jewishly complete, while many marital ones are not, despite the sanctions of the state and the rabbinate.

Avoidance of Illicit Sexual Behavior

In light of our criteria for moral relationships discussed above, we would ask for consideration of sexual relations in the categories of moral and immoral, rather than licit and illicit. The area of Jewish sexual ethics is a complex one and not amenable to easy answers. But in this area, perhaps more than any other, we must tread with great care and concern for individual needs and sensitivities. Traditional Jewish sexual laws are being questioned today, in part because many of them are based on assumptions about the nature of women which are unacceptable. Ancient definitions of adultery and values such as premarital virginity for women were founded on a view of women as valuable property belonging to her husband or father. Our lives and values are so different from those of our ancestors that this area must be subjected to thorough examination by our best minds and souls before we can arrive at an acceptable understanding of how our sexuality should reflect our Judaism. We would start, however, with an assumption that a relationship in which each saw himself and others as the image of God and acted on that understanding is the basis for beginning this crucial exploration.

The question should be raised of whether a heterosexual relationship—or even a sexual relationship—is the *sine qua non* of Jewish completeness. One element of the traditional view of marriage was certainly the belief that men and women are different, incomplete without each other, and can find wholeness only in uniting with their counterparts. This question is a deep and mystifying one and cannot be settled here. We might suggest, however, that as women and men experience their own liberation, they are discovering and exploring parts of themselves that were considered inappropriate in the past. Women are learning about their "masculine" attributes, while men are beginning to explore and value the "feminine" aspects of their personalities. It may be that, in time, we can find complementary masculinity and femininity within ourselves, within a group, and within a series of relationships in combinations and possibilities which are as yet unknown to us. If this were to happen, then it would no longer be true that each of us can complete ourselves only through union with the opposite sex, but can find our counterparts and attain wholeness in a variety of ways.

How can we restructure Jewish institutions so that they will create an environment conducive to the redefinition of completeness? First, we need to acknowledge the extent to which major Jewish institutions are built on a family- and couple-centered model. Consider the synagogue. The family orientation of the synagogue is evident in most of its activities. Most Conservative and Reform synagogues promote the notion of prayer as a shared family experience. It is difficult for a single person to feel comfortable in an environment where family is the dominant value. Family Shabbat services, traditions such as having only a married woman lighting the congregational candles, or a mother and daughter regularly lighting the candles for the congregation—all these alienate the single person. Perhaps it is most painful for the widowed or divorced person to experience such family-oriented rituals and, as a result, many simply leave the synagogue.

Social groups within the synagogue are generally directly related to marital status. Sisterhoods and brotherhoods tend to be—implicitly, at least—the territory of married people. People are organized into couples clubs or singles groups, the main purpose of the latter being to create couples for the couples club as soon as possible. Single people—whether they have chosen that status or whether they view their position as a temporary one that they would like to change —correctly perceive that they are an embarrassment to their synagogue and to their community.

It seems that by setting out the problem, the solution is obvious.

Instead of organizing people around marital status, synagogues and other institutions should organize around interest groups and task-oriented projects. Married people and single people who share similar interests might meet together—to study, to celebrate, to perform some synagogue-related task. The advantage of this alternative is clear. People's need for community would be satisfied at the same time that the basic tasks of the synagogue would be accomplished. This interest group orientation is applicable to other communal institutions as well—UJA-Federation, Y's, volunteer organizations, etc. For those single people interested in meeting potential mates, the odds are considerably increased when people come together out of a common interest rather than out of a common need to end the cause of their embarrassment. This arrangement can ultimately lead to groups of people of different statuses sharing common concerns and eventually common friendships. Within these groups, a person who chooses not to have children can partially satisfy his or her need to parent by interacting with other people's children; while the parents can satisfy their need for time away from their children.

The process of restructuring Jewish institutions must go hand in hand with open-mindedness about all the Jewishly valid options. Obviously, people who choose to marry should be encouraged, for marriage is one way (and the most traditionally acceptable way) to live a complete life. However, those who choose not to marry, who postpone marriage, who are unwillingly single, or who are not sure, also need and deserve support and encouragement. This process is one of reeducation, restructuring, rethinking and reevaluation for single and married people alike.

ON WRITING NEW KETUBOT
Daniel I. Leifer

The immediate concrete reality of working with couples who wish to express their mutual nonsexist relationship in the celebration of their Jewish marriage encouraged me to begin the writing of a new *ketubah*. In the fall of 1971, I began to meet such couples who had a positive and serious attitude toward Jewish tradition and who wanted very much to have a full and complete Jewish marriage ceremony. Interestingly, and of vital importance for this discussion, these people wanted to express the binding character of their relationship, which a marriage ceremony connoted to them, through the instrument of both a Jewish and a legal document. When they turned to the traditional *ketubah,* however, they were disappointed, and therefore sought some new form of this document to express both their traditional Jewish and their modern values.

The traditional *ketubah* was a great advance in its time, at the end of the first century C.E. For the first time, it provided a woman with a legal document that secured her status and bound her husband to make provision for her welfare while they lived together, and for her security, in case he should die, disappear or divorce her. However, this legal document was not a mutual one: it was a document which the man gave to the woman, not a document which the woman could give to the man. He promised to provide food, clothing, sustenance, and sexual rights to the woman and set aside a certain sum of money which would come to her upon the dissolution of the marriage. The woman was simply required to consent and accept this document. Of course, she had the right to refuse to accept the *ketubah* and the marriage; however, she could not function as an equal legal agent and had no legal standing equal to that of the man. The traditional *ketubah* presumed that a woman moved directly from the house of her parents or extended family to the house of her husband. Should the marriage dissolve, it was assumed that she would either return to her father's house or remarry almost immediately. The traditional *ketubah* was not designed to cope with the contemporary situation where a woman lives alone, works, and supports herself, nor with a situation where a woman might contribute the major economic support to the marriage, temporarily (while the man is in school, in job training or unemployed) or permanently (when the woman has a higher earning capacity).

In addition, the detailed economic arrangements spelled out in the extensive second section of the traditional *ketubah* are no longer observed even by many people who operate in an otherwise traditional context. References to the *mohar* (marriage gift) of two hundred silver *zuzim* and to the *nedunia* composed of the wedding outfit, are waived today in many traditional divorce proceedings. They have been a dead letter ever since the Emancipation, when even traditional Jews became subject to the economic laws of the modern secular nation-state. The economic arrangements which govern the dissolution of a marriage today are, even for most traditional Jews, handled by the civil courts. Therefore, this section of the *ketubah* strikes many people as simply meaningless.

For these three reasons: (1) the lack of mutuality and equality of legal status; (2) the change in a woman's economic and social situation; (3) the legal irrelevance of the economic aspects of the traditional *ketubah*, it became imperative to work to create a new traditional Jewish marriage contract.

I have worked with the following guidelines in the creation of new *ketubot,* a couple of which are to be found at the conclusion of this article: (1) A new *ketubah* must presuppose and express the equality of status—both personal and legal—of women and men. Its language and form must express full and complete mutuality in the promises each partner makes to the other. (2) A new *ketubah* should retain, as much as possible, the framework, language and style of the traditional *ketubah*. There must be an obvious parallelism and resonance between the old original form and the new one. (3) The text of the new *ketubah* must be simple and succinct. I do not believe that marriage contracts should say too much. To attempt to spell out in detail the mutual obligations and responsibilities of a man and woman in a marriage relationship is foolish, naïve, and unworkable. Therefore, the language should be general, but should touch upon a sufficient number of areas of life and values to encompass the broad totality of a marriage and mutual living relationship. (4) I believe that for a new *ketubah* to be a meaningful Jewish document, it must include some reference to the following categories: God, Torah-*mitzvot*, People of Israel. In contrast to the traditional *ketubah,* I and the couples with whom I have worked, believe that the *ketubah* should touch upon a relationship to God or to a transcendent dimension in existence in order to express the spiritual dimension of their relationship. Such traditional phrases as *yirat shamayim* (the fear or reverence for God) and *yirat hakodesh* (reverence for the holy) are appropriate inclusions. I believe that the mutuality of obligation and action in everyday areas of life must also be extended to the specific area of Jewish life; therefore, a reference to *mitzvot* and/or good deeds should also be included in a *ketubah.* Some reference to Torah as both instruction-study and commandment should also find its place here. Finally, the couple must express their rootedness in the concrete historical community of the people of Israel. These areas of value and commitment, I believe, should find their expression in every *ketubah,* though the language and details will vary from couple to couple, depending on the personal style of the partners.

Even at the outset of this endeavor, I knew that it would be impossible to create one single document appropriate to all couples and acceptable to all rabbis and members of even the liberal Jewish community. My experience has proved this to be true. Each couple is different and wishes to express their relationship and Jewish commitment and obligations in a different way. I work in the following manner: when a couple asks me to read their marriage service, I explain in detail the nature and historical background of the traditional *ketubah,* giving them a copy to read and discussing the problems inherent in the traditional document. I tell them about the innovations which have been made, giving them copies of some of the new versions which I have shared in creating. The couple has the option of choosing a traditional *ketubah* or an innovative one, a decision which is theirs by right. If they choose to create their own, they then work on their first version, guided by several models and the principles outlined above. We then revise the document together. Although I will exercise some authority in order to assure that the basic threefold Jewish values of God, Torah, Israel are in some fashion expressed in the *ketubah,* I do not censor. Once we have decided upon a text, I then translate it into

Hebrew, choosing, wherever possible, traditional rabbinic language and phraseology to express the thoughts and values of this new *ketubah*. Those couples who wish to have their *ketubah* hand-lettered and painted in the tradition of the illuminated *ketubot* of the Middle Ages are put in touch with a local artist-calligrapher.

The creation and use of a new nontraditional *ketubah* creates serious problems which must be faced by those who create and use such documents. We must recognize that this kind of *ketubah* is a private document, expressing the values of the marriage partners. It has no halakhic standing in the Jewish community. Every legal document, including the *ketubah,* presupposes the existence of a corporate community that recognizes the validity of the document and has the authority to enforce its provisions. Behind the traditional *ketubah* still stands the Orthodox halakhic community which provides the recognition and the sanction, however limited, which makes the traditional *ketubah* a recognized legal document. No such community, however, stands behind these new *ketubot* at present. It is symptomatic of our times that innovation and change occur on an individual or small-group basis and are not the product of a structured and broadly based community. The fragmentation of Jewish life, brought on in part by the Emancipation and the changed juridical status of the Jewish community within the secular nation-state, has made the creation of new halakhic communities almost impossible. Those new quasi-halakhic communities which are part of the *havurah* movement are so loose in their structure and law, and so averse to the concept of having and enforcing sanctions, that they cannot function as the corporate community which could give legal legitimacy to a new form of *ketubah*.

It is therefore my duty to impress upon people that an innovative *ketubah* has no legal authority within the Jewish community. The question then arises as to whether couples who use such a *ketubah* are legally married according to Jewish law. Since Jewish law recognizes common-law marriage, where witnesses can attest to the fact that a man and a woman are living together as husband and wife, that question can be answered affirmatively. Indeed, the halakhic tradition would consider this man and woman married. Should such a couple come before an Orthodox *bet din* (court of law), it would consider the traditional *ketubah* to be in effect even if the couple did not actually have such a document. So these new *ketubot* become, in effect, personal statements and documents rooted in the framework, values, and language of the traditional *ketubah*.

I do not believe that the legal problematics of new *ketubot* in any way invalidate the legitimacy of the creation and utilization of such documents. Ritual and halakhic innovation and creation in the Jewish community today can take place only as personal statement and individual creation. At most, such ritual and halakhic innovations can take place within the limited boundary of a *havurah* where that small human community provides the legal legitimacy and sanctions for change. Those who think that they can achieve major halakhic change within the existing Jewish community will perhaps be disappointed by my perspective. I believe, however, that those who are struggling to change Orthodox *halakhah* and/or the minds of the traditional Orthodox decision makers are wasting their time and energy. It is my conviction that change is effected through the creation of new alternate and rival Jewish rituals and halakhic forms which will ultimately affect and bring about change in the traditional forms and the traditional community.

A word should be said about the use of these new *ketubot* in the marriage ceremony. Prior to the marriage ceremony, I conduct a *kabalat kinyan* (legal acquisition of the document) as is done with a traditional *ketubah*. However, in this case, the *kabalat kinyan* is effected with both the man and the woman; witnesses sign the *ketubah* in Hebrew and in English. The witnesses, who must be Jewish and not related by blood to either of the marriage partners, may be either male or female. The *ketubah* is read in Hebrew and English under the *hupah* during the ceremony, either by me or by the couple themselves, reading the parts of the *ketubah* which express their promises to each other.

I think it would be helpful to comment upon the wedding ceremony itself, the context in which the *ketubah* is set. My preference—and that of most couples—is to read the full traditional wedding liturgy, which is brief, simple, and meaningful to most people. The traditional ceremony is very neatly structured—rather like a sandwich, to use a prosaic comparison. There is a prologue and an epilogue which are the wrapping; the slices of bread are represented by the two sets of blessings, the *birkhot erusin* (engagement blessings) and the *birkhot nisuin* or *kiddushin* (wedding or sanctification blessings), also known as the *sheva berakhot* (the seven blessings). Each of these sets of blessings is accompanied by a cup of wine from which the couple drink at the conclusion of the chanting of the blessings. The inner filling of the sandwich is represented by the exchange of rings and the reading of the *ketubah*. Traditionally, the Jewish marriage ceremony involved only one ring, given by the man to the woman. However, in almost all non-Orthodox, and even in some Orthodox weddings, the ceremony is a two-ring one. I fully support the practice of having both the woman and the man say exactly the same liturgical formula when placing the ring on the finger of the mate. In English translation: "By this ring you are made holy to me as my husband (or wife) according to the law of Moses and the people of Israel." Some women, who do not wish to say the full traditional liturgical statement which is said by the man, may choose from several variations of that formula, including one which omits the boldness of the innovation of having the woman state that what she does is "according to the law of Moses and the people of Israel."

The traditional wedding ceremony is built of discrete sections which easily allow for interpolations of prose or poetry selected or written by the couple. These can be read or sung by the rabbi, the couple, or a wedding guest. There are unlimited possibilities for music in the ceremony, my only caveat being that liturgical music from another faith not be used.

It is fascinating that the least halakhic aspect of the Jewish marriage ceremony is the one most tenaciously retained by Jews who are very much secularized and even by those who choose to have a civil marriage ceremony—the breaking of the glass, the epilogue to the ceremony. Beneath its articulated Jewish historical meaning (remembrance of the destruction of the Temple), this act has symbolic sexual-anthropological meaning. It is an obvious representation of the sexual consummation of the marriage by the breaking of the hymen. It also is an act of noisemaking employed to chase away the demons that might attack the couple as they pass through that liminal period between unmarried and married status. At present, the traditional manner of breaking the glass is the groom's stepping on it. This custom disturbs many people due to its violent and sexist character. My goal—of developing a nonsexist way of handling the breaking of the glass—has not yet been realized to my satisfaction, but two innovative suggestions follow: (1) to have both bride and groom step on the glass together, or to have each step on a separate glass; (2) to have them together hold the stem of the glass and break it by hitting it against a hard object such as a table top.

The conscious articulated historical meaning of the breaking of the glass captures a basic dimension of the Jewish marriage ceremony. As is well known, breaking the glass represents the destruction of the Temple in Jerusalem. The Temple is the arch symbol in Judaism for *galut* (exile), not yet redeemed historical time. As the sanctification blessing states, the couple under the *hupah* are viewed as existing in mythic rather than historical time. As Jacob Neusner points out in his article "Coming Together," in *"The Way of Torah: an Introduction to Judaism* (Encino, Calif.: Dickenson Publishing Co., 2d edition, 1974), pp. 15–17, the couple is likened to the first man and woman in the Garden of Eden and to the young men and women in the restored, rebuilt, and redeemed Jerusalem (Messianic time). At the moment of liminal existence, crossing from one stage of life to another, the couple exists beyond time and history. Thus they are protected at this dangerous moment of their lives by *hupah*, family and friends. Breaking the glass returns them to historical time. As they leave the *hupah*, they go out into the real world of their private and Jewish existence, an existence which is yet unredeemed, pre-Messianic, in *galut*. Because it is such a powerful symbol of this profound awareness of Jewish faith, I would argue for the retention of the act of breaking the glass and the finding of a nonsexist way of accomplishing the ritual.

Two marriage rituals remain to be mentioned. First, I recommend to couples that they appropriate and utilize in a traditional or nontraditional manner the custom of saying *viddui*, a personal confessional on the day of their marriage. The traditional Yom Kippur confessional prayer may be appropriate for some couples. However, the act of meditating upon and assessing one's existence up to the moment of marriage—the expression of regret for misdeeds committed and the yearning for wholeness and right deeds in one's new stage of life—is comprehensible and acceptable to all spiritually sensitive people. Second, I recommend that after the marriage ceremony, couples appropriate the traditional custom of *yihud* (uniting). This custom originally meant the immediate sexual consummation of the marriage. However, in traditional circles, it long ago came to mean the brief seclusion of the bride and groom in a room where they can eat together and share each other's quiet company after the ceremony. Given the hectic quality of most weddings, these brief moments of quiet and companionship are a meaningful way of bringing to a close the high seriousness of the marriage ceremony before moving on to the excitement and joy of the wedding celebration. I suggest that couples have prepared some food, such as wine and cheese, in a designated room where they can retire quietly even before taking their places on the reception line.

Many varied innovations have been created by couples in recent years who have sought to have a meaningful and traditional Jewish marriage ceremony. I have touched on but a few of the possibilities. Efforts should be made to collect and share this rich reservoir of new Jewish ritual expression.

Orthodox Ketubah

On the . . . day of the week, the . . . day of the month . . . , in the year five thousand, six hundred and . . . since the creation of the world, the era according to which we reckon here in the city of (name of city, state and country), that (name of bridegroom), son of (name of father), surnamed (family name), said to this virgin (name of bride), daughter of (name of father), surnamed (family name): "Be my wife according to the practice of Moses and Israel, and I will cherish, honor, support and maintain you in accordance with the custom of Jewish husbands who cherish, honor, support and maintain their wives faithfully. And I here present you with the marriage gift of virgins, two hundred silver zuzim, which belongs to you, according to the law of Moses and Israel; and (I will also give you) your food, clothing and necessities, and live with you as husband and wife according to universal custom." And Miss (name of bride), this virgin consented and became his wife. The trous-

בְּאֶחָד (בַּשְּׁלִישִׁי) בְּשַׁבָּת, אַחַד עָשָׂר יוֹם (יָמִים) [1] לַחֹדֶשׁ ......, שְׁנַת חֲמֵשֶׁת אֲלָפִים וְשֵׁשׁ מֵאוֹת וְ...... לִבְרִיאַת עוֹלָם לְמִנְיָן שֶׁאָנוּ מוֹנִין כָּאן ק"ק (עִיר) ...... בִּמְדִינַת אֲמֶרִיקָה הַצָּפוֹנִית, אֵיךְ הֶחָתָן ר' פ' בֶּן ר' פ' (הַכֹּהֵן) אָמַר לָהּ לַהֲדָא [1] בְתוּלְתָּא פ' בַּת ר' פ' הֱוִי לִי לְאִנְתּוּ כְּדַת מֹשֶׁה וְיִשְׂרָאֵל, וַאֲנָא אֶפְלַח וְאוֹקִיר וְאֵיזוֹן וַאֲפַרְנֵס יָתִיכִי (לִיכִי) כְּהִלְכוֹת גּוּבְרִין יְהוּדָאִין דְּפָלְחִין וּמוֹקְרִין וְזָנִין וּמְפַרְנְסִין לִנְשֵׁיהוֹן בְּקוּשְׁטָא. וְיָהֲבְנָא לִיכִי מֹהַר [2] בְּתוּלַיְכִי כְּסַף זוּזֵי מָאתָן דְּחָזֵי לִיכִי מִדְּאוֹרַיְתָא, וּמְזוֹנַיְכִי וּכְסוּתַיְכִי וְסִפּוּקַיְכִי, וּמֵיעַל לְנָתַיְכִי כְּאוֹרַח כָּל אַרְעָא. וּצְבִיאַת מָרַת פ' [3] בְּתוּלְתָּא דָא וַהֲוַת לֵהּ לְאִנְתּוּ. וְדֵין נְדוּנְיָא דְהַנְעֲלַת

seau that she brought to him from her father's house, in silver, gold, valuables, clothing, furniture, and bedclothes, all this (name of bridegroom), the said bridegroom accepted in the sum of one hundred silver pieces, and (name of bridegroom), the bridegroom, consented to increase this amount from his own property with the sum of one hundred silver pieces, making in all two hundred silver pieces. And thus said (name of bridegroom), the bridegroom: "The responsibility of this marriage contract, of this trousseau, and of this additional sum, I take upon myself and my heirs after me, so that they shall be paid from the best part of my property and possession that I have beneath the whole heaven, that which I now possess or may hereafter acquire. All my property, real and personal, even the shirt from my back, shall be mortgaged to secure the payment of this marriage contract, of the trousseau, and of the addition made to it, during my lifetime and after my death, from the present day and forever." (Name of bridegroom), the bridegroom, has taken upon himself the responsibility of this marriage contract, of the trousseau and the addition made to it, according to the restrictive usages of all marriage contracts and the additions to them made for the daughters of Israel, according to the institution of our sages of blessed memory. It is not to be regarded as a mere forfeiture without consideration or as a mere

לֵהּ מִבֵּי אֲבוּהָ בֵּין בְּכֶסֶף בֵּין בְּדַהַב בֵּין בְּתַכְשִׁיטִין, בְּמָאנֵי דִלְבוּשָׁא, בְּשִׁימוּשֵׁי דִירָה וּבְשִׁימוּשֵׁי דְעַרְסָא, הַכֹּל קִבֵּל עָלָיו ר' פ' חֲתַן דְּנַן בְּמֵאָה זְקוּקִים כֶּסֶף צָרוּף. וְצָבֵי ר' פ' חֲתַן דְּנַן וְהוֹסִיף לָהּ מִן דִּילֵהּ עוֹד מֵאָה זְקוּקִים כֶּסֶף צָרוּף אַחֲרִים כְּנֶגְדָּן, סַךְ הַכֹּל מָאתַיִם זְקוּקִים כֶּסֶף צָרוּף. וְכַךְ אָמַר ר' פ' חֲתַן דְּנַן, אַחֲרָיוּת שְׁטַר כְּתוּבְּתָא דָא, נְדוּנְיָא דֵן וְתוֹסֶפְתָּא דָא אֲרַג נְכַסִין וְקִנְיָנִין דְּאִית לִי תְּחוֹת כָּל שְׁמַיָּא, דְּקָנָאי וּדְעָתִיד אֲנָא לְמִקְנָא, נְכַסִין דְּאִית לְהוֹן אַחֲרָיוּת וּדְלֵית לְהוֹן אַחֲרָיוּת. כּוּלְּהוֹן יְהוֹן אַחֲרָאִין וְעַרְבָאִין לִפְרוֹעַ מִנְּהוֹן שְׁטַר כְּתוּבְּתָא דָא, נְדוּנְיָא דֵן וְתוֹסֶפְתָּא דָא מִנָּאי, וַאֲפִילוּ מִן גְּלִימָא דְעַל כַּתְפָּאי, בְּחַיֵּי וּבָתַר חַיַּי, מִן יוֹמָא דְנַן וּלְעָלַם. וְאַחֲרָיוּת שְׁטַר כְּתוּבְּתָא דָא, נְדוּנְיָא דֵן וְתוֹסֶפְתָּא דָא, קִבֵּל עָלָיו ר' פ' חֲתַן דְּנַן כְּחוֹמֶר כָּל שְׁטָרֵי כְּתוּבּוֹת וְתוֹסָפְתּוֹת דְּנָהֲגִין בִּבְנוֹת יִשְׂרָאֵל, הָעֲשׂוּיִין כְּתִקּוּן חֲכָמִינוּ זִכְרָם לִבְרָכָה, דְּלָא כְּאַסְמַכְתָּא וּדְלָא כְּטוֹפְסֵי

ormula of a document. We have fol-
owed the legal formality of symbolic
elivery *(kinyan)* between (name of
ridegroom), the son of . . ., the
ridegroom, and (name of bride), the
aughter of . . ., this virgin, and we
ave used a garment legally fit for the
urpose, to strengthen all that is
tated above,

דִּשְׁטָרֵי. וְקָנִינָא מִן ר׳ פ׳ בֶּן פ׳ (הַכֹּהֵן)
חֲתַן דְּנָן לְמָרַת פ׳ בַּת פ׳ בְּתוּלְתָּא דָא
עַל כָּל מַה דְּכָתוּב וּמְפוֹרָשׁ לְעֵיל בְּמָאנָא
דְּכָשֵׁר לְמִקְנֵא בֵיהּ,

וְהַכֹּל שָׁרִיר וְקַיָם.

נְאוּם פ׳ בֶּן פ׳ עֵד. ....

וּנְאוּם פ׳ בֶּן פ׳ עֵד. ....

**AND EVERYTHING IS VALID
AND CONFIRMED.**

ttested to ....(Witness)

ttested to ....(Witness)

New Ketubot

June 13, 1973

On the fourth day of the week of
e portion ''The Lighting of the
andles,''on the thirteenth day of the
onth of Sivan in the year 5733 since
e creation of the world, according
o our accustomed reckoning in the
ity of Chicago, Illinois,

The groom, Jeremy Alan Brochin,
aid to the bride, Reena Miriam
picehandler, ''Let us make a mar-
age covenant. Be a wife to me ac-
ording to the law of Moses and Israel
nd I will honor and respect you and
ork for our sustenance and will live
ith you in the manner of all the
arth so that we may sanctify our
ves and establish a home in Israel in
oliness and purity, with love of
orah and respect for the Divine and
ith good deeds according to the

בָּרְבִיעִי בְּשַׁבָּת פָּרָשַׁת בְּהַעֲלוֹתְךָ אֶת
הַנֵּרוֹת בִּשְׁלוֹשָׁה עָשָׂר יוֹם לְחוֹדֶשׁ סִיוָן
בִּשְׁנַת חֲמֵשֶׁת אֲלָפִים וּשְׁבַע מֵאוֹת שְׁלוֹשִׁים
וְשָׁלוֹשׁ לִבְרִיאַת עוֹלָם לַמִּנְיָן שֶׁאָנוּ מוֹנִים
כָּאן בָּעִיר שִׁיקָגוֹ בִּמְדִינַת אִילִינוֹי
שֶׁבְּאַרה"ב אָמַר הֶחָתָן יְהוּדָה אַבָּא בֶּן
דוֹב וּבַתְיָה הַמְכוּנֶה בְּרוּכִין שֶׁיִּחְיֶה אֶל
הַכַּלָּה רִינָה מִרְיָם בַּת עֶזְרָא וְשִׁירְלִי
שֶׁתִּחְיֶה הָבָה נִכְרוֹת בְּרִית נִישּׂוּאִין
וְתִהְיִי לִי לְאִשָּׁה כְּדַת מֹשֶׁה וְיִשְׂרָאֵל
וַאֲנִי אַעֲרִיץ וְאוֹקִיר אוֹתָךְ וְאֶעֱבוֹד
לְפַרְנָסָתֵנוּ וְאֶחְיֶה אִתָּךְ כְּאוֹרַח כָּל אַרְעָא
לְמַעַן נְקַדֵּשׁ אֶת חַיֵּינוּ וְנָקִים בַּיִת
בְּיִשְׂרָאֵל בִּקְדוּשָׁה וּבְטַהֲרָה בְּאַהֲבַת תּוֹרָה
וּבְיִרְאַת שָׁמַיִם וּבְמַעֲשִׂים טוֹבִים וּבִשְׁמִירַת
מִנְהֲגֵי יִשְׂרָאֵל בֶּאֱמוּנָה.

customs of Israel." And the bride Reena consented and became a wife to Jeremy, entering into a marriage covenant with him.

And the bride, Reena Miriam Spicehandler, said to the groom, Jeremy Alan Brochin, "Let us make a marriage covenant. Be a husband to me according to the law of Moses and Israel and I will love and respect you and work for our sustenance and live with you in the manner of all the earth so that we may sanctify our lives and estalish a home in Israel in holiness and purity, in love of Torah and respect for the Divine, with good deeds, according to the customs of Israel." And the groom Jeremy consented and became a husband to Reena, entering into a marriage covenant with her.

This contract has been legally acquired and accepted by the groom, Jeremy Alan Brochin, and by the bride, Reena Miriam Spicehandler. And everything is valid and confirmed.

Attested to by .... Witness

Attested to by .... Witness

Groom ....

Bride ....

וְהַכַּלָּה רִינָה מִרְיָם בַּת עֶזְרָא וְשִׁירְלִי
שֶׁתִּהְיֶה הִסְכִּימָה לִדְבָרָיו וּבָאָה בִּבְרִית
נִישׂוּאִין עִם הֶחָתָן יְהוּדָה אַבָּא בֶּן דוֹב
יִבַתְיָה שֶׁתִּחְיֶה.

וְאָמְרָה הַכַּלָּה רִינָה מִרְיָם בַּת עֶזְרָא
שִׁירְלִי הַמְכוּנָה שְׁפַּייהֶנְדְלֶר שֶׁתִּהְיֶה אֶל
חָתָן יְהוּדָה אַבָּא בֶּן דוֹב וּבַתְיָה הַמְכוּנָה
רוּכִין שֶׁיִּחְיֶה הָבָה נִכְרוֹת בְּרִית נִישׂוּאִין
תִהְיֶה לִי לְבַעַל כְּדַת מֹשֶׁה וְיִשְׂרָאֵל
אֲנִי אֱעֱרִיץ וְאוֹקִיר אוֹתָךְ וְאֶעֱבוֹד
פַּרְנָסָתֵנוּ וְאֶחְיֶה אִתָּךְ כְּאוֹרַח כָּל אַרְעָא
מַעַן נְקַדֵּשׁ אֶת חַיֵּינוּ וְנָקִים בֵּית
יִשְׂרָאֵל בִּקְדוּשָׁה וּבְטָהֳרָה בְּאַהֲבַת תּוֹרָה
בְּיִרְאַת שָׁמַיִם וּבְמַעֲשִׂים טוֹבִים וּבִשְׁמִירַת
וְנֶהֱגֵי יִשְׂרָאֵל בֶּאֱמוּנָה. וְהֶחָתָן יְהוּדָה
אַבָּא בֶּן דוֹב וּבַתְיָה הִסְכִּים לִדְבָרֶיהָ
בָּא בִּבְרִית נִישׂוּאִין עִם הַכַּלָּה רִינָה
רְיָם בַּת עֶזְרָא וְשִׁירְלִי שֶׁתִּחְיֶה.

וְקַיֵּימְנוּ קִנְיָן מִן הֶחָתָן יְהוּדָה אַבָּא
ן דוֹב וּבַתְיָה לַכַּלָּה רִינָה מִרְיָם בַּת
זְרָא וְשִׁירְלִי וּמִן הַכַּלָּה רִינָה מִרְיָם
ת עֶזְרָא וְשִׁירְלִי לַחָתָן יְהוּדָה אַבָּא בֶּן
וֹב וּבַתְיָה עַל כָּל מַה שֶׁכָּתוּב וּמְפוֹרָשׁ
מַעֲלָה וְחָתַמְנוּ עַל שְׁטַר כְּתוּבָּה זֶה
כֹּל שָׁרִיר וְקַיָּים
נְאוּם .... עֵד
נְאוּם .... עֵד

On the first day of the week, the ?enth day of the month of Hesh-? , in the year five thousand seven ?dred and thirty-six since the crea-? of the world, according to our ?customed reckoning in the city of ?icago, Illinois, in the United States ? America.

As is the custom of the people of ?ael and under the laws of Moses, ?, JONATHAN MATTHEWS ?BIN and GRETTA SPIER, stand be-?e family and friends to affirm our ?tention to be husband and wife: ?rtners in marriage. We will estab-? and maintain our home amidst ?e community of Israel, guided al-?ays by reverence for God which we ?pe to instill in our children.

We see loving relationships ?ound us and we will learn from ?em. In particular, we plan to share ?y and drudgery; to be responsible ? and for each other; to be one and ?t remain individuals; and to strive ?r growth, intellectual and emo-?nal, individually and together.

This contract has been legally ac-?ired and accepted by the groom, ?NATHAN MATTHEWS RUBIN, ?d the bride, GRETTA SPIER. And ?erything is valid and confirmed.

?tested to by ....Witness

?ttested to by ....Witness

?room ....

?ride...

?abbi...

October 12, 1975

בְּאֶחָד בְּשַׁבָּת, בְּשִׁבְעָה יָמִים לְחֹדֶשׁ מַרְחֶשְׁוָן, שְׁנַת חֲמֵשֶׁת אֲלָפִים וּשְׁבַע מֵאוֹת וּשְׁלֹשִׁים וְשֵׁשׁ לִבְרִיאַת עוֹלָם, לַמִּנְיָן שֶׁאָנוּ מוֹנִים כָּאן בָּעִיר שִׁיקָאגוֹ, בִּמְדִינַת אִילִינוֹי, שֶׁבְּאַרְצוֹת הַבְּרִית.

כְּמִנְהֲגֵי עַם יִשְׂרָאֵל וּכְדַת מֹשֶׁה, אֲנַחְנוּ, יוֹנָתָן מַתִּתְיָהוּ בֶּן מְנַחֵם מֶנְדְּל וִיטָא, הַמְכוּנֶּה רוּבִּין, וְחַנָּה בַּת אַבְרָהָם וְשָׂרָה, הַמְכוּנָּה סַפִּיר, עוֹמְדִים בְּנוֹכְחוּת מִשְׁפַּחְתֵּנוּ וַחֲבֵרֵינוּ לְאַשֵּׁר אֶת כַּוָּנָתֵינוּ לִהְיוֹת בַּעַל וְאִשָּׁה, שׁוּתָּפִים בִּבְרִית נִשּׂוּאִין. אֲנַחְנוּ נָקִים וּנְקַיֵּים בֵּיתֵינוּ בְּתוֹךְ עֲדַת עַם יִשְׂרָאֵל וְיִרְאַת שָׁמַיִם שֶׁיָּאִיר אֶת אוֹרַח חַיֵּינוּ כָּל הַיָּמִים, אוֹתָהּ נִטַּע בְּתוֹךְ לִבְבוֹת צֶאֱצָאֵינוּ.

אֲנַחְנוּ רוֹאִים יַחֲסֵי אַהֲבָה סְבִיבָתֵינוּ וְנִלְמַד מֵהֶם, בִּמְיֻחָד, אֲנַחְנוּ מִתְכַּוְונִים לְשַׁתֵּף שִׂמְחָה וַעֲבוֹדָה מְיַגַּעַת, לִהְיוֹת אַחְרָאִים אֶחָד לַשֵּׁנִי וּלְמַעַן הַוִּלַת, לְהִתְיַחֵד אַךְ לְהִשָּׁאֵר יְחִידִים, וּלְהִתְאַמֵּץ לְהִתְפַּתְּחוּת הַשֵּׂכֶל וְהָרֶגֶשׁ בְּנִפְרָד וּבְצַוְותָּא.

וְקִיַּמְנוּ קִנְיָן מִן הֶחָתָן, יוֹנָתָן מַתִּתְיָהוּ בֶּן מְנַחֵם מֶנְדְּל וִיטָא, לַכַּלָּה, חַנָּה בַּת אַבְרָהָם וְשָׂרָה, וּמִן הַכַּלָּה, חַנָּה בַּת אַבְרָהָם וְשָׂרָה, לַחָתָן, יוֹנָתָן מַתִּתְיָהוּ בֶּן מְנַחֵם מֶנְדְּל וִיטָא.

וְהַכֹּל שָׁרִיר וְקַיָּם.

נְאוּם .... עֵד

נְאוּם .... עֵד

TUMAH *AND* TAHARAH: *ENDS AND BEGINNINGS*

Rachel Adler

And death shall have no dominion
Dead men naked they shall be one
With the man in the wind and the west moon;
When their bones are picked clean and the clean
    bones gone,
They shall have stars at elbow and foot;
Though they go mad they shall be sane,
Though they sink through the sea they shall rise again;
Though lovers be lost love shall not;
And death shall have no dominion.

——Dylan Thomas

In water everything is "dissolved," every "form" is broken up, every-thing that has happened ceases to exist; nothing that was before remains after immersion in water, not an outline, not a "sign," not an event. Immersion is the equivalent, at the human level, of death at the cosmic level, of the cataclysm (the Flood) which periodically dissolves the world into the primeval ocean. Breaking up all forms, doing away with the past, water possesses the power of purifying, of regenerating, of giving new birth. Water purifies and regenerates because it nullifies the past, and restores—even if only for a moment—the integrity of the dawn of things.

——Mircea Eliade

All things die and are reborn continually. The plant which bows its head to the earth leaves its life capsulized in the dormant seed. In our own bodies, death and regeneration proceed cell by cell. Our finger-nails grow, die, and are discarded; our hair also. Our skins slough off dead cells, while a tender new layer forms below the surface. Within us our organs repair and renew themselves repeatedly. Throughout each teeming and dying body, moreover, flows an undying spirit. It is confined to no single area, but, as the Sages taught, it "fills the body as the ocean fills its bed." That spirit is the soul. Only a conscious being has a soul. Of what is such a being conscious? He is aware of himself. He is aware also of his own growth process and of his history. Our consciousness tells us that we are created beings and so are mortal. Our soul tells us that we are the image of the Creator and so cannot be mortal. Our knowledge of ourselves, then, is paradoxical. How do we reconcile it and make ourselves whole? Jews solve the paradox with the ritual cycle of *tumah* and *taharah,* in which we act out our death and resurrection.

II

> O dark dark dark. They all go into the dark,
> The vacant interstellar spaces, the vacant into
> the vacant . . .
>
> ——T.S. Eliot

Tumah is the result of our confrontation with the fact of our own mortality. It is the going down into darkness. *Taharah* is the result of our reaffirmation of our own immortality. It is the reentry into light. *Tumah* is evil or frightening only when there is no further life. Otherwise, *tumah* is simply part of the human cycle. To be *tameh* is not wrong or bad. Often it is necessary and sometimes it is mandatory.

It was not so for the primitive religions, the soil out of which our *tumah* and *taharah* symbolism grew. For them, *tumah* was pollution. The source of pollution was a source of danger, and a polluted person was both endangered and dangerous.

> A polluting person is always in the wrong. He has developed some wrong condition or simply crossed some line which should not have been crossed and this displacement unleashes danger for someone.
>
> ——Mary Douglas, *Purity and Danger*

Thus the menstruating woman might have the power to cause illness or death. The corpse, in some societies, was so dangerous that the dying had to be carried outside the village to breathe their last. Or the corpse had to be mutilated to prevent it from doing harm. In other societies, those who had the task of burying the dead were permanently polluted.

In a Jewish society, however, *tumah* was not perceived as causing physical consequences, nor was it viewed as dangerous in any way. Since some of the basic human functions and behaviors caused *tumah*, every member of the society regularly underwent the cycle from *tumah* to *taharah*. Nor were even the most intense sources of *tumah*, such as a corpse, treated with dread and avoidance. Everyone, even the *kohen*, who otherwise had to avoid the *tumah* of corpses, was obligated by the Torah to participate in the burial of a parent, sibling, spouse, or child. Similarly, it was a special *mitzvah* to bury an unburied corpse which one found. If no other person was available to perform this *mitzvah*, a *kohen* was obligated to do so. The *kohen* also contracted special forms of *tumah* in the purification rituals in which he officiated. Thus *tumah* was an accepted component of the human condition. Neither fear nor disgust is associated with *tumah* in Jewish law. The Prophets made such associations when they saw the *tumah* of the Jewish people as detached from its place in the cycle. They saw a *tumah* for which there seemed to be no *taharah*, and they hid their eyes before the vision of everlasting darkness.

How, then, does one contract *tumah?* Its most powerful source is a human corpse. Touching this inanimate shell, we recall that a person inhabited it, willing it to sing, to make love, to pray. Whoever touches a human corpse sees in its face his own. Whoever is in the presence of death is in the presence of his own death. For that reason, whoever comes into contact with a corpse or is in the same room with one himself becomes a source of *tumah* and imparts *tumah* to others upon contact. An animal carcass also is a source of *tumah*, although its *tumah* is less powerful than that of the corpse. Nevertheless, it breathed, it moved upon the earth, and now it is still. We recognize its stillness as our own. *Tumah* is also caused by the Biblical disease *tzaraat*, usually translated "leprosy." The person who had *tzaraat* had to withdraw from society until he was cured, and that, perhaps, is why the Sages compared him to a dead man.

"In my beginning is my end," writes T.S. Eliot. In all creation is the seed of destruction. All that is born dies, and all that begets. Begetting and birth are the nexus points at which life and death are coupled.

They are the beginnings which point to an end. Menstruation, too, is a nexus point. It is an end which points to a beginning. At the nexus points, the begetter becomes *tameh*. The fluids on which new life depends—the semen, the rich uterine lining which sustains embryonic life—the departure of these from the body leaves the giver *tameh*. The menstrual blood, which inside the womb was a potential nutriment, is a token of dying when it is shed. Menstruation is an autumn within, the dying which makes room for new birth. Semen has always symbolized man's vital force. That is why in so many cultures the idea existed (and still exists) that a man's semen supply is limited, and when it is depleted he will die. Men may have associated this old belief with the feeling of exhaustion which follows sexual intercourse, or perhaps it is simply the feeling of one's consciousness being yielded up and borne on an overwhelming tide which has caused poets of all nations and all times to link love and death. Such an association must underlie the Elizabethan slang term for orgasm, "dying."

The nexus points are those in which there appears to be a departure or a transfer of vital force. One of the most powerful nexus points, therefore, is childbirth. The infant who passes from the womb into the world undergoes a transition from potential life into life itself. The womb of woman is associated with the womb of earth. Living things grow out of the earth; dead things return to it and are buried in it. Seeds must be buried to bring them to life. The womb is the dark warm place in which we do not live, but live *in potentia*. We think of death as a return to the womb because the womb is the place of birth.

III

What we call the beginning is often the end
And to make an end is to make a beginning.
The end is where we start from . . .
. . . And any action
Is a step to the block, to the fire, down the sea's throat,
Or to an illegible stone: and that is where we start.
We die with the dying:
See, they depart and we go with them.
We are born with the dead:
See, they return, and bring us with them.

——T. S. Eliot

What were the practical consequences of *tumah?* When one became *tameh,* he acted out his own death by withdrawing from the great life-affirming Jewish symbols. A *niddah*—a menstruating woman—could not engage in sexual intercourse; a person with *tzaraat* was isolated from human society; and no person in any category of *tumah* could enter the great Temple at Jerusalem. It is easy to see why the great Temple would have been interdicted for the *tameh.* There was the dwelling of the Master of time, the God whose dread and unarticulated name meant "was-is-will be." Who but the deathless can stand in the presence of the undying King? The laws of *taharah* teach men to impersonate immortality. It is a mask we assume, this *taharah,* just as *tumah* is a mask of death. Even after the Israelites and the sanctuary have been readied for the Shekhinah by means of the rites of *taharah,* the Torah still speaks of the Tent of Meeting—the earthly resting-place of the Shekhinah—as abiding "with them in the midst of their *tumah*" (Leviticus l6:l6). Ultimately our *taharah* is but a mime of *taharah,* a shadow of the *taharah* of God, a semblence of our own *taharah* which is to be.

The duration of *tumah* is divided into two parts; the duration of contact with that which renders one *tameh,* and a period of dormancy whose length is determined by the type of *tumah* contracted. At the end of the dormancy, the one who is *tameh* immerses himself in a *mikveh.* For those with *tzaraat* or the *tumah* of corpses, there was an additional purification ritual which is no longer extant.[1] The *mikveh* is what is referred to in the Bible as *mayim hayyim*—literally, "living water;" that is, running water as opposed to stagnant water. Any natural gathering of water at least forty *seah* in volume constitutes a natural *mikveh.* This would include ponds, lakes, rivers, and seas.

There is also a way to make a legally valid approximation of a natural *mikveh,* using water collected only through the force of gravity. The water—usually rainwater—is permitted to fall into a huge container called the *bor,* or pit, since it usually extends beneath the ground surface. Around this *bor* a building is built containing small sunken pools, each sharing a wall with the *bor.* Each shared wall has a hole cut in it which can be plugged up or left open. In order to make the adjoining pools into legally valid *mikvaot,* they are "seeded" with *bor* water and then filled with regular tap water. When the hole between the pool and the *bor* is unplugged so that the waters are touching (or as the sources put it, "kissing"), the pool becomes a valid *mikveh.*

The *mikveh* simulates the original living water, the primal sea from which all life comes, the womb of the world, the amniotic tide on which the unborn child is rocked. To be reborn, one must reenter this womb and "drown" in living water. We enter the *mikveh* naked, as an infant enters the world. We stand in the water, feet slightly apart, arms outstretched frontward and fingers spread. The lips, too, should be loosely compressed and the eyes loosely closed. Then we bend the knees so that the entire body including the head and all the hair are simultaneously covered by water, and we reemerge. At this point, a *niddah* says a blessing. So does a convert, since immersion in a *mikveh* is the final step in conversion, the rebirth of a Gentile as a Jew. The blessing is followed by a second immersion. We emerge from the *mikveh tahor,* having confronted and experienced our own death and resurrection. *Taharah* is the end beyond the end, which constitutes a beginning, just as the Messianic "end of days" is in actuality the beginning of days.

> Rabbi Akiva said: Happy are you, Israel! Before whom do you make yourselves *tahor,* and who makes you *tahor?* Your Father in heaven. As it is written, "The *mikveh* of Israel is the Lord" (Jeremiah 17:13). Just as the *mikveh* makes *tahor* those who are *tameh,* so the Holy One makes Israel *tahor.*   —Mishnah Yoma 8:9

Sources

Biblical:
  Leviticus 12:1-18; 13; 14; 15:1-33
  Numbers 19:1-22

Talmudic: Mishnayot Negaim, Parah, and Niddah

Post-Talmudic:
  Miamonides *Mishneh Torah,* Book of Toharah; esp. Hilkhot Tumat Met, Hilkhot Tzaraat, Hilkhot Metameh Mishkav Umoshav, and Hilkhot Mikvaot. *Shulkhan Arukh:* Yoreh Deah: Hilkhot Niddah, sec. 183-200

Notes

1. The purification rituals for corpse *tumah* and *tzaraat* present excellent examples of symbolism using life-death nexus. These two types of *tumah* represent the most concrete experiences of death, and therefore, immersion in a *mikveh,* while necessary, is in itself insufficient to remove the *tumah.* The

ceremony for removing the *tumah* of corpses utilized the ashes of a red heifer which was slaughtered and burned with scarlet wool, cedar and hyssop added to the fire. The ashes were mixed with *mayim hayyim*, "living" water, and sprinkled upon the *tameh* with a spray of hyssop. Among those things which are burned, the color red predominates. Red is the color of blood, which itself symbolizes both life and death. Blood is the vehicle through which life pulsates through the living body. To kill someone is to "shed his blood." Ashes, a death symbol, are mixed with *mikveh* water, a life symbol. Hyssop is a plant, and probably symbolizes vegetative life. The mixture itself, then, becomes one of the fluids associated with the life-death nexus and thus, it creates a bridge over which the dead travel toward life and the living toward death. That is why the *tameh* person who is sprinkled with the mixture becomes *tahor*, while the *tahor* who sprinkles or touches it becomes *tameh*.

Similarly, the purification ritual for *tzaraat* utilizes nexus symbolism. The *kohen* was to take two birds of a *tahor* species. One bird was to be killed and its blood mixed with "living water." Then the *kohen* was to take scarlet, cedar, hyssop, and the living bird, dip them in the blood and water, and sprinkle the *tzaraat* victim with the mixture. The living bird was then freed and allowed to fly away. Clearly the two birds represent life and death. The cedar and scarlet wool both enhance the blood symbolism. The mixture of blood and "living water" is another life-death amalgam, while the hyssop, again, may represent vegetative life.

Editorial Note

The laws of *niddah* raise several issues of concern to women—and particularly to feminists—which are, however, left untouched in Ms. Adler's article. Perhaps the most vexing is: Why were the restrictions imposed upon the menstruating woman retained after the destruction of the Temple, while all other forms of *tumah* were allowed to lapse? Women of childbearing age are thus the only Jews regularly *tameh* fifty per cent of the time. It is difficult to avoid the implication that we are dealing here with the potent residue of an ancient taboo based on a mixture of male fear, awe, and repugnance toward woman's creative biological cycle.

Furthermore, is there really no stigma attached to the concept of *tumah* especially as practiced in the isolation of the *niddah*? She is treated, after all, as though bearing a rather unpleasant contagious disease. The prolongation of her period of *tumah* for seven days after the cessation of her menstrual flow reinforces the impression that the menstrual blood itself has powerful contaminating properties which must be guarded against.

If the concept of the life-death nexus inherent in the menstrual cycle is to be stressed, rather than the *tumah* of the female, the time of nexus should be observed by the couple who together embody the potential for creating new life. This could be achieved most meaningfully not merely through joint sexual abstinence, but through joint or simultaneous visits to the *mikveh* when the period of *tumah* is ended.

In response to a letter from the editors, Ms. Adler wrote the following additional explanation of her article:

When we consider the meaning of *niddah*, we encounter two equally well documented but exactly opposite contentions. The first contention—the one to which I devoted my article—is that viewed in context within the symbol system of *tumah/taharah*, *niddah* is not a ritual which oppresses or denigrates women. Indeed *tumah/taharah* constitutes one of the few major Jewish symbolisms equally accessible to men and women.

The second contention is that Jewish women experience *niddah* as prejudicial. It seems to express a paradoxical loathing on the part of men for the rich uterine lining which was both food and cradle to them during nine fetal months. If *niddah* is not singled out for especially punitive treatment, women ask, then why is it the only form of *tumah* to which days were added by the rabbis? They might add that anyone who doubts rabbinic hostility toward female functions and anatomy should read tractate Niddah, making note of terminology like *bet hatorfa* (literally, place of rot) designating the uterus (Niddah 57b) or halakhic exegesis from prophetic passages filled with sexual disgust (Niddah 4lb). Finally, *niddah* exemplifies a halakhic method in which woman is viewed purely as an object with which the truly human (man) may do *mitzvot* or commit *averot* (sins).

Both these contentions are true. Originally *tumah/taharah* was simply a way of learning how to die and be reborn. A dominant strain in Talmudic thought, however, stresses woman's alienness, her differentness from man. Some sages, moreover, were influenced by a powerful asceticism. Hence, the Talmudic elaborations upon *tumat niddah*. History, too, served to isolate *niddah*. After the destruction of the Temple, most of the laws of *tumah* applying to men were no longer in force. The red heifer ritual was lost, and many authorities ruled that men need not go to the *mikveh* after the loss of semen, but might remain in their state of *tumah*. *Niddah* survived because the Biblical prohibition against intercourse with a *niddah* applies whether the Temple stands or not. In a world in which everyone was *tameh*, women, ironically, became the only visibly impure people.

A newly created legal category, the Purity of the Family (*taharat ha-mishpahah*) made *tumah* a special condition afflicting only women. The *mitzvah* itself was reinterpreted, not as an individual spiritual experience born out of the metaphor of one's own bodily cycle, but as an enabling activity through which women safeguarded the purity of husbands and children: the purity of the *family*.

Yet all this evidence, damning as it is, does not invalidate the original *mitzvah*. *Tumah/taharah* remains one of the few major Jewish symbolisms in which women had a place. Having so few authentic traditional experiences on which to build, is it worthwhile to reject *niddah*, because later generations of men have projected their repugnance for women upon it? Ought we not, rather, to urge men to recognize the process of death and renewal in their own bodies, not simply by joining us in our immersions, but by reappropriating immersion after the loss of semen, as the tradition offers precedent for them to do?

PORTNOY'S MOTHER'S COMPLAINT: DEPRESSION IN MIDDLE-AGED WOMEN

Pauline Bart

> A young man begs his mother for her heart, which his betrothed has demanded as a gift. Having torn it out of his mother's proffered breast, he races away with it; and as he stumbles, the heart falls to the ground, and he hears it question protectively, "Did you hurt yourself, my son?"
> ——Jewish folktale

Mrs. Gold is a young-looking Jewish housewife in her forties. A married daughter lives about 20 miles away. Her hyperactive brain-damaged thirteen-year-old son has been placed in a special school even farther away. After his departure she became suicidally depressed and was admitted to a mental hospital. I asked her how her life was different now, and she answered:

> It's a very lonely life, and this is when I became ill, and I think I'm facing problems now that I did not face before because I was so involved, especially having a sick child at home. I didn't think of myself at all. I was just someone that was there to take care of the needs of my family, my husband and children, especially my sick child. But now I find that I—I want something for myself, too. I'm a human being, and I'm thinking about myself.

Although she believes her life was "fuller, much fuller, yes, much fuller" before her children left, she used to have crying spells:

> But in the morning I would get up, and I knew that there was so much dependent on me, and I didn't want my daughter to become depressed about it or neurotic in any way, which could have easily happened

because I had been that way. So I'm strong-minded and strong-willed, so I would pull myself out of it. It's just recently that I couldn't pull myself out of it. I think that if there was—if I was needed maybe I would have, but I feel that there's really no one that needs me now.

Her inability to admit anger toward her children and her perfectionist demands on herself are shown in the following remark: "It was extremely hard on me, and I think it has come out now. Very hard. I never knew I had the amount of patience. *That child never heard a raised voice.*"

Since she had used her daughter as a confidante when the daughter was a teen-ager, she lost a friend as well as a child with her daughter's departure. Mrs. Gold said she didn't want to burden her daughter with her own problems because her daughter was student teaching. The closeness they had now was "different" since her daughter's life "revolved around her husband and her teaching, and that's the way it should be." They phone each other every day and see each other about once a week.

Like most depressives, she feels inadequate: "I don't feel like I'm very much." Between the day of her son's departure and her hospitilization, she spent most of her time in bed and neglected her household, in marked contrast to her former behavior.

I was such an energetic woman. I had a big house, and I had my family. My daughter said, "Mother didn't serve eight courses. She served ten." My cooking—I took a lot of pride in my cooking and in my home. And, very, very clean. I think almost fanatic.

She considers herself more serious than other women and couldn't lead a "worthless existence" playing cards as other women did. She was active in fund raising for the institution her son was in, but apparently, without the maternal role—the role that gave her a sense of worth—fund raising was not enough. Formerly her son "took every minute of our lives" so that she "did none of the things normal women did—nothing."

Mrs. Gold's problem, psychologically and sociologically, is perhaps more dramatically apparent in her response when I asked her to rank seven roles available to middle-aged women in order of importance. She listed only one role: "Right now I think of *helping my children,* not that they really need my help, but if they did I would really try very hard." Thus she can no longer enact the role that had given her life meaning, the only role she considered important for her. Her psychiatrist had told her, and she agreed, that a paying job would help her self-esteem. But what jobs are available for a forty-year-old woman with no special training, who has not worked for over twenty years?

Mrs. Gold has most of the elements that are considered by clinicians to make up the pre-illness personality of involutional depressives: a history of martyrdom with no payoff (and martyrs always expect a payoff at some time) to make up for the years of sacrifice, inability to handle aggressive feelings, rigidity, a need to be useful in order to feel worthwhile, obsessive, compulsive supermother, superhousewife behavior and generally conventional attitudes.

Some of my friends have asked me what I am doing studying depressed middle-aged women. The question, implying that the subject is too uninteresting and unimportant to be worthwhile studying, is itself evidence for the unfortunate situation these women find themselves in. But a society's humanity may be measured by how it treats its women and its aged as well as by how it treats its racial and religious minorities. This is not a good society in which to grow old or to be a woman, and the combination of the two makes for a poignant situation. In addition, there are practical and theoretical reasons why such a study is important. Practically speaking, women today live longer and end their childbearing sooner than they did in the last century. They are more likely now to reach the "empty nest" stage or the postparental stage (a term used by those investigators who do not consider this life-cycle stage especially difficult). Moreover, in clinical terms, depression is the most common psychiatric symptom present in adults, but, like middle age, it, too, has been generally ignored by sociologists.

Problems of middle age are important theoretically for several reasons. In the first place, there is contradictory evidence on the question of whether middle age is in fact a problem for women. After a study of middle age in thirty-five different cultures, for example, I found that most women in most of these cultures do not think of middle age as being a particularly stressful time. This would seem, at the very least, to refute such biological determinists as Hubert Humphrey's physician adviser, who, in a celebrated exchange with Representative Patsy Mink, declared that women ought to be barred from positions of serious responsibility because of the "raging hormonal influences" that overwhelm them at menopause. Nevertheless, it is a fact that many women in American society do undergo a painful period with the onset of middle age, and it is also a fact that some of these women collapse in a state of clinical depression, like Mrs. Gold.

This raises some serious questions. Why is it that one woman, whose son has been "launched" says, "I don't feel like I've lost a son; I feel like I've gained a den," while another mother reports that the worst thing that ever happened to her was

> When I had to break up and be by myself and be alone, and I'm just—I really feel that I'm not only not loved but not even liked sometimes by my own children . . . they could respect me. If—if they can't say good things, why should they, why should they feel better when they hurt my feelings and make me cry and then call me a crybaby or tell me that I—I ought to know better or something like that. My worst thing is that I'm alone, I'm not wanted, nobody interests themselves in me . . . nobody cares.

The role one has in life and one's image of himself are intimately interconnected. When people are given the "Who Are You?" test, they usually respond by naming their various roles—wife, doctor, mother, teacher, daughter and the like. As a person goes from one stage of life to another, however, or from one step in a career to another, he or she must change his self-concept because the relevant or significant others, the people with whom he interacts, change. A loss of significant others can result in what Arnold Rose called a "mutilated self." One woman put it to me this way:

> I don't—I don't—I don't feel like—I don't feel that I'm wanted. I don't feel at all that I'm wanted. I just feel like nothing. I don't feel anybody cares, and nobody's interested, and they don't care whether I do feel good or I don't feel good. I'm pretty useless . . . I feel like I want somebody to feel for me, but nobody does.

Another woman stated:

> I don't feel like I'm doing anything. I feel just like I'm standing still, not getting anywhere.

The traditional woman bases her self-esteem on a role—motherhood —that she must finally relinquish. Some do this with ease; some others, especially those with inflexible personalities, cannot. But the problem is not hers alone; society has provided no guidelines for her, no rites of passage. There is no bar mitzvah for menopause. The empty nest, then, may prompt the extreme feelings of worthlessness and uselessness that characterize depressives. One can think of these women as overcommitted to the maternal role and then, in middle age, suffering the unintended consequences of this commitment.

But there is more to it than that. Ideally, a mother should be flexible enough to stop mothering adult children, but if her personality is rigid, as depressives' usually are, she can't, and she can't expect them to stop acting like dependent children either. When the children do not act this way, she may feel resentful. But since a woman is not "allowed" to be hostile to her children, she may turn the resentment inward and become depressed.

Moreover, a woman who overplays her role as mother may consciously or unconsciously want to place her children morally in her debt. Dan Greenburg's best-selling satire, How to Be a Jewish Mother, refers to guilt as the mother's main method of social control. It is no accident that his second book, How to Make Yourself Miserable, begins with the sentence, "You, we can safely assume, are guilty." It is the "supermother" who feels she can legitimately expect her children to be more devoted to her, more considerate of her, bring her more satisfaction than would otherwise be the case. Furthermore, in this situation, there may even be some payoff in the depressive collapse. When that happens, once again she gets the attention, sympathy, and control over her children she had before they left.

I should make clear at this point why I have been quoting so extensively from Jewish empty-nest mothers, women, moreover, who had been hospitalized for clinically defined depression. The most obvious reason is that in terms of the larger study I have done on the problems of middle-aged women cross-culturally, Jewish women in America occupy a pivotal place.

The literature on the Jewish mother is practically unanimous in painting her as "supermother," especially vulnerable to being severely affected if her children fail to meet her needs, either by not making what she considers "good" marriages, not achieving the career aspirations she has for them or even by not phoning her every day. Not only is the traditional Jewish mother overinvolved with or overidentified with her children, but the children are viewed as at the same time helpless without the mother's directives, and as powerful, being able to kill the mother with "aggravation." As one depressed empty-nest woman says, "My children have taken and drained me." In a sentence completion test, she filled in the blank after the words "I suffer" with "from my children."

Now, the theory governing my larger study of middle-aged women can be stated plainly enough. First, depression in middle-aged women is not due to the hormonal changes of the menopause, as is implied, for example, in the psychiatric diagnosis of "involutional melancholia." Rather, it is due to sociocultural factors that drastically reduce a woman's self-esteem. Second, depression is linked to actual or impending loss of a significant role; therefore, depression in middle-aged women will be linked with maternal role loss. Third, certain roles and attitudes toward them increase the effect of loss. For example, "supermothers" will have a higher rate of depression than normal mothers, and full-time housewives will have a higher rate than working women.

Obviously, one of the things that this theory would lead you to expect to find in "real life" is a higher rate of depression among Jewish mothers than among Anglos or among blacks. For, as everyone knows, the stereotypical Jewish mother is almost by definition an exaggerated version of the "supermother." Moreover, again according to the theory, one would expect to find that Jewish women would be more prone to depression than to other mental illnesses, and that European-born Jewish women, being presumably more traditional, would have higher rates of depression than American-born Jewish women.

These were my suppositions; to test them out I examined the records of 533 women between the ages of forty and fifty-nine who had had no previous hospitilization for mental illness. The women were in hospitals, ranging from an upper-class private hospital to the two state hospitals that served people from Los Angeles County. I compared women who had been diagnosed "depressed" (using the following diagnoses: involutional depression, psychotic depression, neurotic depression, manic-depression) with women who had other functional (nonorganic) diagnoses.

I made every effort to overcome diagnostic biases on the part of the doctors and myself. First, the sample was drawn from five hospitals. Second, "neurotic depressives" were merged with the "involutional" and "psychotic depressives" and "manic-depressives" since I suspected that patients who would be called neurotic depressed at an upper-class hospital would be called involutional depressed at a lower-middle-class hospital— a suspicion that was borne out. Third, I used a symptom checklist and found that depressed patients differed significantly from those given other diagnoses for almost all symptoms.

Fourth, a case history of a woman with both depressive and paranoid features was distributed to the psychiatric residents at the teaching hospital for "blind" diagnosis. In half the cases, the woman was called Jewish and in half Presbyterian. The results showed no difference in number of stigmatic diagnoses between the "Jews" and "Presbyterians" since the most and least stigmatic diagnoses (neurotic depression and schizophrenia) were given to "Presbyterians." Fifth, 39 MMPI personality profiles at one hospital were obtained and given to a psychologist to diagnose "blind." He rated them on an impairment continuum. The results supported the decision to combine psychotic, involutional, and neurotic depressives, because the ratio of mild and moderate to serious and very serious was the same for all these groups.

Next, I conducted 20 intensive interviews at two hospitals to obtain information unavailable from the patients' records, using questionnaires already used on "normal" middle-aged women. I also gave them the projective biography test—a test consisting of 16 pictures showing women at different stages in their life cycle and in different roles. These interviews provided an especially rich source of information. I did not read their charts until *after* the interviews so as to leave my perception unaffected by psychiatrists' or social workers' evaluations.

Maternal role loss was recorded when at least one child was not living at home. I considered an overprotective or overinvolved relationship to be present when the record bore statements such as "my whole life was my husband and my daughter" or if the woman entered the hospital following her child's engagement or marriage. Ratings of role loss, relationship with children and with husbands were made from a case history which omitted references to symptomatology, ethnicity or diagnosis, and high intercoder reliability was obtained for these variables. (Jewish coders were more likely to call a parent-child relationship unsatisfactory than non-Jewish coders. Categories were refined to eliminate this difference.) A woman was considered Jewish if she had a Jewish mother and regardless of profession of faith. The attitudes and values I am discussing need not come from religious behavior. For example, Mrs. Gold didn't attend religious services and was unsure of her belief in God. But she taught her daughter that "we just don't date Gentile boys" and considers herself very Jewish, "all the way through, to the core."

My suppositions were confirmed: Jews have the highest rate of depression, Anglos an intermediate rate and blacks the lowest rate (see Table 1). Jewish women are roughly twice as likely to be diagnosed depressed as non-Jewish women. Moreover, the very small group of Jewish women whose mothers were born in the United States had a rate of depression midway between that of Jewish women with European-born mothers on the one hand and Anglo women on the other. The low rates for black women suggest that their family structure and occupational roles tend to prevent depression. However, when I controlled the data, holding patterns of family interaction constant, the difference between Jews and non-Jews sharply diminishes (Table 2). To be sure, overprotection or overinvolvement with children is much more common among Jews than among non-Jews. But it is clear that you don't have to be Jewish to be a Jewish mother. For example, one divorced black woman, who had a hysterectomy, went into a depression when her daughter, an only child, moved to Oregon. The depression lifted when the woman visited her and recurred when she returned to Los Angeles. Yet these results may simply reflect a greater unwillingness to hospitalize depressed black women in the black community. Depressives are not likely to come to the attention of the police unless they attempt suicide. Therefore, if the woman or her family do not define her condition as psychiatric, she will remain at home. Only a prevalence study can fully test the hypothesis about the black family.

Any doubts about the validity of my inferences from the hospital charts were dispelled by the interviews.

Even though they were patients and I was an interviewer and a stranger, one Jewish woman forced me to eat candy, saying, "Don't say no to me." Another gave me unsolicited advice on whether I should remarry and to whom, and a third said she would make me a party when she left the hospital. Another example of extreme nurturant patterns was shown by a fourth woman who insisted on caring for another patient who had just returned from ECT (shock) while I was interviewing her. She also attempted to find other women for me to interview. The vocabulary of motives invoked by the Jewish women generally attributed their illness to their children. They complained about not seeing their children often enough. Non-Jewish women were more restrained and said they wanted their children to be independent.

Two of the Jewish women had lived with their children, wanted to live with them again, and their illness was precipitated when their children forced them to live alone. However, in another study I did, even women who lived with their children were all depressed. As one such woman complained:

> Why is my daughter so cold to me? Why does she exclude me? She turns to her husband . . . and leaves me out. I don't tell her what to do, but I like to feel my thoughts are wanted.

All the mothers, when asked what they were most proud of, replied, "My children." Occasionally, after this, they mentioned their husbands. None mentioned any accomplishment of their own, except being a good mother. This was reflected also in the ranked answers to the question of what was most important to them: being a homemaker, taking part in church, club and community activities, being a companion to one's husband, helping parents, being a sexual partner, having a paying job or helping children. Needless to say, "helping children" was most frequently ranked first or second by these postnest mothers. Since it is difficult to help children who are no longer home, women who value this behavior more than any other are in trouble. (Interestingly, "helping parents" was ranked first by only one. No woman listed "being a sexual partner" first, and three married women did not even include it in the ranking.)

Those interviewed were also given the projective biography test—16 pictures showing women in different roles and at different ages. The clinical psychologist who devised the test and analyzed the protocols without knowing my hypothesis noted they were "complete mothers." One of the pictures, showing an old woman sitting in a rocking chair in front of a fireplace, got overwhelmingly negative reactions. As one put it:

> And this scene I can't stand. Just sitting alone in old age by just sitting there and by some fireplace all by herself [pause] turning into something like that. And to me this is too lonely. A person has to slow down sometime and just sit, but I would rather be active, and even if I would be elderly, I wouldn't want to live so long that I wouldn't have anything else in live but to just sit alone and you know, just in a rocking chair.

Another woman who was divorced and had both her children away from home said, "This could look very much like me. I'm sitting, dreaming, feeling so blue." When she chose that as the picture not liked, she said, "Least of all, I don't like this one at all. That's too much like I was doing—sitting and worrying and thinking." Two women even denied the aging aspects of the picture: "Here she is over here sitting in front of the fireplace, and she's got her figure back, and I suppose the baby's gone off to sleep, and she's relaxing." This woman interpreted every picture with reference to a baby.

It is very easy to make fun of these women, to ridicule their pride in their children and concern for their well-being. But it is no mark of progress to substitute Molly Goldberg for Stepin Fetchit as a stock comedy figure. They are as much casualties of our culture as are the children in Harlem whose IQs decline with each additional year they spend in school. In their strong commitment to and involvement with their children, they were only doing what they were told to do; what was expected of them by their families, their friends and the mass media. If they deviated from this role, they would have been ridiculed. (Ask any professional woman.)

Moreover, what I am really talking about here is what happens to women who follow the cultural rules, who buy the American Dream, who think there is a payoff for good behavior, who believe in justice, and who therefore suffer depression, a loss of meaning, when they discover that their lives have not turned out the way they expected. We even find the same syndrome in men. Men who have involutional psychosis are usually in their sixties, the retirement age. I would predict that these are men whose occupational roles were "props." Like the women who derive their identity almost exclusively from their role as mothers, there are men whose identity is completely wrapped up in their work. With retirement, then, one could expect to find symptoms of depression. And in fact, the director of admissions at the teaching hospital where I worked reported that it was not unusual for army officers to suffer involutional depression on retirement. And a 1965 study on involutional depression in Israel found loss of meaning a factor among old pioneers who believed "that the values so dear to them were fast disappearing. Current ideals and expectations were now alien to them and the sense of duty and sacrifice as they knew it seemed to exist no longer. They felt different, isolated and superfluous."

But the cases of these women tell us something else that is important. Two psychoanalysts, Therese Benedek and Helene Deutsch, state that menopause is more difficult for "masculine" or "pseudo-masculine" women. The former describes this woman as one whose "psychic economy was dominated—much like that of a man's—by strivings of the ego rather than by the primary emotional gratifications of motherliness." Deutsch states that "feminine, loving" women have an easier time during climacteric than do "masculine, aggressive ones." However, my data shows that it is the women who assume the *traditional* feminine role—who are housewives, who stay married to their husbands, who are not overtly aggressive, in short who accept the traditional norms—who respond with depression when their children leave. Even the MMPI masculine-feminine scores for women at one hospital were one half a standard deviation *more* feminine than the mean.

Until recent years, a common theme of inspirational literature for women, whether on soap operas or in women's magazines, has been that they could only find "real happiness" by devoting themselves to their husbands and children and by living vicariously through them. If one's sense of worth comes from other people rather than from one's own accomplishments, it follows that when such people depart, one is left with an empty shell in place of a self. If, however, a woman's sense of worth comes from her own interests and accomplishments, she is less vulnerable to breakdown when significant others leave. This point is obscured in much of the polemical literature on the allegedly dominant American female who is considered to have "lost" her feminity. It is, after all, *feminine* women—the ones who play the traditional roles, not the career women—who are likely to dominate their husbands and children. This domination, however, may take more traditional female forms of subtle manipulation and the invoking of guilt. If, however, a woman does not assume the traditional female role and does not expect to have her needs for achievement, or her needs for "narcissistic gratification," as psychiatrists term it, met vicariously through the accomplishments of her husband and children, *then* she has no need to dominate them, since her well-being does not depend on their accomplishments. It is unreasonable to expect one sex in an achievement-oriented society not to have these needs.

The Women's Liberation movement, by pointing out alternative life-styles, by providing the emotional support necessary for deviating from the ascribed sex roles and by emphasizing the importance of women actualizing their own selves, fulfilling their own potentials, can help in the development of personhood, for both men and women.

This investigation was supported in part by a predoctoral research training fellowship from the National Institute of Mental Health

Table 1

Jewish mothers are more depressed than mothers of other groups.

Ethnicity	Percent Depressed	Total Number
Jews	84	122
Anglos	51	206
Blacks	22	28

The percent depressed among all non-Jews was 47 percent. Further investigation at one of the five hospitals showed 67 percent (six) of Jewish women with native-born mothers and 92 percent (thirteen) of Jewish women with European-born mothers to be depressed. Although the cases are few, the findings are suggestive.

Table 2

Overinvolved mothers who lose their maternal role are the most depressed group.

Condition	Percent Depressed	Total Number
Role Loss	62	369
Maternal Role Loss	63	245
Housewives with Maternal Role Loss	69	124
Middle-Class Housewives with Maternal Role Loss	74	69
Women with Maternal Role Loss Who Had Overprotective or Overinvolved Relationships with Their Children	76	72
Housewives with Maternal Role Loss Who Have Overprotective or Overinvolved Relationships with Their Children	82	44

THIS MONTH IS FOR YOU: OBSERVING ROSH HODESH AS A WOMAN'S HOLIDAY

Arlene Agus

In 1972, after serious exploration of the nature of women's spirituality and the role of women in Jewish ritual, a small group of women discovered that the celebration of Rosh Hodesh—the Festival of the New Moon—had traditionally held unique significance for women, perhaps dating back as far as the Biblical period. We began observing the day with a special ceremony and feast, combining traditional practices associated with the holiday with additions from contemporary sources.

The discovery came in the wake of a struggle for spiritual self-knowledge and expression, a struggle which left unanswered many basic questions regarding the relationship between a woman and her God within the context of a community.

Formal equality with men was not so much at issue as was the need to delineate those aspects of the ritual role of the Jewish male which held intrinsic value for a Jew and which, therefore, merited adoption by women. In addition, it was necessary to find those practices which were not only permitted, but even incumbent upon women (such as daily prayer) which, out of ignorance or habit, were not being performed.

There were three options available to us to expand womens' ritual role: to retain the traditional role and attempt to enrich it, to adopt the male rituals and hope to find spiritual satisfaction in them, or to create new or parallel rituals.

It was because none of these options was wholly satisfying that the celebration of Rosh Hodesh immediately seemed so appealing. It offered unlimited opportunities for exploration of feminine spiritual qualities and experimentation with ritual, all within the framework of an ancient tradition which has survived up to the present day. As we shall see, the celebration of Rosh Hodesh is the celebration of ourselves, of our uniqueness as women, and of our relationship to nature and to God.

Historical Overview of Rosh Hodesh

The association of the moon and women began as early as the Creation story. Since that time, Jewish literature has portrayed the moon, in its relationship to the sun, as symbolic of women, of the Community of Israel *(Knesset Yisrael),* and of the Shekhinah, the feminine aspect of the Godhead. The divine promise to the moon that she is destined to become an independent luminary like the sun,[1] parallels the promise to women that in the world to come they will be renewed or rejuvenated like the New Moon and the promise to the Shekhinah that when the world is redeemed she will receive direct emanations of divine light.[2]

On the fourth day of Creation "God made the two great luminaries." According to the Talmud (Hullin 60a), the two stars were originally of equivalent size, prompting the moon to ask God, "Sovereign of the Universe, can two kings share a single crown?" He answered, "Go and make yourself smaller." "Sovereign of the Universe!" the moon cried, "Because I presented a proper claim, must I make myself smaller?" And God, realizing the justice of her plea, compensated for her diminution by promising that the moon would rule by night, that Israel would calculate days and years by her, and that the righteous would be named after her. He also decreed that a sacrifice be instituted to atone for his sin in making her smaller. And finally, that in the future, he would intensify her light to equal that of the sun.[3]

It was a similar challenging of God's judgment in creation, in creating two equal human beings, which led to the diminution of woman's status. On the sixth day of Creation, "God created man in his image . . . male and female he created them." According to the Midrash, Adam's first wife, Lilith, having been created equal to Adam, refused a role of subservience and was replaced by Eve.

Lurianic *kabbalah* claims that, like the two lights and the first two humans, the male and female aspects of the Godhead were equal in the embryonic stage. But as a result of Eve's sin and the subsequent banishment from the Garden, the moon became smaller and the Shekhinah went into exile. It is only when the world is redeemed that the two will be restored to their rightful places.[4] A similar destiny is promised to women.

The source for this promise—and the halakhic basis for observance of Rosh Hodesh by women—is a passage in the Babylonian Talmud[5] discussing the laws of work on Rosh Hodesh. Rashi and Tosafot comment that while men are permitted to work on the New Moon, women are not, as explained in *Pirke DeRabbi Eliezer* (Chapter 45):

> The women heard about the construction of the Golden Calf and refused to submit their jewelry to their husbands. Instead they said to them: "You want to construct an idol and mask which is an abomination, and has no power of redemption? We won't listen to you." And the Holy One, Blessed be He, rewarded them in this world in that they would observe the New Moons more than men, and in the next world in that they are destined to be renewed like the New Moons . . . (*shehen atidot lehithadesh kemotah*).

This is later echoed in *Mekore Haminhagim:* "Women were enthusiastic about the *Mishkan* (Sanctuary) and reluctant about the Calf, and were therefore rewarded with the observance of Rosh Hodesh as a minor festival."[6]

Why was Rosh Hodesh chosen? Because the three major festivals had already been assigned to the forefathers[7] and, according to the Or Zaruah, because Rosh Hodesh is an obvious reference to the monthly cycle after which women renew themselves like the moon through immersion.[8]

But what exactly does it mean that in the world to come "women will be renewed like the New Moons"? Women already experience a physical renewal each month. What further renewal or rejuvenation will they experience in the world to come? The promise is rather unclear, but can be understood as a parallel to the future renewal of the moon. Just as that star will be elevated in size and brilliance without becoming identical to the sun, so women will ascend in function and status without becoming identical to men.

In what way were Jewish women to observe the day? By refraining from work. Rashi says that women specifically refrained from spinning, weaving and sewing on Rosh Hodesh[9] which were the very skills women so enthusiastically contributed to the *Mishkan*.

The authoritative source confirming the validity of the women's abstinence from work is the Palestinian, or Jerusalem, Talmud which says: "It is an acceptable custom for women not to work on the New Moon."[10]

At one time, work may have been prohibited on Rosh Hodesh because of the Musaf sacrifice in the Temple on that day.[11] Some say there was no real prohibition on work, but during the period in which the Sanhedrin would notify the people of the beginning of the new month through a system of torch relays, no work would be done while everyone awaited notification. After the Exile, the celebration of Rosh Hodesh more closely resembled *hol ha-moed*, the intermediate days of a festival, and gradually fell only to the women.

It appears that the custom of abstaining from work was widely observed by Jewish women, although there was some disparity among the forms of work which women permitted themselves on that day. The Tashbetz (thirteenth century) describes the differentiation between types of work; for instance, the women were strict regarding spinning but lenient with sewing, a simpler task.[12] A ban on gambling was declared in the Middle Ages partly because "mischievous Jewish women" were squandering family money to engage in the practice during their free time on Rosh Hodesh.

The following lecture on *musar* (ethics) regarding Rosh Hodesh was written in the seventeenth century:

> Women should appreciate the glorious, majestic splendor of the day, in that they observe Rosh Hodesh more than men. Although it is proper for them to completely refrain from work because of their refusal to join the men in the sin of the Golden Calf, there is no actual prohibition of work, as on a holiday, so as not to embarrass the men. Women of every rank and status must observe the day.
>
> It is horrifying that there are women who do laundry on Rosh Hodesh. Moreover, some even save time on work days by leaving the laundry for the holiday. These women are clearly misguided and should abstain from this wretched, depressing task. Hard work is prohibited even to men on Rosh Hodesh. Men should make their wives aware of the wisdom and value of the day so that they may glorify it and behave modestly and perform the most virtuous deed of the day—the collection of *tzedakah*(charity)—from among the women. Rosh Hodesh is not for licentiousness and tempting others in sin. Modest God-fearing women will act properly. If not, they will cause a "stain on high" and are not permitted to refrain from work.[13]

The *Shulhan Arukh* states that women's abstinence from work on

Rosh Hodesh is a good custom. The Beur Halakhah describes at length the rabbinic opinions regarding the binding nature of the custom. He points out that despite considerable feeling that Rosh Hodesh is simply a custom for those who adopt it or follow in their maternal tradition, it is in fact a tradition from our foremothers from ancient times and the *mitzvah* still applies to all Jewish women. A woman may not treat the day as if it were a regular weekday. However, depending on her family custom, she is permitted to perform light work.[14]

Before we discuss a comtemporary Rosh Hodesh ceremony, we will examine some of the many laws and customs, past and present, associated with the holiday, so as to draw from the tradition the significant elements of the day.

Rosh Hodesh is introduced in Exodus (12:2) in the verse, "This month is for you the first of months;" and is the source of the *mitzvah* of observing Rosh Hodesh. In Numbers (10:10, 28:11), Rosh Hodesh is described as a day on par with the other festivals, requiring the blowing of trumpets and special sacrifices. Several of the prophets equate Rosh Hodesh with the Sabbath or the three major festivals.

In the days of the Second Temple, when the declaration of the New Moon by the sages depended on its being sighted by two witnesses, a feast was held for these witnesses in order to encourage their coming.[15] From this and from King Saul's feast,[16] we derive the *mitzvah* of holding such a meal on Rosh Hodesh.[17]

The day preceding Rosh Hodesh is called a Yom Kippur Katan—a minor Day of Atonement—and was traditionally a day of repentence and mourning over the destruction of the Temple. Rosh Hodesh itself is similar to Rosh Hashanah; on it we pray for blessings of renewal, are judged for our sins, and are purified.

The theme of renewal recurs throughout the many customs of Rosh Hodesh—in fact, it is called the Day of Good Beginnings. As such, it was an appropriate day for holding housewarmings, dedications, and other "simchas," a day for wearing new clothes and shoes, for saying Shehehiyanu over a newly ripened fruit, and for beginning a new book in school. Joy and song are associated with the day and no fasts are permitted.[18]

After the torch relays were discontinued by Rabbi Yehudah Hanasi, the practice of lighting a special candle for Rosh Hodesh remained. In Yemen, candles would be lit in the synagogue and at home. In Algiers, gold coins or rings were placed inside the burning lanterns for good luck. Different traditions vary on the number of candles to be lit on

Rosh Hodesh: some require one more than Shabbat, some, one less; but all agree that a differentiation should be made.

Today, Rosh Hodesh is observed by the recital of special holiday prayers, partial Hallel, the Additional Service and reading from the Torah. In addition, Yaaleh Veyavo is included in the Silent Prayer (Amidah) and the Grace After Meals.[19] The *haftarah* portion on Rosh Hodesh is of particular interest here because, in this prophecy of redemption, Isaiah uses the imagery of fertility in describing God and Zion as life-bearers, providing nurturance to the people of Israel.[20]

The link between women and the moon is strong and far-reaching, touching Jewish law, custom, mysticism, and even superstition. Let us now turn to an actual ceremony of Rosh Hodesh.

The Rosh Hodesh Ceremony

Rosh Hodesh is celebrated only eleven times a year. Tishre, the month Rosh Hodesh coincides with Rosh Hashanah, is omitted. If Rosh Hodesh falls on two days, the ceremony may be performed on either one or both days, though the second is the more important.

The ceremony is a celebration of divine creation and of those characteristics which women share with the moon—the life cycle, rebirth, renewal. Just as the Jewish calendar sanctifies time annually through the holidays, weekly through Shabbat, and daily through prayers, so Rosh Hodesh sanctifies time monthly. And just as birth ceremonies, *brit milah*, bar and bat mitzvah, weddings and funerals mark each nexus point in the life cycle of members of the religious community, so Rosh Hodesh corresponds to and celebrates the life-giving monthly cycle of the community's women.

The symbols of water, spheres, circles, representing monthly purification and rebirth in the *mikveh*, the shape of the moon and the cyclical nature of life, as well as foods containing the seeds of life, will recur throughout the ceremony.

The following is not meant to be a standard text for the observance of the holiday. The creative process, exemplified in this ceremony, should be enhanced and developed by the creativity and imagination of individual women. Naturally, the traditional parts of the ceremony, e.g. the giving of charity, the candle, the feast and the special Rosh Hodesh prayers, should be given special emphasis and lend some uniformity.

The Ceremony Itself

All are dressed in nice clothing, or, if possible, in new clothes saved for the occasion. A *pushke* can be available for the giving of charity before the ceremony begins.

A. Light a candle to burn for twenty-four hours.
   A floating light closely resembles the moon floating in the sky.
B. Read the following poem/prayer by Hillel Zeitlin:

   CREATE ME ANEW

   Father,
   O great and holy Father of all mankind,
   You create the world, Your child, every instant.

   If for an instant You withdrew
   The loving gift of Your creation
   —All would be nothingness.

   But You shower Your children, Your creatures,
   With blessing every moment.

   Once again the morning stars appear,
   Singing a song of love to You,
   And once again the sun bursts forth,
   Singing a song of light to You.

   Once again angels sing of holiness to You,
   Once again souls sing of yearning to You
   And once again grass sings of longing to You.

   Once again birds sing a song of joy to You,
   Once again orphaned nestlings sing of loneliness to You
   And once again a brook whispers its prayer.

   Once again the afflicted, faint, pours out his complaint to You,
   Once again his soul-prayer splits Your heavens, rising to You,
   Once again he trembles in awe of Your glory
   And once again he hopefully awaits You.

   One ray of Your light and I am immersed in light,
   One word from You and I am reborn,
   One hint of Your eternal Presence and I am refreshed
         with the dew of youth

For You create everything anew.
Father, please, create me, Your child, anew.
Breathe into me of Your spirit
That I may begin a new life.

C. Usher in the Upcoming Month

This can be done in several ways: Focus on the Jewish holiday occurring in that month, learn a text concerning the laws or customs pertaining to that holiday, observe the *yahrzeit* of a famous Jew due to occur that month, commemorate the anniversary of a historical event, etc.

D. Kiddush

A traditional holiday Kiddush is not appropriate, since the holiness of Rosh Hodesh more closely resembles the interim days of a holiday when one is permitted to work, than the festivals, when one is not. The text used is the same one chanted at the blessing of the New Moon. Note its references to those who are carried in the womb, and to the divine promise that they are destined to be renewed like the moon.

Blessed is he who created the heaven by his word, and by the breath of his mouth all of its hosts. He appointed for them a time and a limit, so they might not alter their rounds [but rather be] happy and joyous doing the will of their Creator. Trustworthy Creator whose creation is trustworthy. And to the moon he said, that she might always be renewed, as a glorious crown to those borne in the womb, who themselves are destined to be renewed like her, and to praise their Creator for his glorious kingdom.

בָּרוּךְ אֲשֶׁר בְּמַאֲמָרוֹ בָּרָא שְׁחָקִים,
וּבְרוּחַ פִּיו כָּל־צְבָאָם, חֹק וּזְמַן נָתַן
לָהֶם שֶׁלֹּא יְשַׁנּוּ אֶת־תַּפְקִידָם, שָׂשִׂים
וּשְׂמֵחִים לַעֲשׂוֹת רְצוֹן קוֹנָם, פּוֹעֵל
אֱמֶת, שֶׁפְּעֻלָּתוֹ אֱמֶת, וְלַלְּבָנָה אָמַר,
שֶׁתִּתְחַדֵּשׁ עֲטֶרֶת תִּפְאֶרֶת לַעֲמוּסֵי בָטֶן,
שֶׁהֵם עֲתִידִים לְהִתְחַדֵּשׁ כְּמוֹתָה, וּלְפָאֵר
לְיוֹצְרָם עַל שֵׁם כְּבוֹד מַלְכוּתוֹ.

Raise a cup of wine, recite the following blessing:

Blessed are you, Lord our God, Sovereign of the universe, creator of the fruit of the vine.

בָּרוּךְ אַתָּה יְיָ אֱלֹהֵינוּ מֶלֶךְ הָעוֹלָם, בּוֹרֵא פְּרִי הַגָּפֶן:

E. The Feast

It is a *mitzvah* to eat in abundance on Rosh Hodesh. As is traditional with Jewish feasts, two rolls or *hallot* are used. For Rosh Hodesh, it is appropriate to use round or crescent-shaped rolls. It is customary to buy a new fruit for Sheheheyanu. The first course may consist of a special Rosh Hodesh dish like the egg soup eaten traditionally on Passover, the holiday which celebrates the birth of the Jewish people. (Again the seed of life is being immersed in liquid.) Sprout salad is another possibility. The main course should be festive, preferably containing two cooked dishes, as is customary on Sabbath and holidays. You may also wish to use nut loaf, for the seeds, and quiche for its circular shape.

During the meal, Rosh Hodesh songs,[21] Hallel songs, or songs from the forthcoming holiday should be sung. Grace After Meals following the feast includes Shir Hamaalot and Yaaleh Veyavo for the New Moon. If Rosh Hodesh falls on Sabbath, it is customary either to add a special dish to the Sabbath meal in honor of the New Moon, or to have a feast for Rosh Hodesh during the Shalosh Seudot (the third Sabbath meal), and to extend it until after the Sabbath.

Earlier we read that the Biblical source for the *mitzvah* of Rosh Hodesh is "This month is for you," about which the Midrash comments that God granted the Jewish people the authority to sanctify the New Moons—unlike the Sabbath, which is sanctified in heaven. The acronym of *roshe hodoshim* (New Moons) spells *rehem* (womb). The revival of Rosh Hodesh as a holiday for Jewish women is an opportunity for spiritual development, an occasion for speaking to the Creator and experimenting with the dialogue. It is offered here as a pause in which to thank God for creating us women.

Notes

1. *Pirke DeRabbi Eliezer,* Chapter 51, See also *Midrash Konen* pp. 25–26.
2. *Sefer Hemdat Yamim,* Vol. 1, p. 25. This and other mystical references courtesy of Rabbi Daniel Shevitz.
3. Isaiah 30:26.
4. Gershom Scholem, *Major Trends in Jewish Mysticism,* pp. 231–32.
5. Megillah 22b.
6. *Mekore Haminhagim,* no. 38.
7. *Sefer Hahasidim,* no. 121.
8. J.D. Eisenstein, *Otzar Dinim Uminhagim,* p. 377.
9. Megillah op. cit.
10. Taanit 1:6.
11. Haggigah 18a; Tosefta and J.Taanit 1:6.
12. Tashbetz sect. 3, no. 244.
13. *Sefer Hemdat Yamim,* Vol. 1, pp. 23b–24a.
14. *Shulhan Arukh/Mishnah Berurah* no. 417.
15. Rosh Hashanah 2,4.
16. Samuel 1, 20:5–6.
17. Rambam, *Mishneh Torah,* Chapter 8.
18. Taanit 15b.
19. *Shulhan Arukh/Mishnah Berurah,* nos. 421–24
20. Isaiah 61.
21. A collection of traditional and modern prayers and songs is available from the author.

JEWISH WOMEN'S HAGGADAH

Aviva Cantor Zuckoff

Several years ago a group of young Jews in New York constituted themselves the Jewish Liberation Project. We came from a variety of backgrounds—Old and New Left, Zionist, religious, Yiddishist—and in time we came to define ourselves as Socialist-Zionists. We became involved in a variety of work within the American Jewish community and on the left. We talked a lot about "alternative politics" and "alternative life-styles."

A family feeling definitely existed among us in those early years. When Pesah came around, we wanted to be able to hold a Seder that reflected both our politics and our feeling of community. Thus the Jewish Liberation Seder was born. It was written by three people: Itzhak Epstein, Yaakov (then Jerry) Kirschen, and myself. I wrote the basic draft, drawing on much research and on long discussions with my two collaborators; they helped me cut, refine, and polish it. Kirschen did all the art.

What we wrote was a ceremony that was both Jewish and radical in values and concepts, traditional in ritual, and modern in its pace and language. We tried to tie in the struggle for Jewish liberation today with struggles of our people in the past and to draw on Jewish experience and Jewish sources to speak to what we ourselves were going through.

We began at the obvious point: we cut a lot of what we considered excess verbiage that related to medieval scholastic debates—but added a lot of our own verbiage! We added material on the Holocaust, Israel, and Soviet Jewry. One of the main things we did was to infuse old rituals with new content and meaning. For example, while retaining the four cups of wine that must be drunk at the Seder, we attached new meaning to each one, making each stand for a particular struggle against oppression.

A couple of years later, while wandering through a bookstore, I picked up Beverly Jones's and Judith Brown's paper, "Toward a Female Liberation Movement." On reading it I experienced a flash of recognition and identification and promptly became a feminist. More reading and thinking followed. Later I began to do research on the Jewish woman; I lectured on the subject and taught a course on it at the Jewish Free High School.

About two years after that, as more women were also trying to synthesize their new Jewish consciousness and their feminist consciousness, one woman sent out a circular to all her friends and acquaintances, calling them to a meeting to discuss how we feel and think as Jewish women. Several large meetings followed. A core group of five women eventually became my Jewish women's consciousness-raising group, which met for over two years. In our weekly meetings we tried to understand how our Jewish background made us what we are, and explored what it meant to be a Jewish woman.

The first year, having become close and loving friends, we decided that we wanted to hold a Jewish Women's Seder. We felt that we were a family and that we could use this most Jewish of ceremonies to bring us and other Jewish women closer to each other and to our history and values. What follows are excerpts from the Seder I put together for this occasion. In true Pesah spirit, the seder was written in haste (like the matzah baked by the Jews escaping Egypt).

Because of the rush, I did not write the Haggadah from scratch. I took the Jewish Liberation Haggadah, used it as a basic framework, cut some material and then added feminist material. My first shock came in rereading the Jewish Liberation Haggadah. First, I was bothered by the obvious things: the four sons, the "he" all over the place not followed by "and she." But even more disturbing—especially since I was the main author of the Haggadah—was the almost complete absence of women, our invisibility. Except for one poem, there was very little to indicate that Jewish women had been active participants in Jewish life and struggles.

So I rewrote the Haggadah, first taking care of the minor changes: making God "ruler of the universe" instead of "king," adding the names of Jacob's wives to the Exodus narrative, and changing "four sons" to "four daughters." The major change was to utilize the four-cups ritual and to dedicate each cup of wine to the struggle of Jewish women in a particular period. The Haggadah's aim was to provide connecting links between Jewish women of the past and us here in the present. A great deal of material came from Jewish legends and historical sources, some only recently discovered. Although the Seder proved enjoyable to us and our friends, I still feel quite dissatisfied with it and in no way regard it as complete.

The first and most obvious problem is the fact that this Seder is based on another Seder and is therefore not really "original." Although beautiful in many respects, it represents an almost verbatim takeover of its "predecessor's" account of the Exodus. Then, too, changing "four sons" to "four daughters" while leaving the rest of the segment (written by Itzhak Epstein) largely intact makes that excerpt less relevant than it might be if it were completely rewritten.

However, there is a more fundamental problem involved in writing a Seder for Jewish women and that is the tension between the very nature of the Seder and the needs of the participants. I think this tension cannot be fully resolved, and whoever writes such a Seder should be aware of it.

On the one hand, the Seder is a *Jewish* celebration. It marks a *specific*—national—liberation from a *specific*—national—oppression. The Jewish woman, however, cannot celebrate this liberation with a whole heart because she knows that *her* oppression continues. This might lead us to want to incorporate into the Haggadah a whole lot of material on the oppression of women in Jewish life, and indeed my first draft did just that. But that would bring us into conflict with the essential nature of the Seder, which is joyous and emphasizes those things that unite Jews rather than divide them (for example, at a Seder we do not stress the class struggle).

Thus the women's Seder is in danger of becoming irrelevant to the needs of its participants. The only solution I could see was to draw on Jewish history, extracting material about the participation of Jewish women in the struggles for Jewish liberation (which is the theme of the Seder). Emphasizing our participation in Jewish struggles, however, creates two problems: (1) It makes it seem as if the Haggadah is our "entrance card" to Jewish society, as if through it we were saying, "Look, we're *real Jews* after all." (2) It makes it seem as if Jewish women have never had any problem at all in Jewish society, as if they have always been allowed to participate as equals, and, this, of course, is untrue. So the question remains: how to deal with the oppression of the Jewish woman *within the context of the Seder as a ceremony marking Jewish national liberation.* As yet I have no anwer to this question; perhaps women can find the solution together.

My final reservation about the Jewish Women's Haggadah is even more basic. As much as I loved a Seder with my sisters, what gnawed at me was my memory of the Seders I had at home, in my parents' house, Seders of men and women of several generations, with children running underfoot and spilling the wine. The Seder has always been a family celebration and, for me, a Seder just for women seems incomplete.

What I would like to see—and for me it has not yet crystallized—is a Seder that focuses on the oppression of Jews and on Jewish liberation *from a Jewish feminist viewpoint.* Such a Haggadah would deal honestly with the oppression of women while keeping the main focus on Jewish liberation. It would be a Seder for families of all kinds, whether by blood or by choice. In such a Seder, women would be as "visible" as men, but neither men nor women would be the entire focus of the Seder. This is the kind of Seder I would like to take my children to—if and when I ever have children. I would also, of course, invite my dear friend Nadia Borochov Ovsey who celebrated her ninety-second birthday in October of 1975, the woman of valor to whom I dedicated this Haggadah.

Jewish Women's Haggadah

Haverot, shalom.

We have gathered here tonight to celebrate Pesah, the festival of the liberation of the Jewish people. Pesah is the night when all the families of Israel gather to celebrate and to strengthen their ties—to each other and to all Jews. We too are a family, a growing family. We too have ties we hope to strengthen. For while we are not related by blood, we are related by something perhaps even stronger: sisterhood.

Then follows the blessing on the wine, the dipping of the greens in salt water, the breaking of the middle matzah, *the Four Questions, and the core of the Seder—the telling of the story of the Jews' struggle for liberation from slavery in Egypt. As the first cup of wine—dedicated to the first uprising of the Jews against oppression and the first liberation—is lifted, the following is said:*

As we hold this cup of wine, we remember our sisters in the land of Egypt who fearlessly stood up to the Pharaoh.

Our legends tell us that Pharaoh, in the time-honored pattern of oppressors, tried to get Jews to collaborate in murdering their own people. He summoned the top two Jewish midwives, Shifra and Puah—some legends say one of them was Yocheved, who was also Moshe's mother—and commanded them to kill newborn Jewish males at birth and to report the birth of Jewish females so that they could be raised to become prostitutes. Pharaoh tried at first to win over the midwives by making sexual advances to them. When they repulsed these, he threatened them with death by fire. The midwives did not carry out Pharaoh's command. Instead of murdering the male infants, they took special care of them. If a mother was poor, they went around to the other women, collecting food for her and her child. When Pharaoh asked the midwives to account for all the living children, they made up the excuse that Jewish women gave birth so fast that they did not summon midwives in time.

Like our Jewish sisters through the ages, those in Egypt were strong and courageous in the face of oppression. Our sages recognized this when they said: "The Jews were liberated from Egypt because of the righteousness of the women."

The parable of the four sons is here retold as "The Four Daughters," in language reflecting our struggle to find ourselves as Jewish women. The nature of oppression is also defined and the Holocaust described in "Go and Learn":

Go and learn how the enemies of the Jews have tried so many times and in so many places to destroy us. We survived because of our spiritual resistance and our inner strength. Throughout the ages Jewish women have provided much of this strength, courage, and loyalty. During very desperate times, Jewish women were allowed to show their strength openly. Yocheved, Miriam, Deborah, Yael, Judith,

Esther—who was called a "redeemer"—how few are the names of the heroic Jewish women which have come down to us! How many more were there whose names we will never know?

We speak of rebellion as the only way to overthrow oppression. The Ten Plagues are mentioned one by one. Then we raise and dedicate the second cup of wine to the ghetto fighters.

We drink this second of four cups of wine to honor the glorious memory of the Jewish fighters in the ghettos, concentration camps, and forests of Nazi Europe. They fought and died with honor and avenged the murder of our people. Their courage and hope in the face of unutterable brutality and despair inspires us.

As we hold this cup of wine, we remember our glorious and brave sisters who fought so courageously against the Nazi monsters. We remenber Hannah Senesh and Haviva Reik, who parachuted behind enemy lines in Hungary and Slovakia to organize resistance and rescue Jews. We remember Vladka Meed, and Chaika and Frumka Plotnitski, who served as couriers and smuggled arms for the ghetto fighters. We remember Rosa Robota who organized the smuggling of dynamite to blow up a crematorium in Auschwitz. Chaika Grossman, Gusta Drenger, Zivia Lubetkin, Gisi Fleischman, Tosia Altman, Zofia Yamaika, Niuta Teitelboim—these are but a few of the names we know. Their willingness to sacrifice their lives for their people shines through the words of Hannah Senesh, written shortly before her execution (Nov. 7, 1944):

> Blessed is the match that is consumed
>   in kindling the flame
> Blessed is the flame that burns
>   in the secret fastness of the heart
> Blessed is the heart strong enough to
>   stop beating in dignity
> Blessed is the match that is consumed
>   in kindling the flame.

We sing the traditional Dayeynu, *eat* matzah *and the bitter herbs and discuss their symbolism, and then talk of liberation and the importance of the Jewish homeland.*

In every century Jews longed to return to Zion. In our own day, many Soviet Jews are struggling for their right to settle in Israel. Ruth Alexandrovitch, Raiza Palatnik, and Sylva Zalmanson were imprisoned for their part in this struggle.

When the Prophet Jeremiah watched the Jews being led away into Babylonian captivity, he saw a vision of our Matriarch Rachel, a symbol of this tragedy and of the yearning to return to Eretz Yisrael:

> A voice is heard on high
> A keening, mournful wail.
> Rachel is crying for her children
> Refusing to be consoled
> For their loss.
>
> The Lord says:
> Hold back the cries in your throat
> And the tears in your eyes
> For there is a future of hope for you:
> Your children shall return
> To their own land. (Jer. 31:15–18)

The third cup of wine is blessed.

We drink the third cup of wine to honor the Jews of our own time who fought and died to establish Israel.

As we lift this cup of wine, we also bring to mind our many sisters in Israel who started the "first wave" of feminism there. We remember the *halutzot,* the women pioneers who won their struggle to work in the fields and as laborers in the cities—as equals in the upbuilding of Israel.

We remember our sisters Manya Schochat, Sarah Malchin, Yael Gordon, Techia Lieberson, Hannah Meisel, and so many others, who set up women's collectives and women's agricultural training farms and organized the working women's movement in Eretz Yisrael. We remember two of these organizers, Sarah Chisick and Dvora Drachler, who fell in the defense of Tel-Hai with Yosef Trumpeldor. We remember our many sisters who fought in the underground and in the army during the War of Independence.

In Passover of 1911, the first meeting of working women in Eretz Yisrael was held. Ada Maimon wrote:

"The girls who had the opportunity to work in the fields were few and far between and even within the pioneering, revolutionary labor movement in the Land of Israel, women were relegated to their traditional tasks—housekeeping and particularly kitchen work. . . .

The girls wanted very much to discuss ways of changing and improving the situation. A meeting of their own, they felt, was absolutely necessary, for it had become clear that women would not raise their voices at general conferences and that the male delegates would not put the special problems of women workers on the agenda.

The first meeting of the working women took place in Kvutzat Kinneret. There were 17 participants. . . . The proceedings went on behind closed doors; no men were allowed to attend.

Emotional outpouring rather than systematic analysis of problems characterized the meeting. From this meeting the Working Women's Movement was born.

We talk of what Jewish identity means and how assimilation is self-oppression. We bless and then drink the fourth and last cup of wine.

We drink this fourth and last cup of wine on this Seder night to honor our Jewish sisters who are struggling to find new and beautiful ways to say "I am a Jew."

We honor all our sisters in the small but growing Jewish feminist movement, here, all over North America, in Europe and Israel; our mothers and our grandmothers whom we have so often misunderstood and fought with; our daughters and granddaughters.

We are liberating ourselves from the assimilationist dream-turned-nightmare and moving toward creating Jewish life-styles, rediscovering our history and our traditions, our heritage and our values, and building on them and from them. It is possible that in struggling to free ourselves, we shall at one and the same time be instrumental in the struggle to liberate the Jewish people as well. That, too, is our goal.

Now we speak of what we've been waiting for—the food! We eat, sing, share the afikoman, *say Grace After Meals, and sing the traditional* Had Gadya—"One Goatling." *After singing "Next Year in Jerusalem," we conclude:*

We have talked on this Pesah night about our liberation from oppression and thus we conclude the formal part of the Seder. Just as we have been privileged to join with our sisters in holding this Seder, so may we be privileged to join with them in struggling for our liberation as Jewish women. May we carry out our self-liberation soon, joyously returning to our heritage and our homeland and our people—to be redeemed and to participate in the redemption of the Jewish people.

Next Year in Jerusalem!

WOMEN IN JEWISH LAW

The dynamic character of the *halakhah*—the legal code—has made it not only possible, but mandatory, for Jews in every age and culture to create an appropriate balance between the traditions of the past and Jewish ideals for the future. One such ideal is *tzelem Elohim*—the image of God—in which human beings were created. The Talmud (Sanhedrin 37a) describes the image of God in terms of the absolute equality, absolute value, and uniqueness of every person. The many laws and customs denying women independent legal status and equal participation in prayer, study, and ritual, the unequal treatment of women in marriage and divorce law, women's exclusion from the legal process itself, prevent the evolution of *halakhah* toward its own ideals.

The authors of the following articles, while pursuing different methods of change, nevertheless recognize the centrality of *halakhah* and the need to couple the mechanisms of change with the sensitivities and values of Judaism in order to achieve equality of rights and obligations for women.

THE OTHER HALF: WOMEN IN THE JEWISH TRADITION

Paula Hyman

In September 1971, a small group of well-educated young Jewish women, all of us personally affected by the renascence of feminism, began to meet regularly to study the position of women in the Jewish tradition and to discuss our specific problems as Jews who are women. We felt in our own lives a tension between our knowledge of Judaism and the limited spheres in which we could put that knowledge into practice in the synagogue and in the community, and we found that many elements of the traditional Jewish attitude to women deeply offended our sensibilities.

As Ezrat Nashim, we have publicly called for changes in Jewish attitudes and law regarding women—primarily full participation of women in religious observance as laymen as well as rabbis and cantors, the obligation of women to perform all *mitzvot,* the recognition of women as witnesses before Jewish law, and the right of women to initiate divorce. These demands are based upon our fundamental conviction that women are intellectually and spiritually equal to men and equally deserving of positions of authority within the synagogue and community. And it is our conviction as well that the biological differences between men and women can no longer justify the outmoded and rigid sex-role division which the Jewish tradition prescribes.

It is this traditional sex-role differentiation which is the central point of the feminist critique of Judaism, as of all other patriarchal cultures.

In patriarchal cultures virtually all social roles and most character traits are ascribed according to sex, with the positions of highest status and the most highly prized characteristics—such as intelligence, initiative, emotional strength—reserved for men. While men are allowed to define themselves through a wide spectrum of activity in the world, women are defined in sociobiological terms as wife and mother and relegated almost exclusively to the home and family life. The only qualities considered "feminine" (and hence approved in women) are those which are useful in the serving, nurturing, and homemaking roles which are the woman's preserve. One need not assume a male conspiracy to explain this social configuration. Obviously biological factors, chiefly the exigencies of childbearing, were critical. However, the biological underpinnings of patriarchal culture have been eroded—childbearing, after all, occupies relatively little of modern woman's time—and the role differentiation which they generated serves only to perpetuate inequality and to deny freedom of choice to men and women alike.

The position of women in Judaism rests upon this patriarchal sex-role differentiation and the concomitant disparagement of women. Thus, the *halakhah* exempts women from all positive time-bound *mitzvot* because of the nature of their family obligations,[1] (though these may be shared with husbands or demand no more time than male occupational responsibilities). Since they are not halakhically required to participate in communal prayer three times a day, women cannot, in traditional Judaism, be counted in a *minyan* nor, as representative of the community, lead a service. Choosing to perform *mitzvot* does not raise one to the halakhic status of those obliged to do so.

But the exclusion of women from ritual activity goes even farther. Within the framework of traditional Judaism, women are not independent legal entities. Like the minor, the deaf-mute, and the idiot, they cannot serve as witnesses in a Jewish court, except for a few specified cases.[2] They do not inherit equally with male heirs;[3] they play only a passive role in the Jewish marriage ceremony; and they cannot initiate divorce proceedings.[4] True, certain communal safeguards were instituted to apply pressure to a recalcitrant husband to compel him to give his wife a *get*. However, the safeguards often failed to serve their purpose, and at all times the woman seeking a Jewish divorce must passively await the male decree. Neither marriage nor divorce is a reciprocal act for man and woman within Jewish law.

By exempting women from time-bound positive *mitzvot*—the three positive *mitzvot* generally considered as women's being *hallah* (the separation of a bit of dough to prepare the Sabbath loaves), kindling the Sabbath candles, and *niddah* (the laws of family purity)—and denying them legal independence, Judaism relegated women to a second-class status. Within the family the woman may have had a necessary and noble task to fulfill. But the heart and soul of traditional Judaism remained communal prayer and study. And prayer and study were the pursuits almost exclusively of men. No wonder, then, that Jewish sages from Rabbi Eliezer to Maimonides considered women as frivolous, ignorant beings, wasting their husbands' time, for they were not engaged in that most worthy and significant of Jewish endeavors, sacred study (the endeavor which according to Maimonides, at least, earned for one eternal life in the world to come).[5] No wonder, then, that the birth of a male child was cause for celebration, the birth of a female, for stoic acceptance. It is a distortion of Jewish history to claim that Judaism was truly ambivalent in its attitude towards education for women. Such equivocation as is reflected in the sources is merely whether women should be left illiterate or not; the *dominant* theme in Talmudic and rabbinic literature is not to educate women to the same level as men. Men and women, after all, were educated for different purposes and different roles. So the *yeshivah* and *bet midrash* were male monopolies.

It is at this point that the apologist will trot out the great women of Sunday School texts, most commonly Deborah, Esther, and Beruriah. The advanced student of Jewish history can add a few more exceptional women, such as Mibtahiah of the fifth century B.C.E. Elephantine colony,[6] or the scholarly daughter of Maimonide's twelfth-century opponent, Samuel ben Ali,[7] or a number of educated women in Renaissance Italy.[8] Thus, we have a handful of token women bearing on their frail shoulders the apologists' argument that within Judaism women could attain positions of authority and influence comparable to those of men. A handful of women throughout a period of some thirty-five hundred years of Jewish history! In historical terms, then, truly the most exceptional of women, born of unique historical circumstances: Deborah, active in the period of early Israelite religion, before strict monotheism eliminated the last vestiges of the female figure from religious life, serving as her people's judge and leader; Mibtahiah, living in a marginal community cut off from normative Judaism, where women could engage in independent business activities in their own right and divorce their husbands; Samuel ben Ali, with no sons to educate, raising his daughter to follow in his footsteps as a rabbinic authority; upper-class Jewish women in Renaissance Italy, profiting from the general rise in status of all wealthy women in this period. Of the oft-cited women in Jewish history, Esther and Beruriah attained immortality by excelling in traditional feminine roles. Esther traded on her beauty and charm to gain the king's favor, and thus was in a position to follow Mordecai's advice, save her people, and earn a position in Jewish history; while Beruriah's reputation rests as much upon her piety and devotion to her scholar husband as upon her scholarship (though the latter, too, was unusual for a woman).[9] Anecdotal references to these singular women cannot substitute for much needed scholarly investigation of the various social and economic roles which Jewish women have played at different moments of Jewish history. Until that scholarship bears fruit, however, we are left with mere token women, colorful and rare though they may be. Their presence in no way changes the status of women in Jewish law and culture.

It is spurious to argue from these "token" women that for the Jewish woman who truly wanted it, success in the man's world was a real possibility. The processes of socialization being what they are, and the socioeconomic conditions under which Jews have lived until the most recent times what they were, it is unlikely that large numbers of Jewish women longed for an equitable place in male society. Our expectations and desires alike are shaped by our vision of the possible, and until modern times, equality of men and women within Judaism would not have been encompassed by that vision. Yet, even if the vast majority of Jewish women throughout history has been satisfied with their role, this alters neither the objective position of women in Judaism nor our modern perception of that position as one of second-class status.

According to the apologists, however, within the Jewish tradition women enjoyed a position of respect and homor. The virtuous woman was extolled; for her the Eshet Hayil was recited every Sabbath evening. Within her sphere, the home, the Jewish woman was placed on a pedestal. Her role was different from the Jewish male's but no less regarded. In fact, however, separate but equal, in this as in other areas, remains an ideal most difficult to realize. Generally it has resulted in the dominant group's defining both the separateness and the equality of the second group, and justifying that separateness by projecting upon the group being defined a radical otherness. What this has meant in male-female relations is that the qualities of femininity have been defined by male culture in polar opposition to masculine traits. And uniquely female biological characteristics—in particular menstruation and childbearing—have been perceived by men as both frightening and awesome, in no small measure because they are alien to male experience.

Within Judaism these attitudes have not precluded treating women with a full measure of humanity in familial relations, as long as they fulfilled their expected role, but they have given rise to the most rigid of stereotypes regarding the nature and duties of women. Thus, the Jewish woman, we are told, is responsible for the moral development of the family, being endowed with an exceptional capacity for moral persuasion. At the same time, however, the female in Judaism is regarded as inherently close to the physical, material world, while the Jewish male is immersed in the spiritual. Thus, conveniently, the male-female role division is perceived in the Jewish tradition as a most natural one, based as it is on the fundamental polarity of the male and female characters. The Jewish woman, therefore, is not spiritually deprived by her virtual exclusion from synagogue and study, for her spiritual capacity is inferior to the man's. Better for her to supply his and his children's needs, while he supplies her spiritual wants. A most efficient division of labor! And one which explains the tendency which existed among Eastern European Jewry to relinquish responsibility for the physical support of the family to wives, while the husbands withdrew to the *bet midrash* to study and acquire spiritual merit for the entire family.

These imposed definitions of male and female, however, seem constraining today, when men and women alike seek to uncover and express both their common humanity and their individual uniqueness. And, within Judaism, they are particularly restrictive for women. The most formidable barrier to change and to the acceptance of women as authority figures and as the equals of men lies in the psychological rather than the halakhic realm. It can be argued that there are few halakhic prohibitions preventing women from taking upon themselves an ever greater role in many aspects of Jewish religious life. Girls can, and do, study much the same curriculum as boys in most institutions of Jewish learning, except for rabbinical schools. There is no halakhic rule barring women from laying *tefillin*. Yet the psychological effects of tradition and upbringing are difficult for both men and women to overcome. Many men delight in a synagogue which is the last men's club, where they can take refuge from a society which has begun to question their natural right to dominance. Many women hesitate to engage in ritual behavior sanctified by time and custom as masculine. A woman who has, throughout her life, come in contact with a synagogue whose ritual is reserved for men, gets the message: she is not needed there. Quite literally, she does not count. Even should she begin to feel the first stirrings of discontent, there is no easy way for her to chart her own course. Within the synagogue she has few role models, and mechanisms for change do not lie within her hands. Thus, the most educated and progressive of Jewish women—who knows full well that her mastery of Hebrew and Jewish knowledge exceed that of the vast majority of Jewish men—feels ill at ease the first time she has an *aliyah*. If the synagogue is to be open to men and women on a basis of equality, then women must take a regular, rather than occasional, part in services as laymen as well as rabbis and cantors, and their participation must ultimately become both normal and normative. Only then will women truly have the freedom to choose, as men do, to participate or not. And only then will women be able to examine their response to male symbolism in liturgy and ritual and perhaps be stimulated to experiment with new material in both areas.

Much has been made of the fact, and rightly so, that the Jewish tradition respects female sexuality and accords the right to sexual fulfillment to male and female alike.[10] While it is well to distinguish the Jewish attitude to sexuality from the negative Christian attitude with which it is often wrongly identified, it is precisely in this area that the second-class status of women within Judaism is highlighted.

Jewish attitudes to sexual relations and to female biology were formulated early in the development of Judaism. The fact that Judaic culture was polygamous for much of its history has, as Dr. Trude Weiss-Rosmarin has noted, profoundly affected the Jewish legal concept of adultery.[11] A married woman commits adultery when she has sexual relations with any man other than her husband, while a married man is legally an adulterer only when he becomes sexually involved with another man's wife! The attitude of the Jewish tradition to the menstruating woman—despite the modern rationalizations that the laws of family purity serve to safeguard the woman's health, to prevent sexual desire from becoming sexual license, or to keep marriage a perpetual honeymoon—reflects a primitive blood taboo.[12] According to halakhic prescriptions, the menstruating woman—or *niddah*—is to have no physical contact whatsoever with a man. Like the person suffering from a gonorrheal discharge, she is impure. Contact with her is permitted only after she has been free of her "discharge" for seven days and has undergone ritual purification in a *mikveh*. During her period of impurity, anything she touches becomes impure. While this state of impurity is a legal rather than a hygienic concept and, according to rabbinic authorities, does not imply that the *niddah* is physically unclean or repugnant, it is clear that simple Jewish men and women throughout the ages have not interpreted the laws of family purity in such a disinterested manner. Even the mere fact of legal impurity for two weeks of every month has involved many disabilities for women. And the psychological impact of the institution, especially in its strictest interpretations, upon a woman's self-esteem and attitude to her own body, would seem to be harmful.

Although irrelevant and even totally unknown to the vast majority of young Jews, the laws of family purity remain fundamental to Orthodox Judaism. In Israel, where the Orthodox rabbinate enjoys a monopoly, each prospective bride receives a booklet instructing her in the importance of family purity and admonishing her that, according to a midrash, death in childbirth is a punishment for the abandonment of the laws of *niddah*.[12] Anonymous medical opinion is invoked to testify that women need to be preserved from any and all disturbance during this two-week period of frailty. To the modern woman who knows that she is indisposed, at most, for a few hours a month, this type of reasoning is not only inaccurate but also offensive.

At the very least, leaders of Orthodox and Conservative Judaism should be willing to confront openly the issues raised by feminists regarding the laws of family purity. If, within traditional Judaism, the symbolic separation of the *niddah* cannot be totally eliminated based as it is on injunctions in the Torah, still, ways must be found to mitigate the restrictions imposed upon the *niddah*. Finally, the rationales for family purity should exploit neither medical fantasy nor sexual mythology.

What Jewish feminists are seeking, then, is not more apologetics but change, based on acknowledgement of the ways in which the Jewish tradition has excluded women from entire spheres of Jewish experience and has considered them intellectually and spiritually inferior to men. Realizing the historical, social, and biological factors which contributed in all generations to Jewish attitudes toward women, we must try to examine the Jewish tradition within its own context and refrain from pointlessly blaming our ancestors for lacking our own insights. But until we all recognize that a problem exists—that the conflict between the objective reality of women's lives, self-concept, and education and their position within Jewish tradition is a most significant one for all of Judaism—we cannot begin to take steps to attain equality for women, both in Jewish law and in Jewish attitude.

Much of the strength of the Jewish tradition has derived from its flexibility and responsiveness to the successive challenges of the environments in which it has been destined to live. In an age when the alienation of young Jews from Judaism is a major concern for the Jewish community, we can hardly afford to ignore fully one-half of young Jews. Thus, the challenge of feminism, if answered, can only strengthen Judaism.

Notes

1. Kiddushin 29a. For a discussion of woman's role in *halakhah*, see Rachel Adler, "The Jew Who Wasn't There: *Halakah* and the Jewish Woman," *Davka* (Summer 1971).

2. The ineligibility of women as witnesses is cited in numerous instances, in particular Rosh Hashanah 22a, which places women in the same category as gamblers, usurers, and pigeon-flyers, and Sotah 47b.

3. For the laws of inheritance, see Numbers 27:8 and Baba Batra 110 a–b. Women were expected to be provided for by their husbands, and in cases of divorce or widowhood, to be provided for according to the stipulations of their marriage contract.

4. The laws of divorce are based on Deuteronomy 24: 1–4, as elaborated in the tractate Gittin. [There is evidence from the Genizah and other sources that in some communities, women were able to initiate divorce proceedings.]

5. It was Rabbi Eliezer who said, "Whoever teaches his daughter Torah teaches her obscenity," (Sotah 20a). Women were considered unfit for study, and the rabbinic comment, from *Tanna debe Eliyahu*, that "women are temperamentally light-headed (*nashim daatan kalot*)," was often cited. See Kiddushin 80b for an example. For Maimonides's attitude towards women's studying Torah, see *Mishneh Torah*, Hilkhot Talmud Torah 1:1 and for his views on the rewards of study, see Ibid., Hilkhot Teshuvah 7:2 and Hilkhot Melachim 21:4.

6. Salo Baron, *A Social and Religious History of the Jews*, Vol. I (Philadelphia: Jewish Publication Society, 1966), pp. 113–14. The classic works on the Elephantine papyri in which Mibtahiah figures are Emil G. Kraeling, *The Brooklyn Museum Aramaic Papyri* (New Haven: Yale, 1953) and Arthur Cowley, *Aramaic Papyri of the Fifth Century B.C.* (Oxford: Clarendon, 1923).

7. *Sibuv Harav Rabbi Petahiah mi-Regensburg* (ed. by Dr. L. Grunhut) (Jerusalem, 1967), pp. 9–10.

8. Cecil Roth, *The Jews in the Renaissance* (Philadelphia: Jewish Publication Society, 1959), pp. 49 –58.

9. Pesahim 52b and Berakhot 10a.

10. For a discussion of the Jewish attitude towards sexuality, see David M. Feldman, *Birth Control in Jewish Law* (New York: Schocken Books, 1973).

11. Trude Weiss-Rosmarin, "The Seventh Commandment," *Jewish Spectator*, XXXVI, 8 (Oct. 1971): 2–5.

12. The basic laws of the *niddah* are to be found in Leviticus 15:19–31 and in the tractate Niddah.

13. For a translation of this booklet, written by Chief Rabbi Unterman, see *Israel Magazine*, IV, 1 (Jan. 1972).

THE STATUS OF WOMEN IN HALAKHIC JUDAISM

Saul Berman

The strident voice of an intelligent, energetic and well-organized minority can often completely overshadow the real expression of the large constituency whom the spokesmen claim to represent.

Jewish women are not an organized constituency: they have no elected spokesmen, no leaders designated to interpret their beliefs and feelings to the rest of the world. Any attempt to generalize about their condition, particularly about a matter as internal as their religious state, is fraught with multiple dangers, not least among which is the ascription to them all of the views of a minority among them.

We would indeed fall prey to this particular danger were we to assume that the voices calling for the liberation of Jewish women from their enslavement by Jewish law and Jewish society, were in truth the expression of the majority of Jewish women today. We may rather assume, certainly within the Orthodox community, that most observant women have been able to discover a life of fulfillment and religious growth within the existing patterns of *halakhah*.

However, relegating the excited voices to a minority does not mean that we can safely, or ought morally and religiously, simply ignore them. Minorities of one generation have a strange way of becoming the majorities of the next.

The purpose of this paper will be threefold. First, I would like to describe the sources of discontent, the issues which have given rise to the public campaign to change the position of women in Jewish law. Second, I would like to offer an analysis of the legal components of the status which Jewish law assigns to women. Third, in the light of my analysis I will attempt to evaluate the justice of the complaints and make some modest proposals for confronting the problems. Given the great complexity of the general area of the status of women in Jewish law, and the paucity of reasoned studies of the matter, I will not presume to offer a comprehensive analysis of the status, nor a thorough proposal as to what changes might ultimately be possible in this area of Jewish law.

I

As I have read or heard them, the basic issues around which the discontent centers are three in number. First, and perhaps most important, is the sense of being deprived of opportunities for positive religious identification. This concern goes beyond just the demand for public equality through being counted to a *minyan* or being given the right to be called up to the Torah. The focus is more significantly on the absence of even private religious symbols which serve for men to affirm the ongoing equality of their covenant with God. The fact that Jewish women are relieved of the obligations of putting on *tallit* and *tefillin,* of praying at fixed times of the day, and even of covering their heads prior to marriage, and have traditionally been discouraged from voluntarily performing these acts, has left them largely devoid of actively symbolic means of affirming their identities as observant Jews.

An interesting byproduct of this absence of covenant affirming symbols is the emphasis which Orthodox outreach groups have placed on dress standards. Not wearing slacks has been treated as if it were a revealed *mitzvah,* equivalent to *tzitzit* as a sign of one's commitment.

The sense of injustice which arises out of the first issue is intensified many fold by the disadvantaged position of women in matters of Jewish civil law, particularly areas of marriage and divorce. From her complete silence at the traditional wedding ceremony, to the problem of *agunah,* the law seems to make women not only passive, but impotent to remedy the marital tragedies in which they may be involved.

The feeling of being a second-class citizen of the Jewish people is almost unavoidable when the awareness exists that men are almost never subject to the same fate, that a variety of legal devices exist to assure that they will be free to remarry no matter what the circumstances of the termination of a prior marriage, and despite the will of the first partner.

3   The third issue has less to do with specific Jewish laws, but is more related to the rabbinic perception of the nature of women and the impact that it has had on the role to which women are assigned. No objective viewer would claim that Jewish women are physically or socially oppressed. However, Jewish women have been culturally and religiously colonized into acceptance of their identities as "enablers."

Jewish society has projected a unidimensional "proper" role for women which denies to them the potential for fulfillment in any area but that of home and family. The Psalmist's praise of the bride awaiting the moment of her emergence to be married to the King, "All glorious is the King's daughter within the palace" (Psalms 45:14), has been taken as if it mandated her remaining "within" her home. Our apologetics have relegated women to the service role; all forces of the male dominated society were brought to bear to make women see themselves in the way most advantageous to men.

The blessing recited by men each morning thanking God "for not having made me a woman," is seen as simply symptomatic of a chauvinistic attitude toward women, intentionally cultivated by the religious system as a whole. Part of that process involves the citing of statements out of context, such as "women are light-minded" (Shabbat 33b).

Taken together, these three issues—deprivation of opportunities for positive religious identification, disadvantaged position in areas of marital law and relegation to a service role—are at the heart of a growing dissatisfaction with their religious condition by an ever-increasing proportion of young Orthodox women.

How are we to respond to this dissatisfaction and implied threat of disaffection?

The first step is to call a moratorium on apologetics. It is one thing to recognize the problems and to attempt to understand the theological, halakhic, economic, and cultural factors which produced them. It is a completely different matter, both dishonest and disfunctional, to attempt through homiletics and scholasticism to transform problems into solutions and to reinterpret discrimination to be beneficial.

To suggest that women don't really *need* positive symbolic *mitzvot* because their souls are already more attuned to the Divine, would be an unbearable insult to men; unless it were understood, as it indeed is, that the suggestion is not really to be taken seriously, but is intended solely to placate women. Could we really believe that after granting women this especially religiously attuned nature, God would entrust to men—with their inferior souls—the subsequent unfolding of his will for man as expressed in the *halakhah?*

It is time to admit that we have attempted through our apologetics to make a virtue of social necessity. We have striven to elicit voluntary compliance by women to a status which men need never accept. It is becoming increasingly difficult for Jewish women to accept the idea that their own religious potential is exhausted in enabling their husbands and children to fulfill *mitzvot.*

It is time to stop talking about the reluctant husband-*agunah* problem and to do something about resolving it. Many women feel that if that same problem affected men, the *halakhah* would long ago have made some ameliorating provisions. The attempt to suggest that refusal by women to pliantly accept the fate to which they are subjected demonstrates a lack of faith in the divine will, would be more convincing if the evil decree fell more equitably among both men and women.

Apologetics will only serve to exacerbate the problem and to convince increasing numbers of women that the rabbis are engaged in an all out battle to keep women subjugated.

The distinguishing line between apologetics and explanation is exceedingly thin. Despite this danger, and while recognizing it, it is vital for us to examine those laws and social practices which seem to be unjust to women.

It has often been suggested that the ethical strength of a legal system and its jurists may be gauged by their treatment of the powerless: the poor, the alien, the widow and the orphans. By any such test, Jewish law and its rabbinic jurists would stand high, if not at the very pinnacle, among the legal systems of the world. It is difficult to conceive of these same jurists setting out with malice aforethought to subject their own mothers, wives and daughters to the most blatant forms of injustice and inequity. It is crucial, therefore, for us to see these laws and practices through their eyes if we are ever to achieve a Jewish perspective as to how to proceed in the future.

II

Any serious attempt to understand the condition of women in Jewish. law must begin with the recognition that womanhood does not merely represent membership in a group like doctors or merchants. Woman-hood, within Jewish law, constitutes an independent juristic status, shaping to varying degrees every legal relationship and being charac-terized by a special set of rights and duties determined extrinsically by law rather than by contractual agreement.[1]

This fixing of the rights and duties of a group through conferring upon them a separate legal status was never an accidental or random occurrence in legal history. The function of status conferral was usu-ally both for the protection of the individual members of the class and for the more comprehensive purpose of determining the basic struc-ture of society and protecting this structure from disturbance.[2] But these purposes can sometimes be so broad as to make impossible the formulation of a single descriptive principle to encompass the reasons for the existence of the status as well as the particular modifications of rights and duties through which those goals would be achieved.[3]

Indeed, the Talmudic sages made not a single attempt to formulate a general principle governing the status of women. The closest they come is in the attempt to define under a single heading the affirmative precepts from which women are exempt. Thus, the Mishnah states:

> All affirmative precepts limited as to time, men are liable and women are exempt. But all affirmative precepts not limited as to time, are binding upon both men and women.[4]

Even this principle, so extensively cited by subsequent Jewish jurists, is found by the Gemara to be inadequate as a general principle.[5] The Gemara rather found that there were affirmative precepts limited as to time which were yet incumbent upon women,[6] and, on the other hand affirmative precepts not limited as to time from which women were exempt.[7] Thus, the statement that, "Women are exempt from affirma-tive precepts limited as to time," is found to be descriptive of some"[8] of the laws regulating the status of women, but is inaccurate as a general description, and is certainly not a useful predictive principle.

Having thus entered into the question of women's exemptions from obligations, let us pursue this matter further. Maimonides lists a total of fourteen positive commandments from which women are exempt.[9] Of those, only eight are affirmative precepts limited as to time,[10] while the other six are not so limited.[11] But beyond these, the Talmud identifies at least six more affirmative precepts, equally limited as to time, from which women are not exempted;[12] to which may be added four affirmative precepts of rabbinic origin, also limited as to time, as to which women are also equally obligated with men.[13]

These facts make it impossible to explain women's exemptions exclusively in terms of the absence of need for time conditional commandments.[14] Women are obligated to fulfill as many positive precepts limited as to time, as the number from which they are exempted. Some other principle or principles must have been operative in determining the specific set of obligations and exemptions which constitute the legal status of women.

As is evident from what I said earlier about the significance of status conferral to the total structure of society, it would be folly for me to attempt to encapsulate the determinants of the status of women in Jewish law in a single principle. There are, aside this, two other major sources of complexity in the treatment of these issues.

The first source of additional complexity is the fact that the Talmud itself records serious debate as to whether women are indeed exempt from the individual positive time-bound precepts. The significance of these debates lies in the implication that for many of the Talmudic sages, neither the world view of Torah, nor the social order of Jewish society, would be totally disrupted by the adoption of what came to be the dissenting opinions. Indeed it was with apparently complete equanimity that the scholars were able to discuss the possibility that women were truly obligated to wear *tefillin* and *tzitzit,* and to recite Shema at the appointed times. Despite the breadth of consequences adoption of such dissenting opinions might have had, the positions were neither written out of the literature,[15] nor attacked as subversive of the accomplishment of divine will. This makes our attempt to define the status of women much more complex.

A second source of complexity in attempting to define the status of women in Jewish law, is the nature of the changes that have been experienced within the law itself. For example, it would appear that during the Tannaitic period there were three distinct positions as to the relationship of women to the *mitzvah* of *talmud Torah*. While the Mishnah[16] reflects the extreme positions of Ben Azzai arguing for obligation,[17] and Rabbi Eliezer propounding that it is prohibited to teach Torah to women,[18] the Tosefta[19] suggests an intermediate position in which women are not obligated to study Torah, but would not be prohibited from doing so. Amoraic discussion already reflects only this intermediate stance, clearly indicating the absence of obligation[20] but not pursuing the prohibitive character of the position of Rabbi

Eliezer.[21] This centrist stance would equate the study of Torah with other *mitzvot,* such as *shofar* and *lulav,* in regard to which women, though not obligated, remained free to fulfill them voluntarily.

However, this position fades during the period of the *Rishonim,* to be replaced with variants of the more extreme position of Rabbi Eliezer.

Among the *Aharonim,* two divergent approaches have manifested themselves. On one hand, the stringencies have been carried even further to the point of serious consideration being given to the possibility that it is even prohibited for women to study the Oral Law by themselves,[22] and for men to teach them even the complexities of the Written Torah.[23] On the other hand, two more permissive lines of thought have also begun to emerge. One such line constructs its case for permission to teach women both Written and Oral Torah on a purely functional base. Thus the Hafetz Hayyim and others have argued that the fact that Jewish women are beneficiaries of a secular education makes it mandatory for us to assure that their knowledge of Scripture and rabbinic thought be sufficient to preserve their identity as Jews.[24]

A second line of opinion developing among the *Aharonim* is even more interesting because for the first time since Ben Azzai it speaks in terms of an obligation of women to study Torah, albeit a limited one. Rabbi Joseph Karo suggests that women are obligated to study those laws which pertain to them.[25] But it is Shneur Zalman of Liadi who formulates a broad principle by which women are obligated to study all laws of the Torah, both Biblical and rabbinic, except those concerning *mitzvot* which they are not obligated to perform.[26]

The flux thus evident in the history of Jewish law makes it a quixotic task to describe in simplistic generalities the position of women within Jewish thought. Indeed, because of the vastness of the material and the paucity of basic legal analyses, much of what I will say in the coming section of this paper will be quite tentative in character.

Despite the inherent difficulty of defining the precise social function of any legal status, and despite the special complexities inherent in debate and legal development, certain broad patterns seem evident as to the status of women in Jewish law. The most striking of the patterns is the absence of a specific role definition for women. Had the Torah intended to preclude for women all roles but that of wife-mother-homemaker, the means of doing so were easily at hand. Much as the law clearly prescribed the obligations of a husband to his wife,[27] the obligations of a father to his child[28] and the obligations of children to their parents,[29] the law could have made mandatory for women not only marriage and procreation but also the entire range of household duties which would have defined an exclusive role for them.

The law ends up mandating for women, neither marriage, nor procreation, nor specific household duties. Jewish law does not then define with any precision whatsoever a "proper" or "necessary" role for Jewish women. While not demanding adherence to one particular role, it is nevertheless clear that since for most of our history, our continuation as a people depended upon the voluntary selection by women of the role of wife-mother-homemaker, the law would and did encourage the exercise of that choice.

Indeed, the Torah modified the civil and religious demands it made upon Jewish women, to assure that no legal obligation could possibly interfere with her performance of that particular role. If a woman elected to discover her fulfillment in the relation to her husband and children and in the shaping of a home, no law would stand in the way of her performance of that trust. It is for that reason, I believe, that the primary category of *mitzvot* from which women were exempted were those which would either mandate or make urgently preferable, a communal appearance on their part.

In the light of this proposition, we can understand why there was complete unanimity as to the Torah's having exempted women from the *mitzvot* of *sukkah, lulav* and *shofar*. These acts were of necessity performed outside of the home. We may likewise understand why it was necessary for the Torah to specifically inform us that women were obligated to attend the reading of the Torah at *Hakhel,* and why it was so obvious that they were included in the mandatory restrictions of Yom Kippur. Finally, we may now better understand the reason for the debates as to whether women are exempted from such *mitzvot* as *tefillin, tzitzit* and the reading of the Shema. For while obligations such as these need not involve communal appearance, and can adequately be fulfilled at one's own home, their very association with communal worship would create, and indeed has created for men, a powerful religious preference for their performance within the context of communal presence.

The underlying motive of exemption would then be neither the attempt to unjustly deprive women of the opportunity to achieve religious fulfillment, nor the proposition that women are inherently more religiously sensitive. Rather, exemption would be a tool used by the Torah to achieve a particular social goal, namely to assure that no legal obligation would interfere with the selection by Jewish women of a role which was centered almost exclusively in the home.

It is admittedly very difficult for an American raised with almost a sense of sanctity of individual rights, to accept a stance which gives not only primacy to the social goal, but then assigns to the individual a status which would encourage the achievement of that goal. Yet, that is exactly what Jewish law seems to do. Placing its emphasis on the communal need for the maintenance of strong family units as the central means of the preservation of the Jewish community both physically and spiritually, the law assures that nothing will interfere with that goal.

We now arrive at the second element of our proposition as to the status of women, that the exemption from obligations results in a loss of rights. While not self-evident,[30] it is clear in rabbinic literature that the exemption of women from obligations of participation in communal worship results in their disqualification from being counted to the quorum necessary to engage in such worship. For each member of the *minyan* must stand equal in obligation and capable of fulfilling the obligation on behalf of the entire *minyan*.[31]

Similarly in civil matters, the fact that women are relieved of the obligation to testify,[32] results in their inability to be part of the pair of witnesses who bind the fact-finding process of the court.[33] The law begins with the desire to exempt women from mandatory public appearances and therefore deprives the courts, in effect, of subpoena power over women. But, in turn, the inability of the court to compel her presence results in the correlative loss on the part of women of the power to compel the court to find the facts to be in accord with their testimony. [34]

III

Much remains to be written on these matters and hopefully some of it will come by the hands of women dealing creatively with the corpus of Jewish law. But if my analyses have been appropriate and I have not overstepped the boundary into apologetics, then we are in a position to at least reach some modest conclusions as to directions in dealing with the problems raised at the outset of this paper. In a status-oriented legal system, the basic laws are those which assure the social interests through status conferral. However, those laws are then modified to assure the highest possible level of individual rights achievable in consonance with the desired social goals.

Thus, in Jewish law, while the goal of family stability seems to be the motive force behind many of the elements of the status of women, the law recognizes that women are disadvantaged by that position and attempts to compensate to the extent possible.

The corrective process is reflected in the assignment of power to the court to act on behalf of a woman in compelling her husband to issue a divorce to her. These steps indicate very clearly that the accomplishment of the underlying social purpose of a particular status should not be viewed as a *carte blanche* for imposing on members of that class all disabilities which flow from their status. Rather, any side effects which are disadvantageous and also are not necessary for the achievement of the social goal, are to be eliminated by secondary legislation.[35]

In the light of this analysis we may suggest that on one hand, the exemption from communal presence seems to be a central element of women's status in Jewish law, necessary to ensure that no mandated or preferred act conflict with the selection of the protected role. But, on the other hand, many of the elements of the three areas of problems delineated at the start of this paper, are accidental side effects of the status conferral, which in themselves contribute nothing, and may ultimately interfere with, the attainment of the central social goal. If such be the case, it is the unavoidable responsibility of religious leaders to do all within their power to eliminate these detrimental side effects.

First, it is vital for religious leadership to recognize the reality of the religious quest of Jewish women. While the law assigns them a distinct status, it does not suggest that their essential religious condition stands at a level any different from that of Jewish men. If a rabbi is concerned with whether a man has prayed three times each day, he must be equally concerned with the daily prayer of women. Women must be made to feel that their own religious development is a vital concern to communal leadership, and that the community will seek out means of enhancing their religious growth.

A small number of religious women have begun donning *tallit* and *tefillin* daily, and have, in so doing, discovered a vital source of religious expression and strength.[36] It seems to me very unlikely that that particular form of religious observance will become widespread among Jewish women. However, constantly increasing numbers of women are attending synagogue services with some regularity, and that trend can be expected to intensify with the increasing liberation of women from the home and with the spread of *eruvin* in religious communities. Under these circumstances, relegating women to the back of the synagogue, both physically and spiritually, will only assure their gradual disappearance from religious life. Building committees must be sensitized to the necessity of designing structures which demonstrate that in the appearance before God, men and women are equal. *Mehitzot,* while crucial for the achievement of proper prayer, must not constitute insurmountable barriers to the approach to the divine presence.

These structural concerns must be accompanied by changes in the expectation from religious women by communal leadership. There is no reason why unmarried women should first make their appearance at some point toward the end of the Torah reading, nor is there any reason why rabbis should be more permissive of talking in the women's section than they are of such demeanor among the men. Lesser demands reflect only one thing: less significance to the endeavor.

Equal in significance with prayer is another mode of worship, Torah study. If Torah study is to occupy such an important place in the lives of Jewish men, how can we expect it to play no role whatsoever in the lives of Jewish women? Whether justified on principled or purely functional grounds, it is clear that when the intellectual development of a Jew in secular areas exceeds his or her intellectual development in Jewish knowledge, it leads at best to fragmented personalities performing mechanical religious duties and at worst to total disillusion and disaffiliation. Aside from this danger to the Jewish identity of women, the failure to educate women Jewishly deprives Jewish scholarship of most valuable resources which we cannot afford to lose.

Most important of all in this area, we must encourage women to develop in a creative fashion whatever additional forms they find necessary for their religious growth. I would not presume to know what new religious developments could emerge from Jewish women's consciously setting for themselves the task of discovering customs expressive of their religious feelings in contemporary society. Their practices might involve their own form of public worship to follow and supplement the standard service, but expressive of women's sensitivities. It might involve the creation of new religious artifacts or of new patterns of communal study. Only one thing is certain, and that is that the creative religious energies of Jewish women remain a major source of untapped strength for the Jewish community as a whole, and those energies must be freed.

The second problem area is that of the position of women in matters of civil law. In the absence of Jewish political autonomy (outside Israel), most issues of this sort are moot. However, the problem of the *agunah* of the reluctant husband continues to plague Jewish ethical sensibilities.

Indeed, this area almost more than any other, cries out for rectification. If it is true that Jewish legal process is completely stymied by this problem, a premise which I am most reluctant to accept, then that still does not absolve religious leadership of their responsibilities. If neither the conditional *get,* nor the conditional *ketubah* are halakhically acceptable, then perhaps we ought to turn to the civil courts to solve our problem for us. Perhaps at this time, every Jewish couple who marry should sign a standard form contract under which both parties agree that in case of dissolution of the marriage by either civil divorce or annulment, each will consent to and execute the issuance and acceptance of the Jewish divorce. If the legalization of such an antenuptial agreement would require enabling legislation, then that course of action is certainly possible.

The third problem area is in one regard the most sensitive of them all: the creation of a preferred role for women. First, there is a critical distinction between a mandated role and a preferred role. Jewish law specifically refrained from mandating for women the exclusive role of wife-mother-homemaker. It may very well be the case that throughout most of human history there were no alternatives practically available. But are we to assume that the Torah did not forsee the current developments and therefore simply failed to make adequate provisions to further eliminate such choices when they would become possible? On the contrary, it would seem to me that we would be compelled to conclude the exact opposite, that the Torah specifically intended to keep alternative options open in expectation of a time when they might become possible.

If such be the case, then we must not wantonly foreclose such choices. Indeed, perhaps we ought to look more closely at the potential for enrichment of the traditional role which becomes possible through its supplementation with meaningful engagement outside the home. It may behoove us as a community to provide for our young women alternative role models to help them integrate the realization that being a good Jewish woman does not mean forgoing creativity and fulfillment beyond the context of the role of homemaker.

On the other hand, the law does protect and thereby indicate a preference for the more traditional role which has home and family as its dimensions. Since society now allows for the election of radically different roles, it becomes increasingly vital for creative religious minds to offer meaningful expositions of why this preferred role ought to be chosen over all other available options. It may very well be the case that the investment of one's total personality in the endeavor of shaping the soul of growing Jewish children is the most fulfilling way in which a person's energies may be used. It may also be the case that women are either inherently or by socialization more capable of making the kind of total commitment necessary for the maintenance of constant love and devotion which form the religious character of a child. All this may be true, but women will have to be convinced—not compelled—to submit to its logic.

Furthermore, we will have to communicate more clearly that election of the traditional role does not mean self-relegation to the service role or the role as enabler. The achievement of the social goal of family stability is not to be at the expense of the souls of Jewish women. Their integrity as religious personalities will have to be emphasized more forcibly both to men and to women themselves.

These steps, small though they be, may lead in the direction of a more fulfilled Jewish womanhood of the future, and as a result, a more perfected total Jewish society.

Notes

1. See G. W. Paton, *A Text-Book of Jurisprudence*, 2d ed. (London: Oxford Press, 1951), pp. 319–24.

2. Julius Stone, *Social Dimensions of Law and Justice* (Sydney, Australia: Maitland Pub., 1966), pp. 138–41. We cannot, however, totally exclude the occasional function of status as a means of exploiting the weak rather than protecting them. See Paton, op. cit., p. 321 and pp. 252–53. Despite the absence, as yet, of systematic studies on this issue in Jewish law, I would suggest that this motive is not present.

3. This difficulty would not arise in relation to the status of the mentally incompetent. There, the protective purpose and the disabilities related thereto could be relatively easily formulated into descriptive principles. The status of the minor might be an intermediate case.

4. Mishnah Kiddushin 1:7 (29a).

5. Kiddushin 33b–34a.

6. E.g. eating *matzah*, rejoicing on festivals, and *Hakhel* (assembling).

7. E.g. study of Torah, procreation and redemption of first born sons.

8. E.g. *sukkah, lulav, shofar*, fringes and phylacteries.

9. *Sefer Hamitzvot*, end of affirmative precepts. These, out of the 60 which are always incumbent upon each individual.

10. 1. Reading Shema.
    2. Binding *tefillin* on the head.
    3. Binding *tefillin* on the arm.
    4. Wearing *tzitzit*.
    5. Counting the *omer*.
    6. Living in the *sukkah*.
    7. Taking the *lulav*.
    8. Hearing the *shofar*.

11. 1. Study of Torah.
    2. For the King to write a Torah for himself.
    3. For *kohanim* to bless the people.
    4. Procreation.
    5. For a groom to celebrate with his wife for a full year.
    6. Circumcision of sons.

12. 1. Kiddush on Shabbat. See Berakhot 20a.
    2. Fasting on Yom Kippur. See Sukkah 28a.
    3. *Matzah* on Pesah. See Kiddushin 34a,
    4. Rejoicing on festivals. See Kiddushin 34a.
    5. Assembling once in seven years. See Kiddushin 34a.
    6. Sacrificing and eating the Pascal lamb. See Pesahim 91b.

13. 1. Lighting Hanukkah lights. See Shabbat 23a.
    2. Reading Megillat Esther on Purim. See Megillah 4a.
    3. Drinking four cups of wine on Pesah. See Pesahim 108a.
    4. Reciting Hallel on the night of Pesah. See Sukkah 38a.

14. Rabbi Emanuel Rackman, "Arrogance or Humility in Prayer," *Tradition* I (1), Fall 1958, p. 17. Cf. Rabbi Norman Lamm, *A Hedge of Roses* (New York: Feldheim, 1966), pp. 75–6.

15. Of course the recording of these dissenting opinions assured that none would confuse them with the approved majority positions, as well as preserving them for the possibility of future adoption by the majority of some subsequent Great Sanhedrin. See Mishnah Eduyot 1:4–6.

16. Mishnah Sotah 3:4 (20a).

17. The texts of both the Jerusalem Talmud and the Babylonian Talmud would seem to support the position that according to Ben Azzai, women are equally obligated with men in the study of Torah. (cf. Tosafot Sotah 21b s.v. Ben Azzai, straining the reading of J.T. Sotah 15b.) This position is further supported by Mishnah Nedarim 35b.

18. The Amoraim lend an aggadic quality to the statement of Rabbi Eliezer through the addition of the word "*Keilu*" ("as if"), Sotah 21b. (See my comments on the usage of "*Keilu*" in *Encyclopedia Judaica*, vol. 10, p. 1484, in article entitled "Law and Morality.") The misogynistic tendencies here implied are made more specific in J.T. Sotah 16a.

19. Tosefta Berakhot 2:12.

20. Kiddushin 29a. cf. Berakhot 22a and the manner in which it omits the references to women's study implied in its source, Tosefta Berakhot 2:12.

21. See Sanhedrin as an instance of women studying Torah in relation to which Rabbi Eliezer's objection is not raised by the Amoraim. Many other such instances reflect the rejection of the position of Rabbi Eliezer.

22. Elijah Gaon, commentary to *Shulhan Arukh, Orah Hayyim*, ch. 47, comment 18.

23. David HaLevi, TaZ to *Shulhan Arukh, Yoreh Deah*, ch. 246, comment 4.

24. Hafetz Hayyim and others cited in *Responsa Tzitz Eliezer*, Rabbi Eliezer Waldenberg, vol. 9, no. 3, p. 32. Indeed the authorities cited limit the distinction between Written and Oral Torah, and function essentially in terms of what is necessary to counter the effects of the society to which Jewish women are exposed.

25. *Beit Yosef* to *Tur, Orah Hayyim* ch 47, s.v. *Vekasav*. His alleged sources are elusive. See Waldenberg, op. cit., p. 31.

26. *Shulhan Arukh HaRav, Laws of Talmud Torah*, 1:15. The *Beit HaLevi* (vol. 1, responsum no. 6), while affirming the possibility of an obligation resting on women to learn all laws necessary for their proper fulfillment of *mitzvot*, denies that such study would constitute a fulfillment of the *mitzvah* of *talmud Torah*.

27. Exodus 21:10. Ketubot 47b.

28. Kiddushin 29a.

29. Kiddushin 30b–31a. Ketubot 46b.

30. This entire area, including the supposed duty orientation of Jewish as compared to Roman law, and the nature of right-duty correlatives in relation to the community, begs further analysis.

31. Based on Mishnah Rosh Hashanah 3:8 (28a). See David M. Feldman, "Woman's Role and Jewish Law," *Conservative Judaism*, vol. 26(4), Summer 1972, pp. 35–6.

32. Leviticus 5:1, Sifre to Leviticus, ch. 11, law 3, *Sefer Hahinukh, mitzvah* 122, indicating exemption from obligation. cf. *Minhat Hinukh* ad. loc.

33. Tosefta Shavuot 3:5. Maimonides, *Code, Law of Witnesses* 5:1–3 and 9:1-2, indicating emphasis on disqualification from the "kat" ("pair") rather than general loss of reliability.

34. The essential function of the "pair" of witnesses is to bind the fact-finding process, unless they are directly contravened. See Maimonides, *Code, Law of Witnesses*, 5:3, 19:1, and 22:1.

35. Further illustration of this process is to be found in legislation "Mipne darke shalom" (Mishnah Gittin 5:8–9) eliminating incidental injuries resulting from status as a non-Jew.

36. For precedent see Eruvin 96a. The practice was approved by Tosafot ad. loc. s.v. *Mihal;* but disapproved by Rama to *Shulhan Arukh, Orah Hayyim*, 38:3. cf. David Feldman, op. cit. note 58, at p. 36.

A MODEST BEGINNING
Esther Ticktin

At a recent conference at which representatives of various "new" Jewish communities (like *havurot, batim,* Ezrat Nashim, Fabrangen) as well as "new" Jews struggling alone, gathered for mutual support and stimulation and the possible formulation of a vital ideology for our day, a number of us ended up saying that it may be time to start thinking and talking about a "new *halakhah.*" We were fully aware of the immense obstacles in the road for even the beginning of such an undertaking. No one had any easy answers to such questions as: *halakhah* for whom? By whom? By what criteria? On what authority? Along what lines of continuity? And yet we all felt that there already exists a new religioethical consciousness, waiting and ready to be brought forward in clear words and deeds. There are values by which many of us live or try to live, clearly Jewish values, though unacknowledged by the rabbinic authorities of our day. But we are timid and hesitant about them because we have not as yet committed ourselves to them as *halakhah*—as the logical outcome of our tradition and our historical experience.

Instead of first trying to make my way through the morass of theoretical issues, I am going to make a beginning by jumping into a concrete problem and proposing four new *halakhot* for our consideration. They deal with a issue close to my concerns: the entry of women into the congregation of Israel as full and equal partners, and what men must do to help bring this about. I chose to begin with these four *halakhot,* not because they are the most important issues for Jewish women today, nor even for women's participation in Jewish religious and intellectual life. I chose them (1) because they are based in already operative *minhagim* (customs), (2) because they are doable, (3) because they are consciousness-raising and sensitizing, and (4) because they involve our own actions rather than mere advocacy (as would *halakhot* dealing with equality in education, opening up the rabbinate to women, changing the marriage and divorce laws, etc.).

The "new" *halakhot* I am about to propose are not new at all. They do not require any new sensibilities not found in the Torah or in rabbinic tradition. In fact, they are solidly based in both, as well as being practiced by a growing number of "new" Jews. What they do require is the recognition and acknowledgement of a new social reality to which the traditional principles have to be applied. The social reality I speak of is the existence of a significant number of new Jewish women: women who have not been socialized to accept the traditional exclusion of women from full and equal participation in the spiritual and intellectual life of Judaism. These new Jewish women now feel like strangers in the house of Israel and are begging, asking, demanding or screaming (depending on their temperament and tolerance for injustice) not to be shunted off behind a *mehitzah* (partition), to be counted as equals in *minyan,* to be called up to the Torah, to be allowed and trained to lead the congregation as *shlihe tzibur,* and to be given the opportunity to study Torah and contribute to its growth and development. The existence of such women and their claims are a new social reality which cannot be denied even by those men and women who deplore it.

My very modest proposals are addressed to those men who are able to hear the claims of the new women. (I will speak of the relevance of these proposals to women later.) But first I must make a distinction between two groups of traditional Jewish men, both of whom are able to hear and understand what the new women are saying, and both of whom should, therefore, feel addressed, if not commanded, by what I am proposing. The only difference between them is that one group feels itself bound by the *piske din* (legal decisions) of the contemporary Orthodox rabbinate, while the other does not. The Orthodox men may, for that reason, be unable to comply with one of the two categories of the *mitzvot lo taaseh* (negative commandments) that I am about to describe. Knowing some of these men to be honest and sensitive souls who are agonizing over these issues, I want to say in all humility, that I hope and pray that their inability to say yes to that category of *mitzvot* be in the realm of the "not yet."

The Biblical basis of both categories of these "new" *halakhot* is: "for you were a stranger in the land of Egypt," and the particular Jewish *galut* (exile) experience that I ask us to remember is the experience of exclusion: exclusion from medical school, Ivy League colleges, professional and social clubs, etc. in the "hospitable" and enlightened countries, total exclusion from the economic and intellectual mainstream in the more benighted ones. If we can at all remember this basic *galut* experience—and doesn't our very Jewishness stand or fall on our ability to remember?—then we also remember what we expected of a decent, sensitive Gentile in that situation. We expected him to express his sense of justice and common humanity by refusing to join a club or fraternity that excluded us as Jews. Is it too much for Jewish women to expect the same kind of decency of Jewish men in relation to us?

The first category of the new *mitzvot lo taaseh*, then, is based on the idea of not being a beneficiary of a policy of exclusion, "for you know the soul of the excluded." It consists of two parts:

(A 1) Do not participate in a *minyan* which separates women behind a *mehitzah* (even if the women assent to such treatment).

(A 2) Do not accept an *aliyah* in a *minyan* which does not call up women to the Torah.

(These are the two *mitzvot* which an Orthodox Jew cannot as yet fulfill—although he might consider the second as a form of self-discipline even today.)

Well-meaning and sensitive Jews are sometimes troubled by the divisive potential of such a *mitzvah*. But to me it seems a double standard and hypocrisy to respect the principled *insistence* on the *mehitzah* by Orthodox Jews, on the one hand, and to make light of the equally principled insistence on justice for female Jews, on the other hand.

The second category of "new" *mitzvot lo taaseh* applies to *all* Jewish men. To many of us it seems a simple matter of *menschlichkeit*—but, certainly, to Jews steeped in a tradition that teaches such extremes in delicacy of feeling as "If there is a case of hanging in a man's family record, say not to him, 'hang this fish up for me' " (Baba Metzia 59b), the relevance of this category should be obvious. But the fact that some of our most spiritually sensitive men are guilty of ignoring these *mitzvot* makes it necessary to state them explicitly.

This category also consists of two parts. The first part says:

(B 1) If, for your own spiritual uplift or social needs, you go to a *farbrengen* with the rebbe, or participate in any other spiritual experience from which women are excluded, do not speak of it to your mother, your sister, your wife, your girlfriend, your female student or counselee, or to your daughter. In fact, do not speak of it to your son either, because he may be less sensitive or less self-disciplined than you.[1]

The cruelty and teasing quality of talking about an experience from which the hearer is forever excluded should be obvious. But, somehow—could it be because the men do not credit the spiritual needs and hungers of Jewish women?—I have heard so much of this teasing that I must assume the men who do it to be unaware of the pain and anger they are causing. I have even heard an otherwise excellent youth leader refuse to organize an alternative *minyan* in which men and women would be equal, not because he had any Orthodox scruples against it, but because in his own words, "the only place *I* can *daven* with *kavvanah* is a hasidic *shtibl*." It so happens that because of where he lives, he can get to that hasidic *shtibl* only once or twice a year, but in the meantime he denies the possibility for *kavvanah* to every woman who hears him.

In light of the first *halakhah* (A 1) I proposed, a non-Orthodox Jew should refuse to go to religious events that exclude his sisters, but if the desire, or the need, or the curiosity is so great that he "must" go, let him, at the very least, keep quiet about it.

The second *halakhah* in this category is based on the same delicacy of feeling required by the tradition as the first, only dealing with action rather than words. The second part says:

(B 2) Do not participate in an exclusively male dancing circle when there are women and female children standing around and forbidden to enter it—regardless of whether the purpose of the joyous dance is Simhat Torah, *seudah shlishit* or a wedding.[2]

I have, myself, cried, and my daughters have cried, about having been excluded from such circles, and we have simply not been able to understand how some of our close male friends could abandon themselves in a joy that deliberately and blatantly excluded us. (By the same token, I shall never forget that my father, *alav hashalom*, refused to participate in the dancing on the Simhat Torah when he took me with him to the rebbe. In fact, that is when he stopped going there himself. It was also my father who first taught me the gemara quoted above. All this took place some forty years ago, but is probably the strongest reason why I continue to believe in the humanizing power of the Jewish tradition.)

I know, of course, that most Orthodox women are socialized from childhood on not to covet such "male prerogatives." My feeling is: how sad for them, their vitality and self-respect! But regardless of how we react to their "willing" acceptance, the new social reality is that there are more and more women who, like Martin Luther King's children at the all-white merry-go-round, ask, "Daddy, why can't we go on it?" And no apology in the world will convince them that the "separate but equal" women's circle is just as good. (We may get to feel that it is *better*, as many Jews and blacks and gay people feel about their communities in America today, but by that time we would be on our way toward creating our separate feminist religious community—hardly a necessary or desirable development.)

The alternative for the non-Orthodox is simple enough: form or join a circle of men *and* women. But what about the Orthodox men? Am I condemning them to mourning or to celebrating behind closed doors where no hungry, longing female eyes can watch them? I think I am. What I think I am saying to them is: "As long as you cannot or will not come up with a solution to the exclusion of women from communal religious celebration, decency and common humanity should keep you from *wanting* to celebrate, yourself. The excluded are not, after all, the unknown and unknowing strangers; they are your mothers, sisters, wives and daughters whose eyes have been opened and who now know that they have been kept out. If you are powerless to bring them *in*—then, maybe, there is no reason for you to rejoice!

But whether or not my Orthodox friends can impose these restrictions on themselves, there is now a community of new Jews in this country, dedicated to a revitalized and spiritualized *Yiddishkeit* which includes women as equal members of the covenant. For them—for us—at least, let me repeat the four *halakhot* I proposed:

(1) Do not—on halakhic, religious grounds—participate in a *minyan* which separates women behind a *mehitzah*.

(2) Do not—on halakhic, religious grounds—accept an *aliyah* where women are not called up to the Torah (and explain your reasons).

(3) If you have to participate in an all-male religious event, and enjoy it or are uplifted by it, do not speak to a woman about it (nor to a man either).

(4) Do not enter a circle of male dancers which excludes women, whether for Simhat Torah, a wedding, or any other religious or secular occasion, for you were a stranger in the land of Egypt.

Do not let the fact that many women assent to their exclusion divert you from the recognition that your participation is perpetuating an evil, an oppression. If your wife, your beloved, or your daughter cannot be in it, neither should you—regardless of whether they would want to or not. The children of Israel did not want to leave Egypt; they had to be dragged out. Oppression can become a comfortable habit for the oppressed. Which does not mean that you have the right to participate in it.

As for women: Except for the first *halakhah* which, of course, I consider obligatory for all women (again, with the possible exception of some Orthodox women, for whom it is "not yet" possible), the other three *halakhot* have to be translated into *mitzvot aseh* (positive commandments) for us. We must actively seek and insist on equality and full participation, certainly avail ourselves of all such opportunities where they exist, and create them where they do not as yet exist. We must work on raising our consciousness so that we can immediately spot the subtle exclusions and put-downs which make us strangers in our own house. And we must become aware of our real power. As mothers, we might consider boycotting camps and religious schools that practice discrimination against our daughters. We must certainly challenge our male friends when self-indulgence or laziness keep them from observing the above *mitzvot* or from helping to create opportunities and occasions in which we can all, together and as equals, seek to find our way to God and Torah.

Some thoughts on process:

The proposed four *halakhot* are, of course, based on already existent *minhagim*. But they are more than *minhagim* made explicit. In proposing them as *halakhot* I imply the principle that whenever a new *minhag* is motivated by a moral and religious insight, that moral and religious insight has a claim on us as *individuals* also. In other words, it has the *potential* of becoming a *halakhah*, a *mitzvah*. But it does not actually become a *mitzvah* until it is proposed to the community as such (i.e., as a potential *mitzvah*), and accepted by a consensus. That not all *minhagim* are in that are in that category should become clear when we think of new *minhagim* like sitting on cushions on the floor for prayer, instead of on chairs, of separating the Kabbalat Shabbat service from Maariv by a meal in between, or other such local customs based on convenience, taste, comfort, esthetics, experiment, etc.

To get back to my concrete proposal. There are a number of communities in this country and in Israel in which women are full and equal participants (at least *de jure*). So far, this participation has been treated, as in Conservative Judaism, as a *minhag*, based more or less on the prevailing mores of the non-Jewish world, for which a *heter* (permission) was sought (and usually found) within the existent *halakhah*. Until now, that is where it has remained: operative as a *minhag* wherever it has become one, but not binding on individuals, not a *mitzvah*. My proposal is to take seriously the religio-ethical basis of these new *halakhot* and move in the direction of making them binding on ourselves.

Notes

1. As proof-text for this *mitzvah*, read the complete mishnah and gemara from which the above quotation is taken (Baba Mezia 58a-59b).

2. Cf. "Bring not your small children to visit one who was bereaved of his small children," *(Sefer Hasidim* 13C no. 103, p. 56), or "Abash not him who has a physical blemish or family stain." (*Orhot Tzaddikim* 15C ch.21). All of which seems to say: "Do not flaunt your privileged status."

MODELS FROM
OUR PAST

Until recently, little of any value has been written on the history of the Jewish woman. Praises of her virtue and talents as the mainstay of the household have been easy substitutes for the serious questioning and analysis which the subject merits. In the past few years, however, scholars—especially women—are beginning to rediscover the real history of the Jewish woman—the different roles she played in different eras and cultures, her economic activity, communal participation, literature, as well as her role in the family. Her mythic history—that she was happily limited to the nurturing role, pious and compliant, transmitter of culture and pillar of the family—is being questioned. It is heartening to note the publication of new works in Jewish women's history, new doctoral studies, and the reprinting of several forgotten classics.

It is impossible in an anthology of this kind to include all of Jewish women's history. We hope that separate works devoted exclusively to this subject will appear. We have, therefore, chosen to highlight several examples from our past which are indicative both of the variety of life-situations and responses of our predecessors, and are models, perhaps, for our present identity and future growth. From them we learn that we are not the first Jewish women discontent with "women's place" and that, concomitantly, Jewish feminism does not, in fact, represent the total break with our past which our critics would have us believe.

BAIS YAAKOV: A HISTORICAL MODEL FOR JEWISH FEMINISTS:

Deborah Weissman

To most of the Jewish world today, the name "Bais Yaakov" ("Beth Jacob") connotes religious orthodoxy, strict observance of modesty requirements, and uncompromising adherence to traditional behavior. Few realize that this network of schools and youth organizations for girls and young women began as a rather radical innovation within the Polish Jewish community. A departure from age-old norms regarding the role of the woman in Judaism, it arose partially in response to the early twentieth-century feminist movement and was attacked on the left by assimilationists and on the right by ultra-Orthodox groups.

The religious Jewish community maintains as its basis a close identification with an historical tradition which is believed to possess eternal relevance. Although innovation is not unknown, it must be legitimated in terms of its connection with tradition. For example, Agudat Yisrael, which, as a worldwide, activist, political organization represents a deviation from older forms of Jewish community life, keeps as its motto, *Masoret avotenu biyadenu,* "the tradition of our fathers is in our hands." Thus, the early leaders of the Bais Yaakov movement, in response to their critics, had to develop an ideological framework to justify their actions. They employed certain techniques common to other social movements—myth-making, the use of kinship terminology, the creation of "total" institutions. In this article, we shall note the "official" Bais Yaakov myth, the historical-sociological reality, the ideological and structural methods of legitimization employed and, finally, the implications all of this may have for contemporary Jewish feminists.

During the interbellum period, the Jews formed the second largest national minority in Poland (second only to the Ukrainians.) There were 3,000,000 Jews, who lived mainly in the large urban centers. In some cities, the Jews accounted for 25 percent to 30 percent of the population. They were primarily involved in middle-class occupations, trades, and commerce, while the vast majority of the non-Jewish population was still agrarian.

The Minorities Treaty signed at the end of the end of the First World War promised support for schools of all cultural minorities in Eastern Europe, but in Poland, each year, subventions to the Jewish schools were diminished. In 1927, the city of Warsaw granted 60,000 zlotys for its Jewish schools; in 1928, 17,000; by 1934, nothing. Originally, there were public schools catering to the children of heavily Jewish neighborhoods. These schools would be closed on the Sabbath and Jewish holidays and open on Sundays and, using state funds, would provide instruction in the Jewish religion. But gradually these were closed down.

About three-quarters of the children attended secular Polish schools and the rest, Jewish schools of different ideological orientations in which the language of instruction was, variously, Hebrew, Yiddish, or Polish. Within the Orthodox community, emphasis was placed on schools for boys.

Traditionally, the commandment of studying Torah is incumbent only on the Jewish male. Women's education had been, for the most part, neglected by the religious community. It would have been considered a frivolous waste of valuable Torah study time for a boy to learn secular subjects. But since no such prohibition applied in the case of the woman, many parents began to send their daughters to secular public schools. Some members of the community felt that because of women's "weaker natures," and certainly because of their superficial knowledge of Jewish sources, they were more receptive to external influences than were their brothers. Yet, paradoxically, these same Orthodox leaders were reluctant to open Jewish schools for girls and young women. Girls were supposed to receive whatever traditional knowledge they needed at home, from their mothers and grandmothers. Some went so far as to quote the words of Rabbi Eliezer: "He who teaches his daughter the Torah virtually teaches her depravity. . . . Better the Torah were burned than to be studied by women."

Thus, many of the daughters of Orthodox parents came to be sent to Polish *gymnasia*. As a result of their exposure to modern, secular culture many of the girls began to question the religious values and traditions which they had been taught by their parents. Some were swept into the small but growing feminist movement in Poland (Polish women achieved political emancipation in 1919); others were influenced by Marxist or other revolutionary ideologies. The legendary intergenerational harmony of the Jewish household was being undermined. Young girls would appear for the family's Sabbath meals in stylish immodest attire, and would respond brazenly to their elders. What was to become of the traditional continuity of Jewish religious life? Where would the dedicated yeshivah students find suitable brides?

Sarah Schenirer, born in Cracow in 1883 to a hasidic family, was a simple seamstress who spent every evening poring over the Bible, the Mishnah, and books of Jewish ethical literature. She envied her father and brothers who were permitted to study Talmud. Her friends mocked her and as children had called her "the little pious one." During the First World War, she temporarily emigrated with her family, leaving Galicia and spending the war years in Vienna. On Shabbat Hanukkah, 1914 she went to the Stumper Gasse Synagogue and heard the rabbi, Dr. Flesch, preach a sermon on Judith and other valiant women in Jewish history. The rabbi called for the spiritual rejuvenation of Judaism through greater devotion and commitment to study on the part of the Jewish woman. Sarah was so inspired that she began to formulate plans for her return to Cracow. She would organize study groups for women and try to instill in them the same fervor that she felt.

Returning to Cracow, Sarah told the parents of the children for whom she had worked as a seamstress that she would now furnish them with "spiritual garments." In 1917 she gathered about forty women and girls in the auditorium of the local Jewish orphans' home for a study session. The older participants seemed to enjoy her lecture, but the young girls mocked her traditional ways. She did succeed, however, in opening a small library for the Jewish women of Cracow.

After several months, Sarah realized that for her vision to become a reality, she would need the wider support of the Jewish community and a more systematic organization. She wrote to her brother in Czechoslovakia, asking his advice. At first he counseled her not to get involved in politics, women's education being a highly controversial issue. Then, he suggested that she travel to Marienbad to consult with the Belzer rebbe. The Belzer Hasidim, although they did not support

Agudat Yisrael, had become politically active in response to the Enlightenment (in contrast to other hasidic groups, such as the Klausenberger, Karliner, etc.) They had begun to use modern mass communications and methods of political organization.

The Belzer rebbe gave Sarah's efforts his blessing. Later, the Hafetz Hayyim, the outstanding halachic authority of his generation, was to answer critics on the religious right by saying that in view of changing social conditions—widespread assimilation and the breakdown of traditional Jewish family life—the historical prohibitions against women's education were to be disregarded and that, on the contrary, it would be a *mitzvah* to teach Jewish girls the fundamentals of their faith.

Encouraged by the rabbinical support, Sarah returned once again to her home and renewed her efforts. In 1918 she enrolled twenty-five young girls in the first Bais Yaakov school. After two months, their number had grown to forty. The name Bais Yaakov ("House of Jacob") was derived from a Biblical expression which had been interpreted by Rashi as referring to the women of the Jewish people and symbolizing their central role in Jewish survival. The motto of the schools, taken from the Book of Isaiah, was *"Bais Yaakov, lekhu venelkha beor haShem,"* ("House of Jacob, come and let us walk in the light of the Lord.")

In 1919 the Bais Yaakov school, which now numbered some 300 students, was taken over as the women's educational arm of the Agudat Yisrael movement in Poland. In 1923 the Agudah convention in Vienna founded Keren HaTorah, an educational fund that would enable Bais Yaakov to expand and establish schools throughout Poland and also in Lithuania, Latvia, Czechoslovakia, Romania, Hungary, and Austria. A teachers' seminary was founded in Cracow and later also in Vienna and Chernovitz. Summer camps were started in several locations in Central and Eastern Europe. Sarah Schenirer established two youth organizations—Batya and Benos (Daughters of Agudah)—for students and graduates of the schools. The three main centers of the movement—Cracow, Lodz, and Vienna—produced textbooks, magazines, and other educational materials. The monthly *Bais Yaakov Journal*, which appeared originally in Polish and Yiddish and later, only in Yiddish, became an important publication in the homes of observant Jews throughout Europe for sixteen years. By 1937 the movement had grown to encompass 250 schools with some

38,000 students. Bais Yaakov fundraising committees existed in many countries, including the United States.

By this time, Sarah Schenirer was no longer the working director of the movement. Her role had been taken over by Dr. Samuel (Leo) Deutschlander, a German neo-Orthodox Jew. She remained as the spiritual symbol of the movement until her death in 1935. Because of her hasidic background, there was undoubtedly some friction between her and the Western European Jews, men and women who were in the chief leadership roles, and whose secular education at the universities of Bonn or Heidelberg had given them a different outlook on the running of the schools. It is important to note that the same East-West tensions existed among the constituent groups within Agudat Yisrael as a whole.

The third and final director of Bais Yaakov before the Holocaust was Yehudah Leib Orlean, a Gerer Hasid. The Gerer Hasidim became, and to this day remain, the dominant group in the Agudah. But the movement still encountered opposition from the right. By the mid–1930s, Bais Yaakov had established a *hakhsharah*, training farm, to prepare its graduates in Poland for immigration to Palestine. Though by no means politically Zionist, its schools in Palestine taught Hebrew as a modern, spoken language. The rift between Agudat Yisrael and what was to become the extremist Neturei Karta group centered largely around the issue of the Bais Yaakov schools. In 1945, when the Neturei Karta gained control of HaEdah HaHaredi, the ultra-Orthodox community council in Jerusalem, one of their first acts was to exclude from membership anyone educating his daughter at a Bais Yaakov school.

The heroism and dedication of Bais Yaakov students and teachers during the Holocaust is worthy of a separate study itself. Ninety-three Bais Yaakov teachers who chose to die a martyr's death rather than be defiled by the Nazi soldiers have already been immortalized in a famous Hebrew poem by Hillel Bavli. Suffice it to say that no one will ever be able to do an adequate analysis of the development of Bais Yaakov, since, as a social movement, it had a truncated life.

Nevertheless, after the Second World War, the movement was rejuvenated. Today, the world center has been reestablished in Jerusalem, and there are now over 150 Bais Yaakov institutions in Israel, the United States, England, Switzerland, Belgium, France, Uruguay, Argentina, and Canada. In addition, the concept of schools for girls has been taken over by the right-wing Orthodox groups which originally expressed vehement opposition to the Bais Yaakov program. The Klausenberger, Karliner, and Satmar Hasidim run schools for girls, called, respectively, Bais Chana, Bais Brocho, and Ohel Rachel. According to Bais Yaakov publications, the schools succeeded in developing several generations of girls who were fully suited to, and comfortable in, their traditional role as Jewish women. Indeed, no longer was the problem finding suitable brides for the yeshivah students but rather suitable husbands for the Bais Yaakov graduates.

So far, we have approached the topic primarily from the perspective of the movement itself, with little sociological analysis. It is necessary at this point, however, to attempt to view the development of the movement in the light of changing socioeconomic conditions of the Polish Jewish community, and the sociology of Jewish feminism.

As a preliminary to the discussion, we shall posit the following basic definition of feminism—a belief in the importance of an independent social, political, or vocational role for the woman, outside of the home. Feminism is thus both an effect and a cause of modernization. A modern mechanized economy calls for a greater labor force outside the home, and thus for women as well as men to be educated into a variety of modern work roles. At the same time, women who are educated and work outside the home bring back with them new ideas and new perceptions of themselves as complete human beings. True equality of the sexes, as can be seen in the modern history of the feminist movement in the United States, can be brought about only where economic conditions facilitate an increased labor force. As J.A. and Olive Banks have noted, the contemporary expansion of the woman's work roles is probably not a result of the ideological success of the Women's Liberation movement, but rather a result of certain sociological factors such as the development of technology, increased use of birth control, greater longevity for women due to improvement of medical facilities, and the like.[1]

Jacob Lestchinsky, in a study of the social structure of Jews in Poland in the period under discussion, wrote:

> It can be unhesitatingly asserted that the Orthodox Jewish family preferred to live in a poorer dwelling or to cut its food consumption rather than have the wife or daughters enter the factory labor market.[2]

But, he continued, under pressure of economic necessity, these cultural sanctions were modified and Orthodox Jewish women began to enter the labor market. Originally, in fact, Jewish girls were sent to the Polish public schools for economic reasons; knowledge of Polish and other languages would help them in business dealings with non-Jews. As part of a broader anti-Semitic campaign, the Polish government legislated that no one could run a business without training. One of the purposes of this law was to make it impossible for the Jewish women, who generally ran their families' businesses, to continue to do so. At the same time, other anti-Semitic measures were making it difficult for Jews to attend Polish schools.

Within the Jewish community, there was a trend towards later marriage and thus a lower fertility rate. The entrance of Poles into the traditionally Jewish middle-class occupations and the world-wide economic depression of 1929 contributed to the increasing pauperization of the Jewish community. The rapid urban population increase far outstripped economic development. Finally, the compulsory Sunday Rest Law, passed in 1919, meant that the businesses of Orthodox Jews could no longer compete on an equal basis with those of their non-Jewish neighbors. Thus, at the very same time that the Jewish community was faced with its greatest need for vocational training, its children were being phased out of the secular school system. Jewish schools were no longer supported by the Polish government. The Jewish community itself, with extensive financial aid from abroad, would have to bear the burden of training its youth.

Thus we can see that the rapid, successful spread of the Bais Yaakov idea may have been due less to the ideological power of the movement or the charisma of its leaders than to the socioeconomic necessity of vocational training for Polish Jewish girls, supported by the Jewish community. But in order to justify and legitimate an innovation of this nature in a community which at least outwardly supported tradition and not innovation, the Bais Yaakov movement had to develop an ideology and a complicated structural framework. It developed, first of all, the romantic legend of Sarah Schenirer. Through the use of pseudo-kinship terminology (e.g., Sarah Schenirer was called "our mother" and the members referred to each others as "sisters") the myth was buttressed. Sarah was made to epitomize the traditional ideal of the "Woman of Valor." It was always emphasized that she remained in her place and never challenged the superior authority of the men. Orlean often stressed in his writings—apparently in response to the fears expressed by certain critics of the movement that the girls would learn too much and begin to compete intellectually with the men of the community—that what was imparted through Bais Yaakov was not so much knowledge as good behavior—modesty, humility, love—the traditional virtues of the Jewish woman.

The movement developed a complete system of slogans, mottoes, symbols, special holidays and celebrations, literature, songs, leadership roles, and other organizational techniques. There were regional and international conventions and conferences at which policies were set. Finally, several "total institutions"—residential schools and seminaries as well as summer camps—were established. Such institutions are often employed for the purpose of solidifying social movements or strengthening educational frameworks.

It is futile but nonetheless fascinating to speculate as to what the future of the Bais Yaakov movement would have been like had its development not been arrested by the Nazis. The Bais Yaakov publications of the 1920s and 1930s are filled with apologetics for the traditional women's role in Judaism and diatribes against the European feminist movement. Still, here and there, we can find articles which speak quite favorably of certain feminist ideas, and, in a poll taken among Bais Yaakov students, the results of which were published in the 1932 editions, a surprising number of respondents stated that they were in favor of the "emancipation of the woman." In the same year, a young girl writes in that her father is pushing her to marry at the age of seventeen, so he can derive some typical Jewish *nakhes* (pride and satisfaction) from her. She writes, "I'm very depressed, I don't know where to turn. . . . My mother was a mother at eighteen, but I still want to live. What's the rush? What is life, if not to be free, independent?" Chana, the letter-writer, is not rebuked for her unorthodox approach. On the contrary, she receives a sympathetic, supportive answer which encourages her to travel and see something of life, but tells her to be careful and to try to understand her father's outlook as well.

Therefore, through deepening their knowledge of classical Jewish sources, through training them for teaching, secretarial functions, bookkeeping, sewing, home economics, settlement in Palestine, and so on, and through providing a framework for organizational activities and international communications for thousands of young Jewish women, Bais Yaakov was functioning to raise the "feminist consciousness" of its students. If the movement had continued to develop (and it is important to note that what happened after the Holocaust is atypical, since the Orthodox community in general made a major move to the right, after that period), it might indeed have developed a new role model for the educated and in certain ways, emancipated, Jewish women.

Interestingly, the movement today is being faced with new challenges. In Israel, the first major challenge was the absorption of thousands of young women of Sephardic and North African background, whose home life and cultural values were very different from those of the previous majority of Bais Yaakov students. The second great challenge to the Bais Yaakov schools in Israel occurred recently when the Israeli Ministry of Education instituted the *reforma* —changes in the standards of accreditation which stipulated that high school teachers had to have an academic university background. The Bais Yaakov network in Israel responded by broadening its scope and furnishing its students with the equivalent of a university education in certain fields.

In the United States, the schools had to respond to a reality more difficult to contend with than that of the interbellum Polish community. Then "assimilated" Jewish girls might continue to speak Yiddish or to espouse a secular Jewish nationalist ideology. In the United States, assimilation might mean total rejection of Jewish identity. The Bais Yaakov schools of New York recently opened new vocational training courses leading to the career of legal secretary. Future plans call for similar courses for dental hygienists and dental and medical laboratory technicians. The advertisements for these courses states that they "will enable girls who have graduated high school to be trained for high-paying jobs without the need to leave the warm Bais Yaakov atmosphere." Will the American schools also begin to offer university-level training? Will the Orthodox community today begin to emulate the model of German Jewry, where observant Jewish women received doctorates from secular universities? And, most important of all, how will all of this affect the women's acceptance of their role in the synagogue, home, and Jewish community?

What can modern Jewish feminists learn from the history of Bais Yaakov? In order to expand the Orthodox women's role today, the Jewish feminist movement must begin to explore historical parallels and models for social and Jewish legal change. Jewish law has been responsive at various points in history to social conditions, but the changes must be deemed of sufficient importance to warrant action on the part of the community. If an ideology of *"et la'asot laShem"* (literally, a time to act for God; figuratively, a social emergency which becomes a religious emergency) can be put forth, rabbis and other leaders may become sensitive to the real personal and sociological needs of contemporary Jewish women.

Obviously, the situation today is different from that of interbellum Poland, since the exigencies are not primarily economic. Nevertheless, some analogies can be drawn. The disaffection of bright, concerned young people is a reality the Jewish community can not afford to ignore. Cutting off a potential source of educational and communal leadership simply because of sex has dangerous consequences for a community already beset by the problems of assimilation and alienation. Jewish feminists who are seeking change must present an awareness, not only of their own personal frustrations and needs, but also of the implications of their movement for the Jewish community at large and, indeed, for the broader context of Jewish history.

With such an approach, the movement can begin to seek rabbinical assistance and approval on a serious level. The women will be taken seriously by halakhic leaders only to the extent that they demonstrate a deep commitment to Jewish life in general and to Torah study in particular.

Notes

1. J. A. Banks and Olive Banks, "Feminism and Social Change." In George Zolischan and Walter Hirsch (eds.), *Explorations in Social Change* (Boston: Houghton Mifflin, 1964), pp. 547–69.

2. Jacob Lestchinsky, "The Industrial and Social structure of the Jewish Population of Interbellum Poland." *YIVO Annual of Jewish Social Science* XI (1957) : 249–50.

BERTHA PAPPENHEIM: FOUNDER OF GERMAN-JEWISH FEMINISM

Marion Kaplan

Bertha Pappenheim was an intense and energetic personality who tried throughout her life to further and integrate feminism and Judaism. She founded the Jewish feminist movement in Germany and led it for twenty years (1904–24), imbuing it with her passionate zeal. Pappenheim educated an entire generation of German-Jewish women in ideas which were considered radical for their time, encouraging Jewish women to demand political, economic and social rights as well as the commensurate responsibilities. In the face of the frequent indifference of women and the hostility or condescension of men, she pioneered in organizing a nation-wide network of Jewish social workers whose primary concern was the protection and emancipation of women. She was the first person to raise publicly the problems of unwed mothers, illegitimate children and prostitutes in the German Jewish community.

Bertha Pappenheim was born in Vienna in 1859, the third daughter of wealthy religious Jews. As "just another daughter" in a strictly traditional Jewish household, Bertha was conscious that her parents would have preferred a male child. Years later she wrote that Orthodox Jews considered a female child to be of secondary importance:

> This can already be seen in the different reception given a new citizen of the world. If the father, or someone else asked what "it" was after a successful birth, the answer might be either the satisfied report of a boy, or—with pronounced sympathy for the disappointment— "Nothing, a girl," or, "Only a girl."[1]

After finishing high school, Bertha was not permitted to continue her education. This was a period in which most universities still excluded women and in which German Jews expected their daughters to prepare themselves exclusively for marriage. Thus Bertha entered what German feminists called "the waiting period," the time a girl spent between graduation and marriage. Bertha's life, in her own words, was "typical" of a *höhere Tochter* (a daughter who did not work) of the "religious Jewish middle class."[2] Besides occasional diversions, most of her time was spent embroidering and daydreaming[3]—an extremely monotonous existence for a girl of her energy and neevven urtvintelligence.

At twenty-one, Bertha began experiencing serious psychological problems, and was referred to the care of Josef Breuer, a well-known physician. Breuer later told his colleague, Sigmund Freud, of his work with Bertha, who became "Anna O.," the patient most often discussed by Freud, although he never treated her. Her case was the best-known example of what was then considered major hysteria.[4]

After her recovery, she and her mother moved to Frankfurt, where her female relatives involved her in charity work. Her sensitivity to injustice and her strong social consciousness were revived further by German feminism. Pappenheim read *The Woman*, a popular feminist periodical and admired its founder, Helene Lange, the main theoretician of the German women's movement. German feminist demands for equal educational opportunities for women probably found fertile ground in the mind of Pappenheim, a markedly intelligent woman who always resented being denied higher education due to the Jewish prejudice which expected girls to marry and boys to achieve scholarly success. Her interest in German feminism fused with her strong identity as a Jew and she henceforth adapted feminist ideology to Jewish life. She applied German feminist propaganda in favor of equal career opportunities and equal political rights to the lot of Jewish women. She read German feminist literature on the historical role of women and developed her own theories about the role of Jewish women in history. The relative successes of German feminism in improving women's status encouraged her to attempt the same for Jewish women.

Pappenheim's writings, begun in the 1890s, reflected her interests and growing concerns. Her first book, entitled *In the Secondhand Shop*, was a collection of short stories which expressed the writer's concern for the poor and her love of children. By 1899 Pappenheim's identity as a feminist was clearly developed. Her play *Womens Rights*

(1899) stressed the political, economic, and sexual exploitation of women. The women in the play—a poor unmarried mother who was arrested for attempting to organize other working women for self-protection, and her friend, a middle-class housewife whose husband had control over her property and prevented her giving money to the poor woman—were victims of male society. The same year, Pappenheim translated Mary Wollstonecraft's *A Vindication of the Rights of Women*, a plea for the education of women, which maintained that women should be men's companions, not their playthings. Intellectual companionship was the main basis for a fulfilling relationship between husband and wife. Her main point was that women had human rights. Pappenheim admired the eighteenth-century English feminist's charm and courage and hung a picture of her in her room.

In 1900 Pappenheim was increasingly aware of the desperate situation of Jews, and particulary Jewish girls, in Eastern Europe. She wrote a pamphlet, "The Jewish Problem in Galicia," in which she maintained that the meager education of Jewish girls led to poverty and vice. Four years later, she repeated this warning in "On the Condition of the Jewish Population in Galicia."

Anti-Semitism and the "epidemic" of Jewish conversions and intermarriage plagued Pappenheim.[5] Her later short stories and plays described either the unhappiness of converts or the plight of religious Jews who preferred death to forced conversions. In one tale a Jewish girl told a convert: "Today, when we Jews are constantly under attack, Jews must stick together. . . . It is cowardly and dishonorable to defect to the side of the attacker."[6] The role of Jewish women was a *leitmotif* in all her stories. One heroine lamented: "I would have . . . enjoyed learning about art and politics, if I had been educated to understand them."[7]

Her interest in Judaism and Jewish women led Pappenheim to translate several works from Yiddish into German. In 1910 she published the diary of a ghetto Jewess, Glückl of Hameln (1645–1724). Pappenheim, a distant relative of Glückl, admired her ancestor's piousness, motherliness, and, particularly, her strength. Although she fulfilled her traditional role as a wife and mother (of thirteen!), Glückl was clearly an equal in the marriage partnership. Her respect for her husband was openly reciprocated, and she referred to him as her best friend. Pappenheim tried to teach women about their cultural and religious heritage by translating the *Tzenah Ureenah*, a sixteenth-century women's Bible, and the *Mayse Bukh*, a collection of medieval folk tales, Biblical and Talmudic stories which had been widely read by Jewish women in the eighteenth century.

Pappenheim's best known publication is *Sisyphus Work*, her study of Jewish prostitution and white slavery (enforced prostitution) in Eastern Europe and the Middle East. she called the book "Sisyphus," because just as the Greek mythical character rolled an enormous rock up a hill only to have it roll down again, Pappenheim felt she was trying to push the sexual abuse of women out of existence, only to be stymied by overwhelmingly strong forces.

Pappenheim was primarily an activist. Her writings, intended to educate and to activate the Jewish community, were only one part of her crusade against injustice. In the early 1890s Pappenheim began her work in Jewish charities, starting by dishing out soup to poor immigrants from Eastern Europe. Her interest in helping the needy —particularly women and children—gradually deepened. She organized a small nursery school, sewing classes, and a girls' club. In 1895 Pappenheim accepted the position of housemother in an orphanage for Jewish girls, which she retained for twelve years, gathering valuable experience as an administrator and educator.

As a social worker, Pappenheim felt that she was fulfilling a religious commandment to help those in need. She spoke of social work as a *mitzvah*. In 1902 Pappenheim founded Care by Women, a Jewish women's society. She did not want to establish a traditional club in which Jewish women ministered to the dead or engaged in well-meaning, but ineffective philanthropic activities. Instead, she hoped to apply the goals of the German feminist movement to Jewish social work. She also recognized the need for modern concepts and techniques of social work within the Jewish community. This need became apparent at the turn of the century when Jewish refugees from czarist pogroms flowed into Gernany, overwhelming the traditional Jewish philanthropies. Jewish charities were outmoded in their methods as well as their organization, often working in isolation, not exchanging information, and dispensing money generously, but inefficiently. Pappenheim objected to the sentimentality, narrowness, and amateurishness of most charities and feared that they did more to satisfy the donors' social consciences than to serve the recipients' needs. While envisioning a national Jewish social service network,[8] Pappenheim began by urging women to "let their reason work alongside their hearts."[9] To this end she taught her followers the principles of modern casework. She formed committees which researched the best methods of child care, the most effective means of finding foster homes, and the most efficient travelers' aid. Her group set up vocational counseling centers and an employment service for women. Gradually she convinced her volunteers that doles were demoralizing. Care by Women accepted the far greater responsibility of rehabilitating and reeducating the poor. Social work of this type, Pappenheim argued, would prevent Judaism's eventual demise in Germany.

Angered by the conspicuous absence of women in the leadership of Jewish philanthropies, Pappenheim accused the Jewish establishment of underestimating the value of women's work and trifling with their interest by refusing to admit them as equal partners.[10] She met with strong male resistance when she demanded that women participate in decision-making positions on the boards of Jewish charities. She warned that the leaders of Jewish community welfare boards were thus losing some of their best women, who were turning to German feminism as an outlet for their energies.

Pappenheim began to convince women of the need to form their own national organization. She turned exclusively to women because she felt that "men always and in every situation follow their private interests."[11] She expected women to volunteer their services for several reasons. A women's organization could not afford to pay professional social workers, of which, in any case, there were very few in the first decade of the twentieth century. Also, Jewish girls and women, most of whom were middle class and did not work, had time to spare, needed no reimbursement and would be educationally and socially enriched by their experience. Furthermore, dreading depersonalization, Pappenheim was apprehensive of professionals; she feared that social work would be dragged down to the level of a business. Even after she began to admit the need for trained workers, she argued that their salaries should remain very low. She told a young social worker that since many other girls did boring mechanical work, unlike social workers who derived satisfaction from their profession, paid social workers should content themselves with salaries considerably lower than typists' or seamstresses'.

The fact that Protestant and Catholic women had their own national organizations encouraged Pappenheim in her interest in a national Jewish women's association. The convention of the International Council of Women, which met in Berlin in 1904, provided the opportunity for Pappenheim to meet with several activists from existing Jewish charities. Together they founded the Jüdischer Frauenbund

(J.F.B.) with Pappenheim as its first president, a post which she held for twenty years, remaining on the board of directors of the organization until her death. To a large extent, the history of the Frauenbund is Pappenheim's story, for she was the driving spirit and main personality in the organization. In fact, the J.F.B. often stood in Pappenheim's shadow and was frequently more timid and cautious than its energetic and impetuous president.

The Frauenbund grew to encompass 430 affiliates, 34 of its own local branches, 10 provincial alliances and a total membership of 50,000 women by 1929.[12] Its members believed that feminism could reinvigorate Judaism in Germany. Like its leader, the J.F.B. insisted that Jews were turning away from their religion because women—the transmitters of culture—were ignorant of Jewish traditions or were alienated from Jewish customs.[13] It blamed the loss of faith on the traditional Jewish treatment of women as second-class citizens. The Jewish women's movement intended to fight for women's equality, which it viewed as an end in itself as well as the means by which women would return to Judaism.

Pappenheim belonged to the board of directors of the largest German middle class feminist organization, the Bund Deutscher Frauenvereine (B.D.F.). She encouraged the J.F.B. to participate in the German movement, asserting that German feminism gave "the shy, uncertain advances of Jewish women direction and confidence."[14] Hers was the only religious organization in the B.D.F. The Frauenbund supported the German movement's efforts on behalf of women's education, career opportunities and political equality, and both organizations attempted to raise the feminist consciousness of women. Yet neither association was militantly feminist; both accepted the conventional view that there were fundamental, natural differences between the sexes which destined them to serve different functions. Women who aped men were considered to be products of a male-oriented society, thwarting their true emancipation and unique development. Women should work for society in a specifically feminine way.

Convinced that women's primal instincts to protect their young endowed them with special qualities for social work, Pappenheim appealed to women's maternal sentiments in her efforts to support orphanages, care for foster children, and help unwed mothers. Pappenheim (like German feminists) regarded motherhood as woman's most important career, because mothers were "above all the educators of future generations."[15] She insisted that J.F.B. members fulfill this, their most significant duty, before participating in organizational activities. She also appealed to the childless by suggesting that "women who have to miss the happiness of real personal motherhood may have an opportunity for spiritual motherhood, if they go the quiet way of helping children and adolescents whose actual mother may fail. . . ."[16] Pappenheim, who never married, missed being a mother and openly admitted that much of her activity was surrogate motherhood. The pure joy she experienced with children was expressed in a short poem that she wrote for a local Jewish newspaper: "A child's hand in my hand/My heart becomes a fairyland!"[17]

Neither German nor Jewish feminists demanded their "rights," preferring to argue that they sought only to add uniquely feminine qualities, such as mildness, patience, and motherly love to male society. The motto of the B.D.F. was: "Women must prove that they are qualified to assume . . . work . . . duties, or rights through their achievements and behavior."[18] Pappenheim also stressed women's duty to help their coreligionists and their accomplishments in the field of social work, believing that women's rights would follow from the services they rendered. The "right" to full citizenship thus had the quality of a reward.

Pappenheim admired the English suffragettes and even rose before dawn on a trip to England to cheer their release from prison, yet she avoided their public political battles. Instead, she petitioned the secular and religious heads of the Jewish community for changes in the status of women, propagandized for feminist goals among women who did not belong to the J.F.B., published essays and a newsletter for women, and at all times fostered the growth of the J.F.B. from which she and other feminists derived a sense of solidarity and strength. These means were designed to court public opinion and win the adherence of Jewish women who were generally conservative. Her moderation was also intended to allay the hostility of Jewish males who shared a strong feeling against women's emancipation. This anti-feminism was led by Orthodox rabbis who regarded any change in the status of women as sacrilegious. They frequently wrote long legal judgments against women's suffrage within the Jewish community, and were not beyond threatening to secede from the community if their views were not respected. Orthodox women did not join the J.F.B. because its stance on suffrage was considered too radical. Liberal rabbis were not overtly hostile to the J.F.B., but they chose to ignore the movement for almost twenty-five years. With very few exceptions, the rabbinical establishment was indifferent to the demands of women.

Other Jewish males were only slightly less antagonistic than rabbis. They assured themselves that Jewish feminists had individual psychological problems and suffered from a group inferiority complex. One writer explained feminism as an attempt by a strange type of woman to lose her will in a mass movement. Some Jewish men assumed that women's demands were the fantasy or sport of a few individuals who had no other concerns. One commentator admitted that women were "crassly" discriminated against in Judaism. He suggested that this was a cause of self-hatred which found its outlet in feminism and social work.[19]

In 1902 Pappenheim attended a conference on white slavery. White slaves were women and girls who were lured, tricked, or forced to go abroad by traffickers who smuggled them across borders and sold them into prostitution. While prostitutes and white slaves had not been unknown earlier in Europe, in the nineteenth century commercialized prostitution had grown into a flourishing enterprise in the expanding urban centers. Pappenheim never forgot her horror upon hearing of the traffic in women: "I remember the time when—despite the fact that I had been involved in social work for several years—the words "white slavery" rang in my ears . . . I did not know what they meant, could not grasp that there were people who bought and sold . . . girls and children . . ."[20] She resolved to found an organization which would fight this vice. Thus, the campaign against white slavery was the original reason for the founding of a German-Jewish feminist organization and was among the J.F.B.'s most important activities. Pappenheim's involvement in the international fight against the traffic in women reflected a concern shared by all German feminists. In addition, she was distressed to learn of the disproportionately high number of Jewish girls from Galicia and Poland who were being victimized, and she believed that by eradicating this evil the J.F.B. would be helping the entire Jewish community.

Jewish reformers—both male and female—who were aware of Jewish prostitutes, traffickers, and pimps,[21] traced the source of these social ills to the recrudescence of active Russian persecution of Jews in 1881. The resulting economic hardships and the desire to emigrate were seen as prime causes of white slavery and prostitution. Pappenheim agreed that the cruel social pressures of poverty were the

prime cause of prostitution. She worried about the inadequate hous-
ing, education and employment conditions of women and the dull
meanness of their daily surroundings. As a feminist, she blamed a
society which condoned a double moral standard as the foremost
criminal in the vicious circle of white slavery. She opposed the regula-
tion of prostitution as hypocritical, demanding that sons as well as
daughters be taught the virtue of chastity. As a Jewish feminist, Pappenheim also understood prostitution to be a result of the low status of
women in her religion and culture. She maintained that women were
seen only as sex objects in the religion and treated as such in Jewish
society. Because Jewish women were not educated, they rarely acquired the skills with which they could support themselves and were
forced to sell their bodies in order to live.

Pappenheim pointed to women's inferior legal status in Judaism as
another cause of white slavery. In Eastern Europe and the Orient,
approximately 4,000,000 Jewish women lived under rabbinical law.
Ritual marriages, performed by rabbis without civil sanction, occurred
frequently. Since only two witnesses are necessary for a Jewish marriage, many young women were tricked into marrying men with
less-than-honorable intentions. The girls followed their "husbands" to
new lands, only to find that the marriage was not legally binding.
Alone and destitute, they worked for these men or entered brothels.
Even when white slavery was not intended, ritual marriages often
resulted in prostitution, because husbands could abandon their wives
easily. Once abandoned, religious women could never remarry unless
their husbands divorced them or died. According to Pappenheim, the
sexist bias of Judaism as found in the laws regarding the *agunah* (the
abandoned wife), further aggravated the white slave problem. A Jewish
woman could not remarry unless her husband ritually released her
before he left her, or unless a Jew witnessed his death. In an era of
pogroms and wars, husbands frequently left home and never returned.
Pappenheim estimated that in 1929 approximately 20,000 Eastern
European *agunot* were living in misery, in danger of being lured or
tricked into fake marriages and eventual prostitution. [22] She petitioned
rabbis to modernize marriage, divorce, and inheritance laws for the
sake of these women. Her pleas went unanswered.

Pappenheim attended every major international conference on
white slavery and participated in the German and international Jewish
movements against the traffic in women. She was not as reticent as
earlier reformers. Her Frauenbund embarked upon an exercise of

social education, rejecting the traditional notion that innocence was protected through silence on subjects related to sex. When cautioned by Jewish leaders who feared the Frauenbund was adding to the arsenal of anti-Semites, Pappenheim responded that the Jewish community would be guilty of complicity if it did not act against these crimes. When confronted by religious leaders who denied that such things existed or who were simply uninterested in the problem, Pappenheim noted that seminaries should teach rabbis about social responsibilities, and added: "I would like to shout in their ears that . . . they are letting the Jewish people rot."[23]

The Frauenbund concentrated on preventing young women from falling into the hands of procurers. It founded girls' clubs in Germany intended to keep girls off the streets and provide them with recreation and religious training. At German ports and railroad stations, which frequently served as stopovers for girls from Eastern Europe who were en route to destinations in the Americas, South Africa, and the Middle East, the J.F.B. set up outposts where women met unaccompanied girls and provided them with money, shelter and counseling. Jewish feminists sent leaflets to Eastern Europe warning both parents and children of the dangers of accepting "job offers" or "marriage proposals" through the mail or press. They also sent teachers and nurses to Galicia, where Pappenheim helped to found a kindergarten and a small hospital. In the interwar years, a friendly relationship grew between the leaders of the Beth Jacob schools for girls in Poland and the Frauenbund. Finally, the Frauenbund established Isenburg, a rescue home and rehabilitation center for unmarried mothers, delinquent girls, and illegitimate children. It was to a large extent Pappenheim's personal achievement and remained of central importance to her. She lived there and ran the home for twenty-nine years. While not condoning premarital sex, Pappenheim felt compassion for the prostitutes she had met on her tours and challenged society's disdain for unmarried mothers and illegitimate children. She believed that these girls could reform and that "no child should be lost to the Jewish community."[24] Isenburg became the first place on the continent where "endangered or morally sick" girls with their babies could find acceptance or care.

Job training was another primary concern of the Frauenbund for several reasons. First, Pappenheim considered career education to be a prophylactic against vice. Second, Jewish feminists encouraged all young women to acquire skills with which they could support themselves; the family had changed from a unit of production to one of consumption and women, who no longer produced goods, should be prepared to supplement the income of a family of consumers. Third, feminists argued that careers were a means to psychological as well as economic independence. Finally, women with careers were useful to their community, and the J.F.B. hoped that their collective importance would eventually be recognized by male society.

Pappenheim and her associates believed that all girls—regardless of their future goals—should learn home economics. They argued that housekeeping was a legitimate career which had been devalued by a male dominated society. The Frauenbund locals provided courses in home economics, and the national organization supported several schools which offered programs in home economics, child care and basic health care, believing that thorough training in this field would raise the standards and the status of the domestic servant and the housewife. Pappenheim also urged the formation of employment services and centers where Jewish girls could receive vocational counseling.

Pappenheim believed that many of the injustices perpetrated on Jewish girls could be rectified if Jewish women played a more prominent role in their community. To this end she sought political equality for women within the Jewish community. This was no small matter, because the Jewish community was a publicly constituted corporation which embraced all the Jews in any one place of residence and was empowered by the state to levy taxes on its members and to administer its own cultural and religious life, religious education, and social welfare.[25]

As in the patriarchal culture of ancient Israel, Jewish women were excluded from positions of communal responsibility. They paid taxes and worked for the community, but they had no voice in running it. Pappenheim remarked angrily that adult Jewish women did not even have the rights of thirteen-year-old boys. Feminists demanded the vote within the Jewish community before—and long after—they had achieved it in secular German politics. Pappenheim approached numerous rabbis seeking favorable interpretations of the Talmud regarding women's rights. In 1919, the year German women achieved full citizenship, she received a note from Rabbi Nobel, a renowned leader of German Jewry, agreeing that women were entitled to complete political equality. Pappenheim considered his decision a milestone on the road to suffrage. However, since each community had to decide the issue independently, the J.F.B. lobbied and petitioned

within the Jewish communities, offered courses on community problems and finances to its members, and encouraged women to learn to
lead meetings, speak in public, and draft constitutions. Eventually
women won their rights in most of the large communities. They were
also represented, albeit in a token manner, on the boards of all the
major Jewish welfare agencies.

Under the Nazi regime, the J.F.B. continued and even expanded its
activities, but its feminist character waned as the condition of Jews
deteriorated. It kept operating its homes and schools and continued to
demand women's suffrage; however it concentrated primarily on social work and on encouraging pride in Judaism. Although Pappenheim
had not been blind to the virulent anti-Semitism of postwar Germany,
her understanding of Nazism was as blurred as that of most German
Jews. Underestimating the nature of German fascism, she discouraged
mass emigration and argued that Jews still had a place in Germany. She
did not admit her error until after the anti-Jewish laws of 1935. She died
in 1936 and was thus spared the agony of watching her world destroyed by the Nazis.

Although Bertha Pappenheim was certainly successful in her career
as a social worker and was recognized by national and international
circles, her stance as a Jewish feminist had been fraught with difficulties and contradictions. She tried to combine feminism with her in-
tensely felt religious identity by asserting that all of her activities
—from fighting white slavery and criticizing Jewish customs to demanding the vote for women in the Jewish community—were meant to
enhance Judaism in Germany. In fact, however, her Jewish faith and
her feminist convictions frequently stood in opposition to one another.
For example, she worried that Jews were not deeply enough involved
in their religion and wrote Martin Buber: "Many Jews in terrible
spiritual need reach for 'their Goethe' before 'their Bible.' " She
wished Jews would emulate Christians for whom the Bible was "a path
to God." (She added, "to God not to him," a reference to the fact that
Buber used the masculine pronoun in place of "God" in his translation
of the Bible.) She criticized Buber's approach to the Bible as too
intellectual: "How awful. Your method is adequate for understanding
Shakespeare or Dante. . . . " She maintained that Jews should learn
to love the Bible, not simply read it as history.[26] Yet this fundamentalist
view contradicted the rationalism of her attitudes on the rights of
women. She found, to her dismay, that it was extremely difficult—if
not impossible—to combine a literal and integral acceptance of the
Scripture with reformism. Orthodox Jews who agreed with her reli-

gious views were adamantly opposed to her feminism, while more progressive Jews accepted her feminist programs, but preferred Buber's conception of the Bible. She was never able to solve this dilemma to her satisfaction.

In evaluating Pappenheim's achievements, we note that despite all her efforts, the poverty, vice, exploitation and inhumanity that she fought remained. She consoled herself by achieving admittedly small victories—she called them "holy small deeds"—in the battle to defend Jewish women. Pleased as she was with the contributions of the J.F.B., as she aged she was "driven by fear" that she would "not . . . accomplish what she felt called upon to do."[27] She again expressed this concern in an ironic obituary that she composed for herself: "In 1904 she founded the J.F.B.—its importance is not yet fully understood. The Jews of the entire world—men and women—owe her thanks for this social achievement. But they withhold it. What a pity!"[28]

Notes

1. Dora Edinger (ed.), *Bertha Pappenheim: Leben und Schriften* (Frankfurt, 1963), p. 118.

2. *Blätter des Jüdischen Frauenbunds* (BJFB) (Berlin), July 1936, p. 11. Even girls from poorer German Jewish families did not work; a working daughter was seen as a sign of inferior social status, which few families wished to acknowledge.

3. Freud later suggested that women who did needlework, a popular pastime, were particularly prone to daydreaming. A harsh psychic trauma could shock them into a state in which their fantasies became their partial or total reality.

4. Sigmund Freud and Josef Breuer, *Studies on Hysteria*, trans. by James Strachey (New York, 1966). See also: H. Ellenberger, "The Story of Anna O.: A Critical Review with New Data," *Journal of the History of the Behavioral Sciences*, VIII, No. 3 (July 1972); Ellen Jensen, "Anna O.—A Study of her Later Life," *The Psychoanalytic Quarterly*, XXXIX (1970). The latter article includes a bibliography of psychoanalytic commentary on Anna O. and on Pappenheim's later life. Since Ernest Jones, Freud's biographer, divulged Anna O.'s identity in 1953, psychologists have turned with particular interest to the case of the hysterical woman who later became a well-known feminist. They have suggested that Pappenheim was sublimating the neuroses that Anna O. had experienced. This interpretation is typical of Freudian psychologists and their popularizers as well as of antisuffragists, many of whom regarded any argument against the sexual status quo as a perversion of psychic normality.

5. *Israelitisches Familienblatt* (Hamburg), January 19, 1911, p. 12. More Jewish men intermarried than Jewish women. In 1901-1904, 8.5 percent of Jewish men and 7.4 percent of Jewish women married out of their faith. *Zeitschrift für Demographic und Statistik der Juden (ZDSJ)*. V, No. 1 (1930): 14. In 1915 the figures were 40.4 percent men, 26.6 percent women. *ZDSJ* (Jan/Feb 1924), p. 25. Between 1921 and 1927, 44.8 percent of all Jewish marriages were mixed. In that period, conversions occurred at the rate of 500 per year, while a similar number of Jews formally "dissociated" themselves from the Jewish community. *Encyclopedia Judaica*, 1971, VII, p. 486. By the early 1930s the number of mixed marriages reached about 40 percent of the total. A. Margaliot, "German Jewry's Struggle for Survival," in *Jewish Resistance During the Holocaust. Proceedings of the Conference on Manifestations of Jewish Resistance* (Jerusalem: Yad Vashem, 1971), p. 101.

6. Bertha Pappenheim, "Ein Schwächling," *Jahrbuch für Jüdische Geschichte und Literatur*, ed. Verbande der Vereine für jüdische Geschichte und Literatur in Deutschland (Berlin, 1902), V, 243.

7. Ibid., p. 242.

8. Pappenheim propagandized for such an agency for years. A national Jewish social welfare bureau (the *Zentralwohlfahrtstelle*) was founded in 1917 and Pappenheim was elected as its deputy vice-president.

9. Schöenwald collection, Leo Baeck Institute (New York), #3896 (II, 11).

10. Schönewald unpublished memoirs, LBI.

11. Pappenheim collection, LBI, #331 (9).

12. In 1933 there were 503,000 Jews in Germany (0.76% of the entire population). Half of the Jewish population was over the age of forty (most J.F.B. members were also middle-aged) and there were slightly more women than men. Thus, the J.F.B. encompassed approximately one-fourth of all eligible Jewish women in Germany.

13. By accepting the role of "transmitters of culture," feminists placed an unfair burden on all women. Even educated and dedicated Jewesses could not hope to forestall the secularization of their children as the family became engulfed by the social and cultural milieu of the twentieth century. Socialization took place largely outside the home. The family was no longer as important as it had been in influencing its young. By concurring with the stereotype of themselves as educators, Jewish feminists set themselves up for final failure.

14. *BJFB* July, 1936, p. 8.

15. Schönewald collection, LBI, #3896 (II,8).

16. Edinger, (ed.,) *Pappenheim, Freud's Anna O* (Illinois, 1968), p. 60.

17. *Frankfurter Israelitisches Gemeindeblatt*, July 1936. Pappenheim's antipathy to Zionism can be traced, in part, to her attitude toward motherhood. She feared that Zionists intended to break up families and disliked their "collective breeding and raising of children." She maintained that a healthy family should bring up its own offspring. In the early 1930s Pappenheim fought Zionist plans to ship children to Palestine, convinced that Youth Aliyah was essentially "exporting children" so that Zionists could populate their land.

18. Margrit Twellman, *Die Deutsche Frauenbewegung, Ihre Anfänge und erste Entwicklung, 1843–1889* (Maisenheim am Glan, 1972), p. 229.

19. Examples of rabbinical opinions can be found in *Jeshurun*, VI (May/June 1919): 262–66; VI (November/December 1919): 515-19. The Frauenbund published some of the anti-feminist comments in its own paper. See: *BJFB* February, 1928, p. 2; June 1932, pp. 4–6.

20. *Official Report of the Jewish International Conference on the Suppression of the Traffic in Girls and Women, held on April 5, 6, 7, 1910 in London* (London, 1910), p. 146.

21. In her *Sisyphus Work* (Leipzig: Paul Linder Verlag, 1924), Pappenheim gave numerous examples from her trip in 1911; a visit to a hospital for venereal diseases in Budapest, where all the patients were prostitutes, and one-third of the girls were Jewish; the acknowledgment by leaders of the community that there were several thousand prostitutes in Salonika; and the admission of a rabbi in Constantinople that there was a synagogue in which prostitutes donateded money to have their pimps called to the Torah on holidays. Ninety percent of the prostitutes and almost all traffickers in that city were Jews. She included reports on Palestine, Alexandria, Warsaw, and Rumania.

Although the exact figures are not known, prominent Jews who were involved in combating white slavery acknowledged a large share of the "merchants, merchandise and consumers" were Jewish. The League of Nations Report of 1927 gives some statistics on Jewish prostitution as well as examples of letters written among traffickers who were obviously Jewish. The letters were written in Yiddish. Jewish leaders who supported the League's report were surprised that the report was not even harsher on Jews.

22. *BJFB* July, 1936, p. 21.

23. Bertha Pappenheim, *Sisyphus Work* (Leipzig, 1924), p. 16.

24. Else Rabin, "The Jewish Woman in Social Service in Germany," in *The Jewish Library*, ed. by Leo Jung, Vol. III (New York, 1934), p. 30.

25. In 1905, 2282 Jewish communities existed in Germany. This number diminished to 1611 communities by 1932. Kurt Wilhelm, "The Jewish Community in the Post-Emancipation Period," in *LBI Yearbook* (1957), pp. 47–75.

26. Letter from Pappenheim, March 18, 1936, in Martin Buber, *Martin Buber: Briefwechsel aus sieben Jahrzehnten*, ed. by Grete Schader, II (Heidelberg, 1973), p. 587.

27. Edinger, "Bertha Pappenheim: A German-Jewish Feminist," *Jewish Social Studies*, XX, No. 3 (July 1958): 185.

28. *BJFB*, July 1936, p. 28.

HENRIETTA SZOLD–
LIBERATED WOMAN
Susan Dworkin

By the standards of her time, Henrietta Szold was blessed with an intellectual and professional freedom which only a handful of women enjoyed in her era.

By the standards of the current Women's Liberation movement, she was exploited and harassed by men throughout the best working years of her long life.

She was born in 1860 to a father whose attitude toward women so far outdistanced his day that most men cannot manage it even in 1976. An impassioned liberal, Rabbi Benjamin Szold of Baltimore steeped his five daughters in secular and Jewish learning, inspiring the best student among them, Henrietta, with ebullient confidence in her capacity to master any discipline she set her mind to, maybe even to reweave the moral fiber of the Jewish world. At the same time, he and her mother impressed indelibly on her young mind the image of a happy marriage in Israel—for theirs was the ideal Jewish home, full of love, learning, shared joys: *shalom bayit!*

Thus Henrietta Szold harbored two ambitions—one for a brilliant career, the other for a brilliant marriage—which any "liberated" woman today will tell you are incapable of peaceful coexistence in a "male-dominated" society.

Denied the crucible of coeducation, she was, for some time, spared the harsh reality of typical nineteenth-century male attitudes toward women. Before she was thirteen, she entered the Western Female High School in Baltimore. At fourteen, she published her first newspaper article. At sixteen, she was contributing political commentary (unheard of for a schoolgirl) to the *Baltimore Elocutionist*. When she graduated high school (with a 99.8 percent average!) she went to work.

"We didn't dare mention Vassar," she told a graduating class two decades later, "except in terms of awe with which one speaks of a remote object one has never seen and dares not hope to approach." She started teaching at the high school from which she had just graduated and at a very proper institution called Miss Adams' School for Girls. She also continued writing.

Now that Henrietta Szold ventured out of the free air of her father's house, the bigotry of men toward gifted women began to choke her. She wrote a column called "Our Baltimore Letter" for *The Jewish Messenger* of New York, and she signed it "Sulamith." With innocent righteousness, she attacked the assimilationism and materialism of the American Jews. The dispersed, meager, and rather wealthy Jewish population was then rife with all manner of movements to dilute and Americanize its origins. The Reform movement, headed by Rabbi Isaac Mayer Wise of Cincinnati, and Felix Adler's Ethical Culture Society offended Henrietta Szold mightily; in fact, they were among the least assimilationist of a number of organizations that progressed downward into outright apostasy.

An article in Rabbi Wise's *American Israelite* criticized traditional elements in both Jewish and Christian practice, infuriating Sulamith. She called it immoral, a breach of good taste. The readers and writers of the *American Israelite* reacted with scathing disdain. What right had a mere "pot and pan scourer" to comment upon the morality of Jewish scholars? Wasn't it logical that she should defend tradition, since "women's hearts and women's bonnets lead them to the house of prayer?"

"They ridicule me on account of my sex," she wrote, "proof positive of the narrow-mindedness of which their thoughtless reform of Judaism is a part. . . . Is telling me that I am a woman, nothing but a woman, refutation of my charges?"

As for the scouring of pots and pans, which contemporary Women's Lib feels should be the equal obligation of men and women, Henrietta Szold never even considered scorning it. She would never, she wrote, "neglect the peculiar privilege of women to attend to the physical comfort of their more awkward fellow creatures."

Funny and eloquent though she might be in these exchanges, she was beginning to realize the vicious emotional pressures on a brilliant woman. In a sketch about the Italian Jewess Sarah Sullam, she offered some comments that probably illuminated her own problems as well:

> Men . . . expect every woman to verify the preconceived notions concerning her sex, amd when she dares not to, immediately condemn her as eccentric and unwomanly. . . . Women themselves have come to look upon these matters in the same light . . . and scarcely find any wrong in submitting to the importunities of the stronger will. . . .

Even an adoring biographer, being a man, allowed a slight lack of sympathy to creep into his account of how she treated the boys she knew. "One thing Papa had not taught her," he wrote, "was how to handle a young man as high-spirited and opinionated as herself. She could not . . . resist the opportunity of showing her superiority in arguments with men."

Consciousness-raising sessions all over America today ring with the bitter complaint of young women whose papas taught them to shut up and dissemble as mindless creatures, with disastrous results. How they would have loved a papa like Benjamin Szold, who had neglected the lesson of feminine self-suppression!

When the Russian-Jewish immigrants began pouring into Baltimore after the repressive czarist May Laws of 1881, Henrietta Szold worked like a demon to organize night-school classes for them. Frantically busy, she wrote to one of her sisters in 1891: "The Russian business so absorbs my thought that I have gone back to my early childhood longing to be a man. . . . I am sure that if I were to be, I could mature plans of great benefit to them."

The letter indicated her own basic belief in the relative incapacity of women that was to halt her own steps from time to time, making her hold back from responsibility, making her instruct other women to hold back—not lest they offend, for she was too sensible to give in to male prejudice, but lest they fail.

In 1893, at the World's First Parliament of Religions, in Chicago, she set forth her ideals of what Jewish women had always been by tradition and what they should be again.

She believed that in the first Jewish family, Abraham and Sarah had shared equally all decisions concerning the education of their children. By making men and women equal in the all-important task of education, Jewish tradition had created "ideals of equality" which were "the basis upon which the position of women in Judaism was fixed." If the position of women in Jewish life was unequal now, that was because Jewish men had succumbed to venal influences of less enlightened cultures and had deserted the teachings of their forefathers. Fortunately, the Patriarchs had provided for this eventuality, protecting Jewish women with a code of "ironhanded" law regarding marriage and divorce.

Henrietta Szold stuck to this idea of tradition as the defender of Jewish women throughout her life; it was a recurrent theme in her letters, in her speeches, and in her battles with both Orthodox and Reform Jews. When a male friend offered to say Kaddish in her behalf after her mother's death in 1916, she wrote:

> I believe that the elimination of women from such duties was never intended by our law and custom—women were freed from positive duties when they could not perform them but not when they could. It was never intended that, if they could perform them, their performance of them should not be considered as valuable and valid as when one of the male sex performed them. And of the Kaddish I feel sure this is particularly true.

The Reform movement offered equal religious training for boys and girls; but since Henrietta Szold did not think the Reform movement had much to teach anyone, she could not accept that girls thus trained were qualified to be successful Jewish mothers. She begged the Jewish establishment to recognize that for better or worse, women were in the home, making or breaking the Jewish consciousness of their children: If Jewish girls were not educated, then Jewish mothers would be unequal to the task of education. If Jewish girls were educated properly, the Jewish people could be guarded against extinction.

In a speech before a Chicago audience in 1893, she offered yet another framework for the modern Jewish woman, a romantic and idealized vision of woman's role in the household which was the legacy of the Szold home.

The Jewish woman, she said

> is the inspirer of a pure, chaste family life, whose hallowing influences are incalculable; she is the center of all spiritual endeavors, the confidante and fosterer of every undertaking. To her the Talmudic sentence applies: "It is woman alone through whom God's blessings are vouchsafed to a house." She teaches the children, speeds her husband to the

place of worship and instruction, welcomes him when he returns, keeps the house godly and pure, and God's blessings resting upon all these things.

Thus her ambitions for women were not political. She recognized that the vast majority of women, like the vast majority of men, could not influence public events. Voting rights did not particularly concern her, although she supported them. The spiritual and moral power that women might have awed her. To Jewish immigrant women in Baltimore she said, "I do not tell you to vote any more than I tell you to wear trousers and coats. But I do tell you to help your sons, your brothers, and your husbands to lead a noble, true life."

Surely a woman with such spiritual ideas of woman's role was no threat to any man! Henrietta Szold was not, after all, like her friend Carry Nation. She did not run away to Zurich to get her Ph.D. when American universities would not have her. She did not set out, like Gertrude Bell, whom she deeply admired, to delve into the politics of exotic nations. She believed that Jewish tradition held a great role for women. She trusted that Jewish tradition would protect her in the world as it had elevated her in her father's house.

However benign her philosophies, her excellence was bound to undo her. When, as she was to say, "Zionism converted me to itself" and she gave her first Zionist speech in 1896, one Jewish weekly found the address "almost too profound for an American woman."

When she moved to New York in 1903, after her father's death, the Jewish Theological Seminary accepted her request for admission to some classes only after she had assured its administration that she would not use the knowledge thus gained to seek ordination.

She was truly a ground-breaker, the first woman ever to take classes with men there. But oh, with what humble steps she entered those halls. And oh, how willingly some of her male classmates allowed her the "peculiar privilege" of editing and correcting and rewriting and otherwise secretarializing over their work, which appeared under their names, and made some of them great men.

In 1893, at the age of thirty-three, she became "literary secretary" of the Jewish Publication Society. She stayed "literary secretary" to the world of Jewish scholarship until her final departure for Palestine in 1920. She was not destined to clean up any man's house, one of the "peculiar privileges" she had always longed for. But she was to spend the best years of her life cleaning up many men's prose, proofreading, revising and, that most difficult and anonymous of literary work, translating into English the scholarship of men who picked her brain and sapped her strength and took her for long walks and partook of long meals at her table while they were thinking through their major creations.

They thanked her with all their hearts, married other women, and when they were through, the brilliant young writer from Baltimore had given them the best of her literary inspiration. Her vast production of letters remains as the evidence of what a writer she might have been in her own right.

Her first visit to Palestine in 1909 left her shocked by the atrocious medical and sanitary conditions existing there. "I should like," she wrote, "to see the women rise up in their might and make demands. I think that such discontent would bring about radical change."

Two years before, she had joined a Hadassah study group. In 1912, the inspiration of her trip invigorating her purpose, she and her friends made that group the nucleus of the Hadassah Organization. "The Zionist Federation looked upon us as organizers of strawberry festivals," she commented wryly, used to it by now. Her vision of the woman's Zionist organization was an expanded version of her concept of the function of the Jewish wife in her household—education, medical service, social service, moral service.

To understand how far she had come in liberating herself from her old self-image, one had only to read her answer to a questionnaire about "Women in the Synagogue" which she had written almost two decades before Hadassah was founded.

> I believe that woman can best serve the interests of the synagogue by devoting herself to her home; by filling any administrative position for which her executive ability is admittedly greater than that of any available man . . . and by occupying the pulpit only when her knowledge of the law, history, and literature of Judaism is masterful, and her natural gift so extraordinary as to forbid hesitation, though even then it were the part of wisdom not to make a profession of public preaching and lecturing. . . . I further believe that, religion being sexless, no necessity exists for Jewish women's organizations. . . .

But in 1917, when Justice Louis D. Brandeis of the Zionist Executive asked her to organize an American Medical Unit in Palestine, she accepted. She did not look around for a better available man.

In 1918 there might surely have been some man available to take responsibility for Zionist educational and propaganda work. When, in the wake of the historic Pittsburgh Convention, Henrietta Szold was chosen, she accepted. In 1919–20, when she was asked to follow the International Zionist Commission to Palestine to take over the Medical Unit's work, she accepted. She was sixty years old. The task ahead excited her.

In all justice, she should have been seated on the Commission. She wrote matter-of-factly to her friend Alice Seligsberg: "We need not fool ourselves. The Commission will not consider seating a woman. . . ." And of course she was right.

The year of her final *aliyah* was 1920, the year of the vote for women in America. Old-guard Zionists in Palestine were not so sure it should be the year of the vote for the women of the *Yishuv* as well. To such men, Henrietta Szold with her forthright espousal of equal political rights for women, equal education for women, equal obligations for women, was a danger. They kept her out of top political office as long as they could; indeed, long after the rights she fought for had been won.

It was not until 1927, when the American Zionist Medical Unit had become the Hadassah Medical Organization with an annual budget of $500,000, that she was elected one of the three members of the Palestine Executive Committee of the World Zionist Organization.

At this extraordinarily late date, when she had created virtually single-handedly a network of health and social welfare agencies for the Jews in their homeland, when she was recognized as one of the handful of prominent Jews in the world who had actually settled in Palestine, she was finally given a major office without the title of "Secretary."

What had kept her from becoming bitter with the male establishment all those years was her own utter lack of vanity, the comforts of sisterhood in Hadassah, and the ecstatic trials and joys of being a mother in Israel—mother to the sick ill-tended children of Palestine and, later on, to the starved, hunted children of Europe.

STAGES
Rachel Janait

1928

From the beginning of her appearance in the country twenty-five years ago, the woman worker has been closely bound up with the general labor movement; and yet the ways of the women workers are peculiar to themselves.

Even at the outset, when workers took their first grip on the land, in the days of the first *kvutzot*—Sedjera, Deganiah, Kinereth and Merchaviah—days of triumph for the workers' ideals, even in those days some of the women workers had already separated off into a special women's *kvutzah* or commune, a *kvutzah* without a home, a wandering *kvutzah* which had neither soil nor plan nor budget.

What brought this thing about?

In the thick of that passionate movement toward the land the women workers suddenly found themselves thrust aside and relegated once more to the ancient tradition of the house and the kitchen. They were amazed and disappointed to see how the cleavage was opening, the men comrades really uniting themselves with the land, but they, though on it, not becoming part of it. The united front was cracking. So that even then a handful of women—all of them very young—set out in a group to build up their own working relationship to the soil.

And quickly enough there began to spring up those early *kvutzot* of women workers—on the shore of Galilee, in the Emek (the Valley of Jezreel) and on the sands of Judaea. And if the *kvutzah* subsisted only for one year, and if the land it worked was only hired—who cared? For the principle issue was not the farm, the economic unit, but the *kvutzah* as such. Nor did they find it so hard to break in the naked soil

171

of the wilderness, if thereby they could slake their thirst for work on the land, and satisfy their passion for a partnership with mother earth.

There was much joking about those early *kvutzot*. No one believed in the success of our idea. But the deep, burning enthusiasm which had caught us up enabled us to ignore the doubts of others. Yes, it is quite clear now to everyone that the temporary *kvutzah* was economically senseless. But in those days it had a deep sense, and because of this it emerged whole from the difficult war period.

Shortly before the close of the war the dream of a Jewish Legion ripened into realisation. The woman worker was caught up in that rush of sacrifice not less than the man; what the *kvutzah* had not been able to satisfy in her, she sought to fulfull in this new phenomenon. It is not easy to write about those sacrificial days. Were the women really caught up in a military emotion—or were they merely imitating the men comrades? No, no. That spirit was absent on both sides. We were enslaved by one idea; one well of feeling sent up its deep, turbulent forces in both of us; the idea was not war, but liberation. But for the men there was the front—and for the women, again, disappointment. There were hundreds of women who reported for duty with the Legion, just like men. Of couse, they were not taken. That rebuff left us flat and wearied; we were not to participate in that great moment. This incident deserves a place of its own in the history of the women workers' movement.

The year after the war those girls' *kvutzot* disappeared; it was something sudden, as if a sponge had wiped them off the slate. Nor was there any struggle about it. The women felt that this form had outlived itself; something new had to answer the spirit of the changed times. Yes, we could no longer form our associations so easily, wander from place to place, take root and uproot every year. The time had come for the permanent settlement, stable, rooted in its own soil.

After the wandering *kvutzah* came, as its natural inheritor, the *meshek hapoalot*, the women's training farm; after group vagabondage came the planned, sensible and stabilised unit.

And so the women's farm was created in Petah Tikvah, the tree nursery in Jerusalem, and the collectives in Nachlath Jehudah and Shechunath Boruchov.

This was in 1921, the time of the big expansion in agricultural work, when the Emek was bought and new forms of land units sprang up, the large *kvutzot,* or communes, the *moshav ovdim,* or workers' individualist-cooperative settlement. In every place the woman worker had her own important role to play.

It does not matter what the exact forces were which brought about the result, whether it was through the pressure of the original women's farms, or through the actual necessities of the life on the land—but as a worker the woman found her role to be richer, fuller and more variegated than ever before. Her place was definite: the vegetable gardening system, the dairy work, chicken-raising and tree-planting. She was gradually relieved from the exclusive claim of the kitchen and laundry; the men learned to give her a hand there. But once she broke into the fuller life of the system, the woman began to understand how much she lacked in training and independent preparation.

A new and complicated question emerged: the question of mother and child in the workers' collectives. The woman began anxiously to seek a way to unite care of the child with productive labor on the soil. And out of this search arose new life-forms in the field of child rearing. If we have been enriched by many values in this field, we must thank the woman worker on the land.

The *meshek hapoalot,* or women's farm settlement, has a distinct purpose: to prepare the woman worker for the general *meshek* or farm settlement. But at first it had an additional purpose: it was a larger school life. There was an educational value in the dividing up of the work, the sharing of responsibility and the adaptation of the individual to the group life. The *meshek* had to be self-supporting: and therefore the comrades in it had to take up all its economic problems. In such surroundings the character of the woman comrade set firm; she developed the necessary independence and initiative. We were amazed sometimes to see the difference which one year made in a woman. Helpless at first, she was at the end of this period an intelligent cooperator, participating in the management and showing a thorough understanding of the complicated economic and administrative problems of the settlement.

Work in the settlement was a joy. Steeped as we were in our labors, the hours of the long day slipped by uncounted and unnoticed. But the purest and most supreme joy was in the tree nurseries—our pioneer contribution to the country.

In old Europe and in new America, which possess such magnificent agricultural institutions, and even in California with its nurseries which number their shoots by the million, it is always the man who directs.

Managers, gardeners, workers—all men—are the creative and responsible elements. The woman worker is hardly to be seen. Here and there
I found a few women wage-workers, or office-workers—in brief, they
were given the inferior or mechanical work, which dulls the individual. Not one single tree nursery did I find created by women.

With our own hands we raised, on our soil, tens and hundreds of
thousands of shoots, and a kind of bond was created between our
fruitful little corners and the wild, bare hills around us. We were
participants in the great task of reforesting the country.

But we share in something more than in the forestry. We play a role
in gardening, chicken-raising and dairy work. It is true that these
activities have not yet taken deep, organic root among us. They still
lack something; here we are short of a breed cow, there the barn is not
completed; elsewhere we lack buildings, or soil—or even water; and
nearly everywhere we are short of quarters for the workers. The universal trouble is that the settlement has not yet established itself on its own
feet.

The critical years 1926–1927 came upon us. Everywhere, unem-
ployment, hunger and suffering—and most of all among the women
workers. The women's farm settlements knew all the bitterness of those
years. So many women workers came knocking at our doors—and
there was no way of admitting them. The settlements were still small,
their absorptive capacity was limited. Two hundred women in the
settlements had food and genuine creative work; two thousand outside
of them were hungry and without employment. And among the latter
one heard dark, bitter remarks about the *meshek*—the darling
women's institution, which picks and chooses and accords its
privileges according to its own rules. . . .

Out of this suffering came creation. The *meshek*, the women's
training farm, gave birth to the *havurah*. The idea was born among the
comrades in the *meshek*, and they transformed it into a reality.

And then new changes come up in the realities of Palestine. Factories and workshops rise in these towns. Thousands of women pour
into the cities and go into the factory or into private homes; and during
those same years, 1926–1928, the country is closed to Jewish immigration.

Just yesterday there were hundreds knocking at the door of the
mesheks and suddenly we are short of hands! And those women
whose lives have been sunk in these institutions feel as if a blow had
struck at them. Something must be done. Out of the new needs come

new ideals: the *meshek* must *give* more. It must be perfected from within. Everyone of its agricultural enterprises must become a model. It is, after all, an institution which educates and trains. But it must not be regarded merely as an institution where women come to learn a trade. It is not a trade, it is a sort of personal destiny we teach. . . . The woman learns to educate herself, and to awaken from within a deep and permanent relationship to the soil. . . .

And one point more, about wage work in the colonies. However difficult it is for the men to find jobs, insecure as these jobs are—yet they have made a place for themselves in every branch of agriculture, in the plantations and fields. But the woman still has to fight out the problem of her right to work in the colony, in the orchard and vineyard; and not merely at the picking of oranges. And how few women get a man's pay for doing a man's work!

Out of this rises doubt, and dissatisfaction and inadequacy; in the workers' settlement, the *kvutzah*, the individualist colony—everywhere the woman feels the same. In no form of Palestinian life does the woman play her proper role economically, culturally and spiritually.

JEWISH WOMEN IN
MODERN SOCIETY

JUDAISM AND FEMINISM

Blu Greenberg

There is much we can learn from the women's movement in terms of our own growth as Jews; there is much that feminism can gain from the perspective of traditional Jewish values. Yet, at this point, the possibility of a positive relationship between the two seems improbable, if not impossible. Traditional Judaism has written off feminism as a temporary cultural fad, if not an extremist movement. Feminists have vilified the rabbis as woman-haters, male chauvinists or, at best, men with ancient hangups. A religion and an ideology which could interact and nurture each other have instead squared off. Why?

The aims, goals, achievements, and even processes of feminism have been revolutionary. Increasingly, public philosophy, policy, and prescription assume that women are full human beings with a potential capacity for achievement in all spheres in which men function. Our secular legal, social, and educational systems are under constant pressure to include women as equals. Our religious systems and institutions, however, lag far behind in the process of recognition.

If, throughout the centuries, Judaism was capable of generating various revolutionary ethical teachings, why should it not incorporate the lessons of feminism easily? Equality in various spheres is a fundamental idea in Judaism[1]—equality before law,[2] equal ownership of property,[3] equality of all men.[4] Logically and theologically, therefore, should not feminist goals be understood as a means to achieving the equality of women and men in the eyes of God and of community?

Oddly enough, the Jewish community, in which many pioneer feminists were nurtured, is one of the last groups to grapple with the challenges of feminism. True, Reform Judaism has taken many steps, beginning with the Breslau Conference's call in 1846 for full equality of men and women in all areas of religion. However, this equalization was largely formal; little substance or leadership was given to women. (Moreover, Reform made fewer religious demands upon both men and women, and the changes it internalized tended to flow from adoption of liberal, modern values, not from Jewish considerations.) Basically, the response of the Jewish community, both male and female, can be characterized in this way: the more traditionally Jewish it was—or the more internally Jewish its orientation (including elements within Reform)—the more it tended to resist the challenges that flowed from feminist ideology.

There are many reasons for this reaction. First, Jewish women, on the whole, have been well treated by Jewish men who have been imbued with strong cultural values sanctioning or demanding good treatment. So Jewish women have been quite content to live with the traditional roles—both religious and social—assigned them. They agreed with the argument that freedom from communal religious responsibilites, such as synagogue prayer, enabled them to better fulfill the familial role which Jewish society had ordained for them.

Second, the halakhic model of Judaism is currently resistant to change, and *halakhah* includes in its all-encompassing rubric the religious institutionalization of social status. What was a sociological truth about women in previous generations—that they were the "second sex"—was codified in many minute ways into the *halakhah* as religio-ethical concepts binding upon future generations as well. What is often overlooked today is that, over the ages, Jewish tradition by and large upgraded the status of women by responding to changes in society at large. One of the virtues of the halakhic system is its attempt to maintain the dialectical relationship of needs between community and individual, Jew and non-Jew, authority and freedom, religion and society. However, in this century, the halakhic authorities have been overwhelmingly resistant to such change.

Third, although it is not always openly articulated, there is a widespread fear that feminist ideology poses a threat to Jewish survival, similar to the threat that modernism in general has posed. Subconsciously or consciously, Jewish leaders fear opening a Pandora's box in exposing Jewish attitudes toward women to the claims of Women's Liberation. This fear is not completely invalid, nor is it restricted to the

Orthodox sector. But feminism will not disappear by ignoring it or rejecting it as a danger. Rather, the dangers posed by feminism should be identified and guarded against in the context of a positive incorporation of feminist virtues into Jewish life.

Today secular society has opened a great new range of roles and psychological expectations to women, while, at the same time, the halakhic status and religious life of Jewish women remain circumscribed. The situation is comparable to sitting in a stationary vehicle alongside a moving one. The net effect upon one is a sense of moving backward; upon the other, a sense of pulling away, of losing connection, of leaving behind. When confronted with harsh, but often valid criticism, religious resistance takes the form of apologetics and defensiveness. Some Jewish women accept these prescriptions—others move closer to the secular pole, abandoning not only observance, but all traditional religious values as well. Since there is no currently sanctioned universe of discourse between feminism and Judaism regarding the religious status of women, the feminist movement has often attacked and rejected the basic structures and values which Judaism has contributed to human society.

What is sorely needed today is the creation of a dialectical tension between Jewish values and the mores of modern society in light of the far-reaching implications of Women's Liberation. One crucial part of the dialectic would be to measure the halakhic and religious status of Jewish women by the feminist notion of equality of women. But there must be a two-way relationship of communication and influence instead of withdrawal and widening of the gap. Thus, an authentic Jewish women's movement would seek to find new approaches within *halakhah* to respond to and express women's concerns. Simultaneously, it would seek to imbue women's concerns with Jewish values.

I would propose that there are four areas in Jewish religious life where the goals of feminism can be applied in a dialectical fashion. This means interaction—not mere aping or assimilation. Though the truth is painful to those of us who live by and love the halakhic system, as I do, honesty bids us acknowledge that Jewish women face inequality in these four areas: in the synagogue and in participation in prayer; in halakhic education; in the religious courts; and in areas of communal leadership. These areas have been examined in depth in the literature of the Jewish women's movement.[5] Here I will touch upon some possible halakhic changes.

What Judaism Can Learn from Feminism

SYNAGOGUE AND PRAYER

The time is long overdue for a serious reanalysis of the principle of exemption from positive time-bound *mitzvot* in light of Rabbi Saul Berman's pioneering analysis of the basis of this exemption.[6] Conceivably, the *halakhah* could obligate women to observe time-bound *mitzvot* equally with adult men, yet allow for exemptions during those years when there are massive familial demands made upon their time and energies. This exemption might be operative until a woman's youngest child is seven, ten, or thirteen. The model to follow here would be *haosek bamitzvah patur min hamitzvah*. (One who is occupied in doing one *mitzvah* is excused from the performance of another *mitzvah* which runs in the same time-span.) A further positive implication of this change would be that once women are attuned to prayer, they might continue to pray even during those times when they are exempt.

Sensitive halakhists must recognize that the general effect of the prayer exemption conditions women to a negative attitude toward prayer. Women hardly ever pray at home; thus prayer becomes a function of intermittent synagogue attendance alone—hardly an incentive to serious prayer. Although the Law Committee of the Conservative Rabbinical Assembly recently allowed the inclusion of women in the *minyan*, it did not take the necessary further step of equating women and men in prayer responsibilities. As a first step in Orthodox synagogues where the *mehitzah* has been used to further the inequality of the sexes rather than to allow separate but equal *tefillah*, women's *minyanim* might be formed as a way of encouraging total development of women in prayer. This means women actually leading prayer, being called to and reading the Torah, etc.[7]

Prayer should not be a vicarious act, but rather one of personal participation. At present, men generally perform for women even those liturgical roles which are binding upon women, such as Kiddush and *Megillah* reading. The woman thus practices them by proxy, and finds herself helpless if the male in her life is absent. Even if the proxy situation were to continue to satisfy Jewish women—which is unlikely as their feminist consciousness changes—it operates only within the family context. Single women, divorcees, and widows cannot enjoy rituals by family proxy and, therefore, are consigned to very tangential roles in communities which organize themselves Jewishly around a synagogue.

Furthermore, traditional life-cycle ceremonies for women are either nonexistent or less significant than those of men. Moreover, ritual responses to biological events which are uniquely female (such as childbirth and onset of menstruation) are conspicuously absent in the tradition. Little by little, and with the help and encouragement of some men, women are beginning to develop religious forms to tie into the tradition and the community the emotions and experiences which currently find no communal halakhic expression.[8] A lot more is needed.

EDUCATION

Halakhic education is the most important area for reaching final equalization of women in the Jewish community. A great deal of leeway for personal judgment is given to *poskim* (halakhic decision-makers) in *halakhah*. Part of human nature as well as the halakhic system is the tendency to find positive solutions to problems with which the judge has the greatest sympathy. Women *poskim* are more likely than men to find sympathetic solutions for women's problems for they share and experience them in the most intense and personal way. Considering how far the *halakhah* will have to grow and stretch to meet women's needs and overcome disabilities, women *poskim* are essential. Until now, only men have studied and understood *halakhah*, and they alone have made all the decisions. Women have been kept ignorant of the sources and processes of the law, although they knew the details which applied to them. Today women must return to the sources and apply themselves seriously to Jewish scholarship. There must be institutes of higher Jewish education such as *kollelim* (communally supported Talmudic institutes) where women can study uninterruptedly with some degree of financial security. Women must be trained to make legal decisions, not only for women, but for the entire Jewish community. And the notion of women rabbis must be accepted in all branches of Judaism, for women *can* make a contribution to the spiritual growth of the Jewish community.

THE RELIGIOUS COURTS

The third area where great pressure must be applied is in overcoming the legal disabilities which deny the dignity of women or cause outright injustice and unjustified suffering to them. The problem of Jewish divorce law (where a woman is altogether dependent on the will of her husband to grant and write a writ of divorce) has led to frequent discrimination, extortion, and innocent suffering. Similarly, the problem of the *agunah* must be reevaluated halakhically. In every generation, rabbis have worked prodigiously to circumvent the harshness of this law. In this generation, however, divorce has become much more prevalent and, therefore, serious. In addition, war is on a vaster scale and wife-desertion is easier. A global solution to the problem of a wife's dependence on her husband is needed. This kind of solution has been offered by Eliezer Berkovits in his work on the use of *tenai* (condition) in marriage and divorce.[9] His proposal has not been treated with due seriousness by halakhic leaders here or in Israel.

Religious courts must change to accept women's testimony. A law which once protected women by preventing them from being subpoenaed into the public sector must now be rethought in terms of equality of men and women. All these changes can be wrought by using the principle of change for the better, which obtains in the history of *halakhah* especially in the area of treatment of women.[10]

COMMUNAL LIFE

In the communal arena, there are still strong obstacles to women's assuming leadership roles in many educational, philanthropic and political institutions. Aside from the question of sexual discrimination, the Jewish community can ill afford to reject out of hand one half of the potential pool of capable leaders.

Thus, many aspects of feminism are relevant to us as Jews and to the total Jewish community. These changes can be wrought in halakhic fashion, within its framework. *Halakhah* need not be asked to conform to every passing fad; neither, however, may the leadership be allowed to hide behind slogans of immutability that are dishonest caricatures of the *halakhah*. Fidelity to the halakhic system demands openness to new realities of life so as to upgrade and enhance our own ethical and religious system. *Torah im derekh eretz* means integrating the best values of society in which we live with our own tradition—especially where they illuminate or coincide with the tradition's own ultimate goals—in this case, the dignity of man and woman as image of God.

However, if we move only in the direction of integrating new (albeit good) values into the tradition, we would not be an authentically Jewish movement. To be Jewish means not only to take and learn from societies in which we live, but to serve as correctives within the broader society as well.

What Feminism Can Learn from Judaism

Since we are Jews, we need not buy the whole package of feminism. Rather, we must infuse a changing society with our own values and check the excesses to which all revolutionary movements fall prey. Further, we must walk a very fine line—continually monitoring even those parts of the new which we have integrated into our lives to see whether they adequately meet the test of Jewish authenticity. This means readiness to reject those aspects of new movements which are antithetical to Jewish values in their very essence. Feminism, for all its worth in upgrading the status of Jewish women, does not bode well in its entirety for Jewish survival. Some of its directions may be wrong—or even destructive—when judged from a Jewish perspective.

FAMILY

One of the by-products of the feminist striving for equality has been a strong attack on the family for having been the locus of abuse of women in all previous generations. Thus, Women's Liberation has escalated the crushing assault mounted on the family by contemporary society. The Jewish family, the most stable of all, is also beginning to crumble. We see signs of this erosion everywhere—increasing divorce rate, lack of communication between parents and children, poor models of family life for the next generation to learn from, etc.

Many young Jewish women today state outright their objections to marriage and having children—in striking contrast to the previous generation whose primary goals were marriage and child rearing. Today we must recognize that not every woman can find happiness in marriage—or in marriage alone. But peer influence is so strong that we risk the danger of having the other option—a traditional marriage and family relationship—being rejected from consideration altogether. This particularly threatens Judaism, where the family is so central to educational and religious life. Much of our religious life takes place within a family context. And the Jewish family has been the primary source of strength and support in coping with the often hostile and dangerous world Jews lived in for two thousand years. The very centrality of the family means that feminists who take Judaism seriously will explore every possible avenue of strengthening the family and correcting its evils before dismissing it. (This includes a willingness to suffer some disabilities, if necessary, and to live at times with frustration for the sake of the greater goal of Jewish survival and stability.)

We must reintroduce into women's consciousness the concept of a total life. Homemaking, childrearing, career and political action need not be seen as competing activities, each demanding total commitment *now*. Each activity can be pursued in turn, at different life-stages. This understanding might help women who respond naturally to the roles of wife/mother to feel less anxious in the face of contemporary pressures to choose one role exclusively or to be superwomen, pursuing everything simultaneously.

Respect for family is important not merely for old time's sake. Despite contemporary desire to believe otherwise, the family remains the most important determinant of educational achievement and religious values and commitment available.[11] The contemporary shift to school and synagogue to do the job of transmission of Judaism for us is mistaken. So central is the family and so effective that I would reverse the modish argument that *havurot* and peer groups are the educational wave of the future, and suggest that the *havurah* can best be understood as growing out of the search of many isolated singles (and couples) for a family to provide the necessary climate for practicing Judaism. In *Sexual Suicide,* George Gilder places the responsibility for the decay of society on the breakdown of the traditional family unit.[12] Certainly, the family survived for so many thousands of years as an institution, even with its imperfections, because it was—and is—the most ethical and viable of relationships.

ENABLING

Although the family was the context in which women functioned as the second sex throughout history, and enabler was the only role open to them, neither of these conditions is axiomatic to a woman's choice of the wife/mother role today. The family was also a source of security, honor, merit, and satisfaction for the majority of women in the past and for most women today who consider their freedom to serve exclusively as wives and mothers a sign of their own liberation.

Thus we should not denigrate the traditional roles, nor those who choose them. Just as women resented the restrictive mold which confined them in the past, so we must not coerce all women into a new restrictive mold—that which excludes enablers. We must check the negative tone which abounds in references to child rearing. More than this, to counteract the current negative stereotype of wife/mother, we must educate others to the excitement, fun, and sweetness of being married and raising children. True, we must bring the husband into a central role in the family, not just as provider, but as childraiser, as involved husband, for the liberation of men and children as well as women. Support of career women, single women, and women involved in political change need not imply denigration of the family.

Another aspect of safeguarding the family is teaching society to open up more to women who have chosen the marriage/family route. One of the subtle indications of the prejudices of the feminist movement has been its ordering of its priorities to campaign for equal jobs and equal pay for full-time careers, while neglecting discrimination in salaries and benefits for part-time jobs, most of which are filled by mothers. Nor has the feminist movement dealt seriously with the adjustments necessary to help reintegrate women, who have been out of the labor market while raising children, back into careers.

SEXUAL FREEDOM

Another new message that should be confronted by Jewish feminists is the "new morality." Although this code of sexual license was on the scene well before Women's Liberation, feminism has extended these messages to the female population, thereby legitimating them for all. Formerly "a man's thing" and oppressive to women, extramarital affairs are now a symbol of the equality of women, undermining family stability and contributing to the soaring divorce rate. Concentrated in urban, higher income, higher educational sectors, Jews are among the most exposed to these new values and their dangers. In previous generations, Jews lived by an internal moral code which may have been based in part on principles coercive to women; however, today's shift in mores is a grim warning of the destructive potential in many well-intentioned feminist clichés—particularly sexual freedom.

Judaism nurtured healthy sexual outlets within marriage, and even recognized them before marriage, yet put very strict curbs on extramarital sexuality. One need not identify with male privilege or the double standard suggested in traditional Jewish definitions of adultery to agree with the main goal of the prohibitions involved. As Jews, we have learned that freedom comes only within an ethical structure. Given human limitations, ethics of interpersonal relationships necessarily involve restraint and frustration. Although Judaism always permitted divorce as a necessary, if regretable, way to end an unsatisfactory marriage, the parameters of the marital relationship, while it was being lived, were, at the least, sexual fidelity and mutual respect. Feminists who claim that now women should have full sexual freedom define freedom as allowing the ex-slave to have the same right to abuse that previously only the master had. Jewish feminists should rather challenge and censure these values in male society; we should press for equal morality, not equal amorality.

ABORTION

Another example of the dialectical relationship between Judaism and feminism is in our attitude toward abortion. In an era when 6,000,000 Jews were killed—and 1,500,000 of them were children—we have to examine both sides of the abortion issue. From our perspective, we must talk about the preciousness of life, not just the right to life. Stressing a woman's right to control her own body, and the legitimacy of considering the quality of life that she and her child will have, should go hand in hand with emphasis on the sanctity of life and on the risk of devaluating it in unthinking or easy medical solutions.

We must ensure that abortion does not become a preferred method of birth control.

The *halakhah* currently opposes abortion on demand. As Jews, we must demonstrate that abortion need not eliminate reverence for life and joy in creating life. On the one hand, this would lead to new halakhic attitudes toward abortion; on the other, *halakhah* could help curb facile and nonchalant attitudes toward abortion and the abuses which have grown out of abortion reform. The protection of the quality of life which is the ethical basis of abortion could be offset or destroyed by a loss of reverence for life.

A further application of this principle would be establishing adoption agencies for pregnant Jewish women who do not want or cannot keep their own babies. The virtual unavailability of Jewish babies for adoption, due to the acceptability of abortion, causes real problems for Jewish couples who wish to adopt.

SOCIETAL VALUES

The feminist movement has bought another unfortunate message of modern society—its materialistic orientation. Men and women's worth are determined by what and how much they produce, what kind of job they hold, their titles, how much they earn—not by what their values and characters are. This has consistently led to dehumanization, worship of success, and rejection of "failures," including the poor. As Jews, we must reject these standards and say that the human being is valuable in his or her very being. As Jews, we affirm that there is value and validity in serving and giving to others—in volunteer action and professional work, in being good family members and friends, in doing good works. The traditional role of enabling is still a valid one; as long as it is not limited to women, or women limited to it. We must attempt to infuse these values into the society we seek to create, rather than simply copy the errors of present male society. The truly revolutionary (and admittedly more difficult) task is to change these societal values and judgments, to overcome the production-value standard and liberate men and women for more human living.

Many interpret Women's Liberation as liberation to fulfill their own personal needs, narrowly defined. This leads to an attitude which values self-actualization to the exclusion of considering others' needs, and a denial that there can be fulfillment in giving to others. Good family situations have been exploded by unreal expectations and demands for immediate and unlimited personal gratification. Capacity to live with frustration has been dangerously weakened. The skyrocketing divorce rate can be explained, in part, by the extreme of the women's movement which attempts to deny the undeniable: that successful marriages and parent-child relationships take time, energy, a measure of sacrifice and generosity of soul—all the very opposites of instant gratification.

Similarly, charity and giving of oneself to others are being undercut in the fight for self-actualization. Volunteerism is under heavy attack by hard-line feminists. Jewish charitable organizations, which rely on volunteer work, are suffering as a result. The slogan that "self-esteem comes from a paying job" or that "if it isn't paid for, it's not taken seriously"—is a half-truth. Not everyone can afford or wish to work without pay—but volunteerism, *tzedakah*, certainly should remain a respected option. Those who find satisfaction in giving of themselves to others should be praised, not scorned.

MEN

We must check the excesses of those feminists who are hostile to men. Jewish women do not need to hate men to liberate themselves; nor should Jewish men be seen simply as crude oppressors of women throughout history. For most of our history, both Jewish men and women suffered from outside persecution and hostility, and their mutual solidarity carried them through. Instead of polarizing, we must try to liberate men so that they will not continue to be slaves to the rat-race, but also strive for a sense of dignity and self-worth. "Making it in a man's world" isn't all that easy for men either. We must also liberate men Jewishly so that they, too, can come to understand and grow in their tradition.

Finally, we must reject the notion that equality means sameness. From the perspective of Judaism, there can be separate clear-cut roles in which men and women function as equals without losing their separate identities. Male and female are, admittedly, difficult concepts to define, but we must be aware in every instance whether we are dealing with the dignity of equality, which is an essential value in Judaism, or identicalness of male and female, which is not.

Those Jewish women who have identified with many of the feminist goals have an added measure of responsibility, for we are in a better position to influence and be heard by both sides. It is no mean task to walk the fine line between old and new, status quo and avant-garde, God's commandments and the emerging needs of society. But one reason Judaism has survived against all odds, and even managed to contribute greatly to world civilization, is that in each era it managed to do exactly that. To keep the fine tension and balance between these opposing forces is probably harder now—the forces are stronger, tension is higher, and society is more open. But our faith in Judaism and the Jewish people gives us the strength to demand and expect the same achievement in our time. It is a task worth the effort.

Notes

l. Emanuel Rackman, "Equality in Judaism," in J. Roland Pennock and John W. Chapman, eds., *Equality* (New York: Lieber-Atherton, 1967).

2. The Jewish legal system enjoins that one is not to be favored in court either because one is the poorer or the wealthier litigant.

3. The laws of sabbatical and jubilee years insured that capital and land would revert to the masses of the population and could not be indefinitely accumulated in ever-enlarged aggregates by a wealthy landowner.

4. Such as freeing the Hebrew slaves in the sabbatical year.

5. See, for example, Rachel Adler, "The Jew Who Wasn't There; Halacha and the Jewish Woman," *Davka*, Summer 1971; Blu Greenberg, "Coming of Age in the Jewish Community," *Tradition*, Spring 1976; Judith Hauptman, "Images of Women in the Talmud," in Rosemary Ruether, ed. *Religion and Sexism* (New York: Simon and Schuster, 1974).

6. Saul Berman, "The Status of Women in Halakhic Judaism," *Tradition* 14(2), 1973: 5–28: An abbreviated version is reprinted in this volume, pp. 114–128.

7. Within Reform and Conservative ritual as well, counting women in a *minyan* and calling them to the Torah will remain cosmetic refinements unless these developments are integrated into a total campaign for developing women's capacities and roles in prayer.

8. See, for example, the articles in the "Life Cycle and New Rituals" section.

9. Eliezer Berkovits, *Tenai Benissuin Uvaget* (Jerusalem: Mossad HaRav Kook, 1966).

10. For example, the development of the *ketubah*, allowing the testimony of one witness to free a woman from *agunah* status, the polygamy ban of Rabbenu Gershom and his requirement that no divorce be given against the wife's will, etc.

11. Geoffrey Bock, "The Social Context of Jewish Education: A Literature Review," paper prepared for the Colloquium on Jewish Education and Jewish Identity of the American Jewish Committee, April 1974. See also Harold S. Himmelfarb, "Jewish Education For Naught: Educating the Culturally Deprived Child," *Analysis*, September 1975.

12. George Gilder, *Sexual Suicide* (New York: Quadrangle, 1973). See also George Gilder, "In Defense of Monogamy," *Commentary* 58 (5), 1974.

THE CHANGING (?) ROLE OF WOMEN IN JEWISH COMMUNAL AFFAIRS: A LOOK INTO THE UJA
Steven M. Cohen, Susan Dessel, Michael Pelavin

> One balmy Alabama night, under a starry Alabama sky, I heard the never-to-be forgotten voice of Martin Luther King ring out in his never-to-be-heard again prophetic cadences as he said, "We are all witnesses together." He did not mean witness as onlooker, witness as voyeur. He meant witness-participant. And so are we women, when we ask to share in communal responsibility, asking to be witnesses, participants, in our own Jewish community. We are asking that there be developed a real community. We are asking that our talents of maintaining Jewish life through the centuries—of caring for our children, of developing a volunteer cadre capable of remarkable achievement, of welding realism with compassion, of developing an understanding of the real priorities a society should have—not be set aside any longer on the grounds of a prefabricated sexual role difference. We are asking, in short, to be treated only as human beings, so that we may be witness to and participants in the exciting challenge of creating a new and open and total Jewish community.
>
> ——*Response* 18 (Summer 1973):65

Thus spoke Jacqueline Levine, a vice-president of the Council of Jewish Federations and Welfare Funds (the umbrella organization for the nation's more than 200 local Community Councils and Welfare Funds) to the more than 3,000 delegates to the CJFWF's annual General Assembly in 1972. She was probably the first to raise the issue of women's involvement in Jewish communal life at a national forum and she reported evidence of pervasive under-representation of women in honorific roles and positions of influence in Jewish fund-raising organizations.

We thank Shifra Bronznick and Natalie Pelavin for criticizing and editing early versions of this manuscript.

Against this background and in light of the growing centrality of the Jewish Welfare Federations in Jewish affairs, we decided to examine the traditional role of women in the local Jewish Welfare Federations (and their parent bodies) and the prospects for change in these roles.

In order to analyze the current status of women, we consulted with the professional and lay leadership of the National UJA as well as the leadership in local Federations. We particularly sought out individuals who have been closely involved with the Women's Division(s) and with the Young Leadership Divisions. Our inquiries were met with occasional hostility, but more often with interest and candor. At first all interviewees asked us to keep their comments off the record, as many seemed fearful of offending professional colleagues or of creating antagonism among lay leadership. The sole exception was Irving Bernstein, secure in his position as Executive Vice-Chairman of the National UJA (the primary fundraising entity for overseas need, e.g. United Israel Appeal, Joint Distribution Committee, Hebrew Immigrant Aid Society, New York Association for New Americans.)

A careful analysis of the role of women should begin with a brief outline of the general structure of the national and local Jewish Welfare Federations and their fundraising apparatus. Locally, each community organizes its own campaign; within that, a separate campaign is conducted by the Women's Division. The overall campaign is headed by a chairman and a campaign committee. Chairmen are never, to our knowledge, referred to as chairpeople; and, if women attain that position, they, too, are referred to as chairmen.

In addition, most communities maintain young leadership or leadership development groups designed to educate potential leaders to the ways and wherefores of UJA and Federation work and to introduce them to the hierarchial structure of the American Jewish community. Most of these groups are composed of married couples. Some are exclusively male or female, and some are composed of both men and women who may or may not be married to each other. In any case, it is rare that single people participate in these groups.

However, gender seems to be less an issue for those participating in these groups than for their older counterparts. Young people participate more often in cross-sex solicitation than do their elders, although most Young Leadership fundraising is still segregated. The trend towards permitting cross-sex solicitation may be the result of changing mores, and may also reflect the greater experimentation permitted with the smaller gifts of younger people.

Once an individual has achieved prominence on the local level, he or she may be drawn into the national activities of the Leadership Development Committee of the CJFWF. Promising young men may be invited to join the Young Leadership Cabinet of the UJA. The YLC now includes nearly 300 men from across the country, who range in age from the early thirties (when most are invited to join) to forty (the mandatory retirement age). Cabinet graduates are found among the officers of UJA's beneficiary agencies and as officers of the National UJA, roles both prestigious and demanding.

Women of all ages who achieve recognition through work in their local Women's Divisions or on the Leadership Development Committees of their Federations may be asked to join the UJA National Women's Division Board or the Women's Communal Service Committee of the CJFWF. Some outstanding women are given the opportunity to serve on other national committees of the CJFWF.

Within the structure of the National UJA, the YLC and the National Women's Division Board perform many of the same functions for and make many of the same demands on their respective memberships. Both expect their members to conduct fund-raising efforts locally, regionally, and nationally. Frequently, national leaders are called into a local community to give advice, to solicit funds (utilizing their expertise or special relationship with potential donors), to speak, and to offer other forms of assistance. Each group develops its own educational program centering around special topics deemed of value to its membership. Each maintains for its members an informal network providing social and moral support. Each aids in perfecting the skills of its members as it provides a channel for upward mobility and national exposure.

Jewish communal leadership on the national level demands a substantial commitment of both time and money. Since lay leaders are expected to function as models, a high level of giving to the cause is a virtual *sine qua non* for national leadership. National involvement brings with it increased pressure for substantial financial commitment, often exceeding that which would be expected by the local community from that particular person. Interestingly, we heard many local leaders complain that national involvement deprives the local community of needed talent.

Membership on these national boards requires a great deal of travel. In addition to community solicitations and consultations, the members are expected to attend at least one annual national retreat, the national conventions of the CJFWF (in a different city each November), and the national UJA convention held in New York in December. Activity on the national level requires at least a minimal level of attendance at committee or board meetings, frequently held in New York. Finally, there is a commitment to participate in at least one Israel Mission—a well-programmed trip designed to offer a view of Israel not encountered by most tourists. All travel costs are, of course, paid for by the participant.

These requirements of time, energy, and money make it extremely difficult for any but the financially comfortable to join the national leadership ranks. There are a few notable exceptions to this generalization; the YLC occasionally has sought out rabbis and professors. Over the past five years, there have been at least two unsuccessful attempts to open the YLC's ranks to women. Various supporters of this effort have included:

(1) Wives of Cabinet members who were eager to participate with their husbands in activities which they both regarded as fulfilling and important.

(2) Husbands of these women.

(3) YLC members who appreciated the talent and commitment of women in their community and who felt the injustice of arbitrarily excluding women (who might, or might not, be wives of current YLC members) from the Cabinet.

(4) Young women leaders in communities who feel that they could make better use of their talents and derive more satisdfaction from their UJA work if they were YLC members.

Steven Offerman, a regional chairman of the YLC Executive Committee, summed up his position, and that of others favoring change, with the following remarks:

> We're not concerned only with injustice to women. Our concern is that many talented Jews are not being utilized to the fullest, and the Cabinet has a lot to offer to help one understand what one's true potential and capacity are. The real injustice is in not using all the people-power available. After all, more than half the wealth in this country is in the hands of women and the Women's Division simply isn't getting the money.

The forces opposing change include:

(1) Men who are afraid of the Cabinet's losing a special male camaraderie they feel at YLC retreats and in other activities.

(2) Husbands and wives who fear that extramarital sexual relations will develop within a male-female YLC in light of the frequent travel and close-knit group experiences. Aside from the impact that this might have on marital relations, some believe that potential sexual relationships would impede the smooth functioning of the Cabinet.

(3) Men whose image of women suggests that (a) women's responsibilities as wives and mothers preclude their traveling extensively; (b) women's infrequent participation in the business world implies a generally weaker comprehension and acuity in financial affairs; (c) potential male donors don't respect women as equals and therefore women's effectiveness as fundraisers is severely limited; and (d) few young women have independent financial resources.

(4) Women deeply involved in the Women's Division of UJA who believe that admitting women to the YLC would threaten the very existence of the Women's Division.

We should note that a new challenge is currently under way to the males-only rule of the YLC, a challenge more potent than those of previous years. For the first time, an entire YLC group has proposed that the Cabinet accept women candidates. Members' views on the matter are now being solicited and the issue will no doubt come to a head in YLC meetings over the next year.

The Women's Division also poses a difficult analytical problem. The Women's Division's *raison d'être* is to create "plus-giving." That is, the general campaign solicits the husband as the "head of the household," with the prestige and status accompanying the contribution accorded to him. The Women's Division provides the woman with the opportunity to make a gift in her own right—from her salary if she is working outside the home, from her personal household funds, or from funds directly under her control.

Many active Women's Division members view the Women's Division as a vehicle for feminist expression. Others see the Women's Division as evidence of the rampant sexism of the UJA.

Those who view the Women's Division as a feminist vehicle feel that Women's Division programs are created by and for local women to satisfy their specific interests in communal work and to utilize their available time. As a result, specific Jewish and personal needs are satisfied which could not be fulfilled without such a structure. The

Women's Division also encourages women to develop their talents and thus to attain positions of leadership. Women are taught to solicit, plan programs, make speeches, and conduct campaigns. As a result of their efforts, roughly $70,000,000—or approximately 15 percent of the total dollars raised in recent years—has been raised by the "plus giving" of the Women's Division.

Those who feel that the Women's Division is inherently sexist offer a number of critical arguments. Some claim the Women's Division is often not taken seriously, nor regarded as a locus of influence or a source of genuine prestige.

One career-minded young woman leader echoed the sentiments of others in stating that the programs of the Women's Division do not fulfill her needs. She finds the separation from men socially artificial and undesirable. She now spends all her local UJA time working together with men in her Young Leadership Division, and she sees no reason for the sexes to be separated on the national level. When pressed for additional reasons for lack of interest in the Women's Division, she cited the older age of most of the women in the Division as well as the small number of career women within its ranks.

Other criticisms of the Women's Division closely follow the arguments advanced by general opponents of women's volunteerism. According to this view, women's free time and needs for social involvement have often led to high levels of volunteer activity on the part of upper- and upper-middle-class women. Usually this volunteer activity is done on behalf of organizations in which men retain most of the positions of influence while women do most of the "dirty work." An argument frequently made against incorporating women into the general structure is that their free time will enable them to outperform the current male leadership and the men will subsequently leave much of the work they now perform to the more energetic women.

Perhaps the most telling criticism of the Women's Division is that, despite its claims, it fails to promote many women into positions of leadership in the general campaigns. In fact, at present, in only a few communities have women attained high office in the Federation or the general campaign. Most of the Board of Trustees or campaign cabinet positions are still filled by men, even if the level of their communal activity compares unfavorably with that of their female counterparts. Our women interviewees reported that women are often taken for granted, suggesting that comnunities are unwilling to recognize that women have the same needs as men for recognition and prestige.

Further evidence of the failure to recognize women's contributions is found in the gross under-representation of women on the National Executive Committee and Campaign Cabinet of the National UJA. The reasons given by Irving Bernstein and others for the scarcity of women in highly visible roles are twofold: many interviewees recognized the open discomfort or hostility of men to sharing influential roles with women; even more stressed the reluctance of women to press their views and promote themselves in the face of opposition. Mr. Bernstein and others conceded that, all things being equal, a woman needs something extra to assure advancement over her male counterpart. It should be reiterated, however, that most of the responsibility for women's under-representation was attributed (by both men and women) to women's continued lack of aggressiveness in seeking advancement.

As the appended document—a draft resolution on women to be brought before the 1975 General Assembly—points out, women have been and continue to be under-represented in key leadership roles. Our informants strongly agreed with this contention. Although in some communities, women are assuming roles they have never held before, often the ascendance of a woman to a previously male-only position bears little relation to feminist forces within these communities, since the woman in question may exhibit little interest in promoting women in the Federation hierarchy.

We uncovered a wide range of sentiment regarding women's roles. The general assessment of our interviewees was that the typical male lay leader is still somewhat uncomfortable with women in traditionally male roles but could be pushed into reluctantly accepting changes in women's status. A middle ground emerges as well in the feelings of passive support for changes in the status of women. This position is best typified by the views of Mr. Bernstein, who sees little need for actively promoting women's advancement. He does not view the issue in terms of morality or equity; rather, he regards the under-representation of women in higher levels of the hierarchy as a pragmatic problem, seriously depriving the UJA of valuable untapped energy and talent. We believe he would genuinely welcome agitation by women for change in their status; agitation which he sees as the critical precondition for significant change in women's roles.

Guided by our interviewees, we agree that Mr. Bernstein's views accurately reflect the strong sentiment of the UJA with respect to the advancement of women. The overriding pragmatism which characterizes American business enterprise flourishes within the UJA. The organization is neither the most progressive force in Jewish or American society with regard to women's rights, nor is it the most traditional or resistant to change. Changing demographics, that is, the increased numbers of single, divorced, and/or professional women, will no doubt create a philanthropic market into which the UJA and Federations will want to expand, and indeed are expanding already. Moreover, the changing attitudes towards sex-derived roles among both men and women should occasion greater assertiveness on the part of Jewish women and greater receptivity to change on the part of Jewish men.

We believe that National UJA and the local Jewish Welfare Federations must assume the responsibility of translating their well-meaning words into action. The business world and academia have developed a successful model for rectifying unjust practices in selection and promotion: the affirmative action committee. If adopted by the Jewish community, these committees could seek out and promote professionals and lay leaders who have suffered the effects of sexist discrimination in the past. These internal pressure groups would compel Jewish organizations to recognize and utilize unrecognized talent within their own ranks. Another benefit of such actions would be a greater appreciation of the problems faced by women within our Jewish community. One such problem is the dearth of Jewish day-care facilities, whose establishment would permit women to participate more fully in communal work.

Concern and sensitivity to the needs of each member of the Jewish community will not only be of benefit to the individual involved, but will improve the quality of Jewish life for all of American Jewry.

Addendum

Draft Resolution: Women in Federation Policy- and Decision-Making

In carrying out a policy of nondiscrimination, selection of persons for highest Jewish communal responsibilities must be on the basis of ability. Women should neither be chosen nor denied such positions because they are women.

While we applaud the efforts of a number of communities to utilize women in the highest policy-making and decision-making roles in Federations, on Agency Boards, in the campaign structure, and in all aspects of Jewish community life, we must again call attention to the fact that as yet the potentials for the involvement of women are far greater than have been realized.

The facts collected by CJF reveal that one of every twenty Federation presidents, one of six vice-presidents, one of six members of executive committees, one of five board members, one of four members of allocations and planning committees, one of three chairmen of these committees or their subcommittees are women.

The pressing tasks at home and abroad which lie before our entire community demand the fullest commitment on the part of each man and woman volunteer in Jewish life. It is essential therefore that the talent of individuals as individuals be recognized and utilized. Women remain our greatest untapped resource.

In the realm of Jewish professional service, we also urge that Jewish women be accorded equal treatment both in employment opportunities and in remuneration by Federations and by member agencies. We endorse and support the policy of equal pay for equal work.

August 29, 1975.

FLIGHT FROM FEMINISM: THE CASE OF THE ISRAELI WOMAN
Carol N. Clapsaddle

Until very recently, the Israeli woman held an unquestioned place of honor in any ranking of liberated women of the world. There was much evidence, in fact, to support the claim that she was the most liberated. Her full participation in the establishment of the State, her early ideological commitment to complete equality, her membership in the army and police services, her attainment of a wide range of rights, and her brash character seemed to confirm the image. In spite of real accomplishments, however, the truth of women's position in Israel, both past and present, is more complex than this and disturbingly less positive.

For the liberation of the Israeli woman was neither as straightforward nor as secure as she and the world had come to believe. From the earliest pioneering years, various forces worked to undermine her achievements. Today a new danger is emerging. It is that, through her complacency, the Israeli woman is forfeiting the equality her mother and grandmother so diligently won. Especially because that equality had once seemed so nearly complete and long established—unlike the comparatively insecure victories of the suffragettes or "Rosie-the-Riveters"—the Israeli woman's gradual retreat is of real concern to us. To attempt a full analysis of why it happened would require an Israeli *Feminine Mystique*. Here, though, are some speculations.

Historically the image of the "liberated" Israeli woman was created by an early secular, leftist, highly political group. By 1924–27, the Fourth Aliyah, 65,000 immigrants arrived in Palestine from Eastern

Europe, of whom only about a third wanted to become *halutzim,* manual laborers. Most were small traders, middlemen, and city dwellers.[1] Another sizable and usually ignored community in histories of the period was the Orthodox. Even before independence in 1948, approximately 15 to 20 percent of the female Jewish population ful- filled only the most traditional feminine roles.

The entire Jewish population before independence was 614,000; after the mid–1950s, it was matched by an influx of over 600,000 Jewish refugees from the Arab countries.[2] Bereft of their cultural and economic leaders, most of whom had emigrated to France, those who came to Israel were, for the most part, destitute, illiterate, and unskilled. They had also completely assimilated the Arab culture's ideas of male supremacy. It was out of the question for a woman to attempt any role but wife-and-mother. If she went out to work, she shamed her husband's honor.

A generation of Jewish girls of Oriental parents has grown up in Israel since the 1950s; and in important respects, such as jobholding and belief in their equality with men, their position has changed considerably. But the force of the old ways persists. Few continue their education beyond the years of high school or work after the first child comes. Fewer still attend universities, even under the special "second chance" programs offered youth from disadvantaged backgrounds.[3] More than for other Israeli girls, then, their only imaginable future is marriage and children.

Israel's Jewish population is now approximately half of Oriental family background, and 30 percent of the total Jewish population are Orthodox[4] (a figure including many Orientals as well as recent immi- grants from the U.S.S.R.) Arabs and other minority women from tradi- tional cultures[5] living within the pre-1967 borders make up another 14 percent of Israel's population. One can understand, therefore, how in 1973 only 30 percent of Israeli women aged fourteen to sixty-five were employed outside the home (33 percent in 1975).[6] The comparable figure in the United States the same year was about 47 percent.[7] More significant even, of the total number of employed women in Israel, only 12 percent (as opposed to 33 percent in the United States) were mothers of preschool-age children.[8]

Even considering the large traditionalist population, the low percen- tage of young working mothers is surprising, since Israeli women have achieved far more in the area of maternity and child-care rights than American women. For example, every working woman employed for one year is entitled to a twelve-week paid maternity leave and every woman, working or not, is entitled to free delivery and postnatal hospitalization.

The Israeli working woman may also have fewer child-care problems. Although the supply is still insufficient, there are many more government sponsored or subsidized day-care centers per capita than in the United States,[9] and the government's policy is to encourage their spread. Most women still prefer to remain home while their children are very young, but my observation is that women who choose work or study have less guilt about leaving their children in day-care centers than do American women. And the society's professed goal is to support them in doing so.

In certain respects, too, Israel is more hospitable to childrearing than is the United States. One never sees a sign saying "no children or dogs allowed" or "no baby carriages allowed." The *Jerusalem Post's* columnist on consumers' affairs, Martha Meisels, writing during a visit in the United States, once commented on the prevalence there of apartments that outlaw children. She noted with surprise the pride apartment complex owners display in their ads about "adult living."[10] This sort of thing is as yet foreign to Israel.

In spite of all these advantages, however, the percentage of working mothers with young children remains low, and the government's obtuseness in certain ways is largely responsible. The Labor Ministry, for example, was "puzzled" by the fact that, in spite of all its efforts, the proportion of working mothers in the population, especially those with young children, has not risen significantly since 1965 (from 1965 to 1975 only 4 percent).[11] Almost any mother who wants to work could dispèl their confusion in a minute. With only one-day weekends, low wages and few opportunities for most working women, and high taxes, it hardly pays for a woman to work. In Israel, child care is not a tax deductible expense, and day care is still often hard to find and expensive. All this—plus the view of a wife's work as just "the second salary"—operates to keep women at home.

In addition, subtle discrimination plays its part in narrowing options. An employer is often reluctant to hire a pregnant or young married woman, since he has to provide generous maternity benefits, equal-pay-for-equal-work laws have little effect if a woman isn't doing "equal work." A major stride a few years ago revealed that the tactic of maneuvering women employees into a lower job classification is resorted to in Israel as in the United States.[12] The efforts of women's rights advocates to improve the situation persist, though so far, as the recent (July 1975) defeat of the Women's Rights Bill shows, without success.

There is, however, one distinct group, mostly Western, secular, well-educated, Israeli women with no overt child-care or discrimination problems, kibbutz women. The kibbutz offers the test case of Israeli social norms and the kibbutz woman, proof of their supposed achievements. But the women of the kibbutz provide most clearly the evidence of a retreat from feminism. Why, with excellent communal child care and ostensibly complete equality with men, did it happen there?

Apparently the insecurity of women dies hard. As kibbutz conditions became easier and more secure, the pioneer woman began to feel the cost of her contribution. "She worked in the fields, and then all of a sudden she realized that in her thirties she looked like an old woman."[13] Her health was often damaged and her beauty gone. There were plenty of younger women around, and perhaps her husband noticed them more than before. According to Yehudah Paz, kibbutz member and researcher, it was the women who called for the introduction of cosmetics and beauty treatments. Kibbutz men often felt uncomfortable with these innovations and objected to them as "violations of kibbutz ideology."

Another and complementary trend was women's abandonment of the "productive" occupations of the kibbutz for the "service" branches. As farm work grew more mechanized and specialized, it became possible to release more hands from the fields. Simultaneously, a demand grew in the kibbutzim for more services and attention to child care, at least partly in response to the increasing seductiveness of urban life. The proportion of workdays devoted to services grew, until today 49 percent of the total adult population works in the children's houses, the kitchen, the laundry, and other similar branches.[14] Older members and women fill these jobs almost exclusively.

The kibbutz committees are also segregated. Having abandoned the "productive" branches, women can claim little expertise in running them. The educational, cultural, and social committees, therefore, are now made up almost entirely of women, while the economic planning and work committees, as well as almost all policy-making bodies, are in the hands of men. Many kibbutzim are concerned about the situation and claim to be trying to place as many women and old people as possible in productive labor. One means has been the introduction of industries of skill into the kibbutz. But progress through this approach remains slow.

A big danger, moreover, is that the present system of education doesn't facilitate a reversal. Kibbutz regional high schools teach the boys welding, soil chemistry, and electrical systems; they teach the girls home economics, sewing, and fashion design. When, on a tour of one of these high schools, I asked the principal whether boys might be encouraged to take dietetics and girls welding or agronomy, he seemed genuinely taken aback. "But they wouldn't be interested," he replied. It did little good to remind him that not so long ago the girls often were vitally interested.

Nobody pushed the women back into the services. Influenced by many factors, including mechanization and, perhaps, guilt over "neglecting" their maternal role, women chose for themselves. The problem is that today, when the kibbutzim are introducing more industrial projects and professionalization, forces are at work which will make it very difficult to reverse that choice. On the kibbutz, a former vanguard of women's liberation, the system is functioning, albeit unintentionally, to ensure that the women will remain in their more traditional roles.

Women's dissatisfaction in the kibbutz rarely arises, however, because of "sexist discrimination." On the contrary, most families leave the kibbutz because the wives want a *more* conventional home life. Their sisters in the cities seem to have a more private and rewarding existence, studying at the university, running their own homes, rearing their own children, and generally, so it appears, having a better time of it. The return to services is, in part, an effort to stem defections from kibbutz. But this strategy may be self-defeating, for it is difficult to see the advantage of working full time in the kitchen or the laundry or the children's house. Such work cannot compete with the variety and sense of running one's own home that causes some women to want to leave the kibbutz. If one must do housework, the housewife's lot is less tedious and offers more opportunities.

The collectivist creed that created the kibbutz also serves to ease the consciences of women returning to the services. That ideology offered only a superficial explanation for and solution to the "problem of the woman;" her full liberation would be achieved once her economic dependence was abolished. The kibbutz ideology's stress on the equal social value of all work, however menial by bourgeois standards, removes any stigma from service jobs. The unfulfilling nature of the work itself—which is, after all, plain old housekeeping collectivized—was never seriously tackled. All work is equally valuable in a true socialist (kibbutz) society. Except, of course, men rarely do housework.

Besides the kibbutz, there is another showcase of Israeli women's liberation, the Women's Army Corps. Under close scrutiny, however, its cracks also become apparent. First of all, because of an inadequate early education, marriage, or Orthodoxy (genuine or feigned), half of all the girls of draft age never serve.[15] Then, while it is true that new recruits do undergo basic combat training, no women ever does the prestigious "men's work." None serves in combat units, pilots a jet, drives a heavy military vehicle, or has any say in tactical decisions. Few, if any, serve in the renowned ground crews for aircraft maintenance, an area in which they could readily be assimilated. The Israeli Army uses women mainly for the support troop divisions, desk jobs, and social work that countries with larger populations fill with men.

No doubt, many young women gain feelings of confidence, independence, and accomplishment from military service; that cannot be underestimated. Some gain useful technical or teaching experience. For the great majority, however, the relative brevity of their service, 24 months as against the men's 36 months, rules out the acquisition of really complex skills. Moreover, their view of the army period as just their "service" and not as the beginning of a possible career, undermines the seriousness of the Women's Army Corps as an instrument of women's advancement.

The Corps has an image problem, too—the problem of the Israeli woman, in spades. During the height of their participation in Israel's defense, in the years, that is, just before and after 1948, Israel's "girl soldiers" were considered tough, unfeminine, and more than a little bizarre by the outside world. Now, after the introduction of a new beauty consciousness, they are merely considered sexy and exotic. It is not only foreign male novelists who see the *hayelot* this way, however. A controversial TV newsclip taken during the Yom Kippur War, for example, showed women soldiers sunbathing and combing their hair. Asked about their contribution to the war effort, all they could say was something about "being good for morale." As a leading Israeli feminist charges, "The Israeli public and the army expect girl soldiers to be 'something nice' but not useful. The girls themselves accept this."[16]

The problem of the female soldier points to what is perhaps the single most powerful force working toward the Israeli woman's flight from feminism, the image of woman which has been beamed at her from abroad for a third of a century. Leon Uris puts it nicely in *Exodus*. Kitty Fremont, the American nurse, in a fight with the beautiful, wild Israeli, Jordana, spits out:

> "Don't tell me what makes a woman—you don't know, you aren't one. You're Tarzan's mate and you behave as though you belong in a jungle. A brush and comb wouldn't be a bad start at fixing what's wrong with you." Kitty pushed past Jordana and threw open her closet. "Take a good look. This is what women wear."[17]

Later on in the novel, the mother of Ari, the Israeli hero, sighs, "Someday our girls may have the time to concentrate on being women."[18]

Well, now they are concentrating—with a vengeance. Once-unshaven armpits and legs are now baby-smooth. Once unfashionably kinky hair is now straightened. Whole months' salaries go for clothes and cosmetics. A reporter covering a recent world congress of cosmeticians in Tel-Aviv found that there are probably more cosmeticians per capita in Israel than in any other country in the world, and over 200 in the kibbutzim alone.[19] This new beauty consciousness is part of Israel's growing "drive toward cosmopolitanism," if one wants to be charitable, or "aping the West," if one does not. It accompanies an increase in conspicuous consumption, Western patterns of leisure, and Western ideas of good living.

Perhaps the most offensive manifestation of the new "feminine" conformism is the rise of the beauty and homemaker contests in Israel. Not only does Israel participate in international beauty contests such as the Miss Universe and Miss World, but it also has its own variety of the Miss America competition. Unlike its American counterpart, however, the Israeli Queen of Beauty contest makes not even the slightest pretense of considering talent or ambitions. The winner is merely a beauty queen. And her beauty, like that of the candidate for Miss Universe or Miss World, is usually of the approved WASP kind: tall, willowy, and fair, despite all the dark, "exotic" North African and Yemenite beauty available in Israel. But international beauty standards, as someone has said, represent perhaps the most insidious and complete triumph of "Western imperialism."

Perhaps even more dangerous than the beauty contest to the Israeli woman's self-image, however, is the plethora of Mrs. America-type competitions. After all, it is reasoned, not every woman can become a beauty queen, but every woman can—and should—become an ideal homemaker. So, in order to stress the Israeli woman's freedeom from such trivial values as physical beauty, various institutions sponsor contests like Woman of Valor, Mother of the Year, Queen of the Kitchen, and Modern Woman. No less a personage than Zena Harman, former member of the Knesset, finds that the contestants in these trials are "authentic representatives of Woman's Lib."[20]

Of course, it is impressive if a contestant is also a sculptor or lawyer, as two winners I can recall have been, but the deciding criteria are still the domestic skills—home management (having ten kids impresses the judges), cooking expertise, home decorating, table-setting ingenuity, sewing ability, and so forth. Professional achievement and volunteer service to the community carry points, but are secondary considerations. In fact, a recent survey by the sponsors of the Ideal Woman contest revealed that Israeli men find civic virtues far less essential to the ideal woman than Israeli women do.[21] The women judged their ideal woman at least as much by her participation in greater society; men said they valued most the excellent cook, mother, and housekeeper.

But let us examine a recent "enlightened" choice, the first winner of Israel's Modern Woman contest.[22] The original title of the competition, an international one held in Italy, was the Ideal Woman Contest. The Israeli sponsors felt, quite justifiably, that this was an impossibly inflated and unrealistic name. The selection criteria remained the same, however—all the usual domestic skills.

Israel's choice was Ronnie Silberschatz, a woman in her late twenties, picture-pretty, with the requisite two children. Ronnie passed the cooking, sewing, and table-setting matches in fine style. But the *coup de grace* was that she is also a "practicing lawyer." Or rather, a nonpracticing lawyer, because she had dropped out temporarily to raise her young children. Israel's Modern Woman, then, is doing nothing at all different from any other Israeli woman; in fact, because she has a prosperous husband and only two children, she is doing a lot less than many. Her life pattern testifies not to Israel's successful efforts to ensure full equality for women; but rather, to Israel's failure to ensure it.

Women in Israel, even those of the formerly most liberated sector, are in full flight from feminism. After so many years of hardship, they see no reason why they should not enjoy the greater luxury and pampering of the Western housewife. There is no strong women's movement to convince them of the costs. But there is the smoke screen of past achievements to convince them that Israel women are equal with men.

The example of Israel supports two conclusions that women all over the United States are drawing: first, that the achievement of a socialist society (the kibbutz) does not in itself guarantee women's full liberation; and second, that liberation, once achieved, must be understood, cherished, and actively guarded, or it may well be lost.

Postscript

Since this article was written in 1972, Israeli life has altered in dramatic ways, mostly as a result of the Yom Kippur War. Israelis are having to think seriously for the first time about the consequences of peace. The great economic boom of 1967–73 has ended. At the same time, public discontent is forcing significant changes in Israel's overcentralized establishment. In surveying the position of women today, however, one is struck by the stubborn lack of real change. This lack is especially glaring when compared with the momentous progress of the women's movement in the United States during the same years.

In the area of women's employment and economic rights, for example, the majority coalition has twice been defeated in its efforts to increase income-tax deductions for nonworking mothers with four or more children. [23] Working women have received no better breaks. As of today, there has been no change in the tax bias against women. A working wife still cannot submit her own return if she is an employee; her wages are treated as part of her husband's in a joint return under his name. At the end of 1974, Tamar Eshel of the Women Workers Council was still charging that many statistics—including various wage rates for men and women—confirm the lack of equality of status for Israeli women.[24]

The war had some effect on the government's thinking. Many vital services and industries were crippled due to a shortage of manpower, while women chafed at their inability to help. But when a call was issued for women to volunteer to work in certain factories during the war and 11,500 responded, many were turned away.[25] Coordination and planning have somewhat improved now. Women are training for Civil Guard duty, bus driving, and various other jobs formally considered "man's work."[26] Whether these measures will force a real alteration in employment attitudes or will simply remain "emergency measures" remains to be seen.

In the institution perhaps best equipped to achieve any reeducation on a mass basis, the Women's Army Corps, there has, again, been little progress. The real attention in Israel continues to center on the pros and cons of drafting Orthodox girls into some kind of national service. The issue of reevaluating women's duties in the army itself, though receiving some recognition,[27] is apparently not of the highest priority. As of 1975, the types of jobs women perform in the army has remained the same and, according to the army spokesman, the question of women's performing new tasks is "still under study."[28] Recently the Committee on Women in the Army of the Israel Feminist Movement, a committee which includes a former head of the Women's Corps, charged that women in the ranks were sadly underutilized.[29] Those willing and fit to serve in combat troops should be allowed, they said, and women should definitely be trained as pilots—at least of transport aircraft. Experiments in the past to encourage the women soldiers to do physical work or in any way "get their hands dirty" failed because of the women's image of themselves. The army should make a conscious effort to change that image, the Committee concluded.

Whether one institution, albeit a most influential one, can counter the attitudes of Israeli society as a whole is questionable. It is certainly an uphill battle. And meanwhile, with relentless regularity, the beauty and kitchen queens are crowned in Tel Aviv.

Notes

1. Walter Laqueur, *A History of Zionism* (New York: Holt, Rinehart and Winston, 1972), pp. 314–15.

2. "Growth of the Yishuv," *Zionist Year Book* (London, 1972), p. 359.

3. Sarah Honig, "Compensating for Environment," *Jerusalem Post Magazine*, October 3, 1975.

4. "Israel—Population," *Encyclopedia Judaica* (Jerusalem, 1971), Vol IX.

5. "Orthodoxy," *Encyclopedia of Zionism and Israel* (New York: McGraw-Hill, 1971), Vol. II, p. 941.

6. Aaron Sittner, "30 Percent of Workers are Women," *Jerusalem Post*, Sept. 21, 1972. The 1975 statistic was given me by Miriam Whartman of the Working Mothers Organization, Jerusalem Branch.

7. U.S. Department of Commerce, Bureau of the Census, *Statistical Abstract of the U.S.*, 1974, p. 336.

8. Sittner, "30 Percent of Workers." U.S. figure from *Statistical Abstract of the U.S.*, 1974, p. 341.

9. Lea Levavi, "Day Nurseries and How They Operate," *J. Post Mag.*, Sept. 22, 1972, p. 23.

10. Martha Meisels, "Marketing with Martha," *J. Post Mag.*, Aug. 18, 1972, p. 20.

11. "Survey Hints Incentives to Working Mothers Are Wasted," *J. Post*, May 25, 1972. The 1965–75 increase is reported in Rinona Tamari, "Israel's Working Women: A Long Way to the Top," *Pioneer Woman*, Sept. 1975, p.8.

12. "'We'll Strike to the End,' Say Elite Women," *J. Post*, Aug. 29, 1972.

13. Kibbutz member, quoted by David Friedman, "Moetzet Hapoalot," *Israel Magazine*, Sept. 1972, p.81.

14. "One-Third of Rural People Work Land," *J. Post*, Sept. 17, 1972.

15. Minister of Defense Shimeon Peres quoted in "Russians Are Defending Damascus, Peres Says," *J. Post*, Dec. 18, 1974.

16. Miriam Tsur quoted in "Girl Soldiers Could Do More, Feminist Committee Asserts," *J. Post*, Aug. 8, 1974.

17. Leon Uris, *Exodus* (New York: Bantam Books, 1969 ed.), p. 350.

18. Uris, p. 420.

19. Arthur Kemelman, "Why Must I look at Ugly People?," *J. Post*, Sept. 13, 1974.

20. Zena Harman on "Woman of Valor contest," *J. Post*, July 14, 1972.

21. "Ideal Woman," *J. Post*, Aug. 5, 1972.

22. Israel's 'Modern Woman,' *J. Post*, Aug. 5, 1972.

23. "Alignment Beaten in Committee on Tax Benefits for Mothers," *J. Post*, Jan. 4, 1974.

24. "No Equality of Status for Women in Israel," *J. Post*, Dec. 15, 1974.

25. "Employment for Women," *J. Post*, Dec. 26, 1973.

26. "Plan to Train Women for 'Man's Work,'" J. *Post*, April 8, 1975.

27. For example, Chief of Staff General Gur's remarks on the underutilization of women soldiers in "No Tactical Advantages for Egypt," J. *Post*, Aug. 31, 1975.

28. "Army Spokesman," J. *Post*, Feb. 18, 1975.

29. "Girl Soldiers Could Do More, Feminist Committee Asserts," J. *Post*, Aug. 22, 1974.

WOMEN
IN JEWISH
LITERATURE

As students in Jewish schools, we learned as children about Biblical women as matriarchs (known for bearing sons) and occasional heroines (whose aggressiveness was approved only when it was good for the Jews). We learned about Talmudic women, if at all, as either *tzidkaniot* who sacrificed their needs to promote their husbands' and sons' piety and scholarship, or temptresses who sought continuously to distract men from prayer and study. Today, women are becoming Biblical and Talmudic scholars themselves and are rediscovering the women in our sacred literature and reevaluating how women have been described by the rabbis and for what purpose. Women are questioning the patriarchalism of the Bible and Talmud, writing their own midrashim, and claiming the Torah, both written and oral, for themselves as full members of the covenant community. The selections in this category are intended to present some of these new studies and suggest ideas for future exploration.

DEPATRIARCHALIZING IN BIBLICAL INTERPRETATION
Phyllis Trible

Biblical faith challenges the faithful to explore treasures old and new. In this context I propose to examine interactions between the Hebrew Scriptures and the women's liberation movement. I am aware of the risks. Some claim that the task is impossible and ill-advised. The two phenomena have nothing to say to each other. As far as the East is from the West, so far are they separated. To attempt to relate them is to prostitute them. Others aver that the Bible and the women's movement are enemies. "Patriarchy has God on its side," declares Kate Millett, introducing her sexually oriented discussion of the Fall. She maintains that this myth is "designed as it is expressly in order to blame all this world's discomfort on the female."[1] Making a similar point from within the Christian faith, Mary Daly writes of "the malignant view of the man-woman relationship which the androcentric myth itself inadvertently 'reveals' and perpetuates."[2] For her this story belongs to a patriarchal religion oppressive to women.

It is superfluous to document patriarchy in Scripture.[3] Yahweh is the God of Abraham, Isaac, and Jacob as well as of Jesus and Paul. The legal codes of Israel treat women primarily as chattel. Koheleth condemns her "whose heart is snares and nets and whose hands are fetters," concluding that although a few men may seek the meaning of existence, "a woman among all these I have not found" (7:23–29). In spite of his eschatology, Paul considers women subordinate to their husbands,[4] and, even worse, I Timothy makes woman responsible for sin in the world (2:11–15).[5] Considerable evidence indicts the Bible as a document of male supremacy. Attempts to acquit it by tokens such as

Deborah, Huldah, Ruth, or Mary and Martha only reinforce the case.

If these views are all which can be said or primarily what must be said, then I am of all women most miserable. I face a terrible dilemma: Choose ye this day whom you will serve: the God of the fathers or the God of sisterhood. If the God of the fathers, then the Bible supplies models for your slavery. If the God of sisterhood, then you must reject patriarchal religion and go forth without models to claim your freedom.[6] Yet I myself perceive neither war nor neutrality between Biblical faith and women's liberation. The more I participate in the Movement, the more I discover my freedom through the appropriation of Biblical symbols. Old and new interact. Let me not be misunderstood: I know that Hebrew literature comes from a male-dominated society. I know that Biblical religion is patriarchal, and I understand the adverse effects of that religion for women. I know also the dangers of eisegesis. Nevertheless, I affirm that the intentionality of Biblical faith, as distinguished from a general description of Biblical religion, is neither to create nor to perpetuate patriarchy but rather to function as salvation for both women and men. The women's movement errs when it dismisses the Bible as inconsequential or condemns it as enslaving. In rejecting Scripture women ironically accept male chauvinistic interpretations and thereby capitulate to the very view they are protesting. But there is another way: to reread (not rewrite) the Bible without the blinders of Israelite men or of Paul, Barth, Bonhoeffer, and a host of others.[7] The hermeneutical challenge is to translate Biblical faith without sexism.

Themes Disavowing Sexism

One approach to translation is through themes which implicitly disavow sexism. Israel's theological understanding of Yahweh is such a theme. Here is a deity set apart from the fertility gods of the ancient Near East; a deity whose worship cannot tolerate a cult of sexuality; a deity described as one, complete, whole, and thus above sexuality (cf. Deut. 6:4). To be sure, the masculine pronoun regularly denotes this God, but just as faithfully the Hebrew Scriptures proclaim that Yahweh is not a male who requires a female. There is no *hieros gamos* in Yahweh religion.[8] Moreover, the danger of a masculine label for Deity is recognized. While depicting Yahweh as a man, Israel repudiates both anthropomorphisms and andromorphisms. God repents, we read in some passages.[9] According to others, God is not a man that he should repent.[10] In his poem on Israel the faithless son and Yahweh the loving deity, Hosea beautifully presents this paradox of affirming while denying anthropomorphic language (11:1–11). Yahweh is the parent who teaches the child to walk, who heals tender wounds, and who feeds the hungry infant. Strikingly, these activities belonged to the mother, not to the father, in ancient Israel.[11] Like a human being, Yahweh agonizes, struggles, and suffers over the wayward child. Then as love overcomes anger, this Deity accounts for a verdict of mercy by denying identification with the male. Thus comes the wonderful climax, "for I am God (El) and not man (ish), the Holy One in your midst" (11:9).

Feminine imagery for God is more prevalent in the Old Testament than we usually acknowledge.[12] It occurs repeatedly in traditions of the Exodus and Wanderings. The murmuring themes focus often on hunger and thirst.[13] Providing food and drink is woman's work, and Yahweh assumes this role. Even as women fetch water for their families,[14] so the Lord supplies water in the desert for the people.[15] As mothers feed their household,[16] so Yahweh prepares manna and quail for the children of Israel.[17] But the children continue to complain, and an angry Moses reproaches God in a series of rhetorical questions:

> Did I conceive all this people? Did I bring them forth, that thou shouldst say to me, "Carry them in your bosom, as a nurse carries the sucking child, to the land which thou didst swear to give their fathers"? (Num. 11:12)

This extraordinary language indicates that Yahweh was indeed mother and nurse of the wandering children.[18] Further, the recital of Heilsgeschichte in Nehemiah 9 introduces Yahweh as seamstress:

> Forty years didst thou sustain them in the wilderness, and they lacked nothing; their clothes did not wear out and their feet did not swell. (Neh. 9:21)

The role of dressmaker is not unique to the God of the Wilderness. This same Deity made garments of skin to clothe the naked and disobedient couple in the Garden (Genesis 3:21). As a woman clothes her family,[19] so Yahweh clothes the human family.

Second Isaiah boldly employs gynomorphic speech for God. Yahweh speaks of her birth pangs:[20]

> Now I will cry out like a woman in travail,
>> I will gasp and pant. (42:14b)

The Deity compares her loving remembrance of Zion to a mother nursing her child:

> Can a woman forget her sucking child,
>> that she should have no compassion
>> on the son of her womb?
> Even these may forget,
>> yet I will not forget you. (49:15)

Third Isaiah continues the maternal picture. Yahweh is like Zion in labor, bringing forth children:[21]

> Shall I bring to the birth and not cause
>> to bring forth?
>> says the Lord;
> shall I, who cause to bring forth, shut the womb?
>>>> says your God. (66:9)

Yahweh is a comforting mother:

> As one whom his mother comforts,
>> so I will comfort you. (66:13)

The maternal Deity may also be a midwife:[22]

> Yet thou are he who took me from the womb;
> Thou didst keep me safe upon my mother's breast.
> Upon thee was I cast from my birth. . . .
>> (Psalm 22:9–10a; cf. Psalm 71:6; Job 3:12)

Midwife, seamstress, housekeeper, nurse, and mother: all these feminine images characterize Yahweh, the God of Israel.

To summarize: Although the Old Testament often pictures Yahweh as a man, it also uses gynomorphic language for the Deity.[23] At the same time, Israel repudiated the idea of sexuality in God. Unlike fertility gods, Yahweh is neither male nor female; neither he nor she. Consequently, modern assertions that God is masculine, even when they are qualified,[24] are misleading and detrimental, if not altogether inaccurate. Cultural and grammatical limitations (the use of masculine pronouns for God) need not limit theological understanding. As Creator and Lord, Yahweh embraces and transcends both sexes. To translate for our immediate concern: the nature of the God of Israel defies sexism.

The Exodus speaks forcefully to women's liberation. So compelling is this theme of freedom from oppression that our enthusiasm for it may become unfaithfulness to it.[25] Yet the story does teach that the God of Israel abhors slavery; that Yahweh acts through human agents to liberate (agents who may not even acknowledge him; agents who may be *personae non gratae* not only to rulers but also to slaves); that liberation is a refusal of the oppressed to participate in an unjust society and thus it involves a withdrawal; and that liberation begins in the home of the oppressor. More especially, women nurture the revolution. The Hebrew midwives disobey Pharaoh. His own daughter thwarts him, and her maidens assist. This Egyptian princess schemes with female slaves, mother and daughter, to adopt a Hebrew child whom she names Moses. As the first to defy the oppressor, women *alone* take the initiative which leads to deliverance (Exod. 1:15–2:10).[26] If Pharaoh had realized the power of these women, he might have reversed his decree (Exod. 1:16, 22) and had females killed rather than males! At any rate, a patriarchal religion which creates and preserves such feminist traditions contains resources for overcoming patriarchy.

A third theme disavowing sexism is corporate personality.[27] All are embraced in the fluidity of transition from the one to the many and the many to the one. Though Israel did not apply this principle specifically to the issue of women, in it she has given us a profound insight to appropriate. "For the wound of the daughter of my people is my heart wounded," says Jeremiah (8:21). To the extent that women are enslaved, so too men are enslaved. The oppression of one individual or one group is the oppression of all individuals and all groups. Solidarity marks the sexes. In sexism we all die, both victim and victor. In liberation we all live equally as human beings.

Exegesis: Genesis 2–3

Another approach to translation is the exegesis of passages specifically concerned with female and male. With its focus on the concrete and the specific, this method complements and checks the generalizing tendencies of themes. Hence, I propose to investigate briefly the Yahwist story of creation and fall in Genesis 2–3. Many feminists reject this account because they accept the traditional exegesis of male supremacy. But interpretation is often circular. Believing that the text affirms male dominance and female subordination, commentators find evidence for that view. Let us read with an opposing concern: Does the narrative break with patriarchy? By asking this question, we may discover a different understanding.

Ambiguity characterizes the meaning of adam in Genesis 2–3. On the one hand, man is the first creature formed (2:7). The Lord God puts him in the garden "to till it and keep it," a job identified with the male (cf. 3:17–19). On the other hand, adam is a generic term for humankind. In commanding adam not to eat of the tree of the knowledge of good and evil, the Deity is speaking to both the man and the woman (2:16–17). Until the differentiation of female and male (2:21–23), adam is basically androgynous: one creature incorporating two sexes.

Concern for sexuality, specifically for the creation of woman, comes last in the story, after the making of the garden, the trees, and the animals. Some commentators allege female subordination based on this order of events.[28] They contrast it with Genesis 1:27 where God creates adam as male and female in one act.[29] Thereby they infer that whereas the Priests recognized the equality of the sexes, the Yahwist made woman a second, subordinate, inferior sex.[30] But the last may be first, as both the Biblical theologian and the literary critic know. Thus the Yahwist account moves to its climax, not its decline, in the creation of woman.[31] She is not an afterthought, she is the culmination. Genesis 1 itself supports this interpretation, for there male and female are indeed the last and truly the crown of all creatures. The last is also first where beginnings and endings are parallel. In Hebrew literature the central concerns of a unit often appear at the beginning and the end as an inclusio device.[32] Genesis 2 evinces this structure. The creation of man first and of woman last constitutes a ring composition whereby the two creatures are parallel. In no way does the order disparage woman. Content and context augment this reading.

The context for the advent of woman is a divine judgment, "It is not good that adam should be alone; I will make him a helper fit for him" (2:18). The phrase needing explication is "helper fit for him." In the Old Testament the word helper (ezer) has many usages. It can be a proper name for a male.[33] In our story it describes the animals and the woman. In some passages it characterizes Deity. God is the helper of

Israel. As helper Yahweh creates and saves.[34] Thus *ezer* is a relational term; it designates a beneficial relationship; and it pertains to God, people, and animals. By itself the word does not specify positions within relationships; more particularly, it does not imply inferiority. Position results from additional content or from context. Accordingly, what kind of relationship does *ezer* entail in Genesis 2:18, 20? Our answer comes in two ways: (1) the word *neged,* which joins *ezer,* connotes equality: a helper who is a counterpart.[35] (2) The animals are helpers, but they fail to fit *adam.* There is physical, perhaps psychic, rapport between *adam* and the animals, for Yahweh forms (*yatzar*) them both out of the ground *(adamah).* Yet their similarity is not equality. *Adam* names them and thereby exercises power over them. No fit helper is among them. And thus the narrative moves to woman. My translation is this: God is the helper superior to man; the animals are helpers inferior to man; woman is the helper equal to man.

Let us pursue the issue by examining the account of the creation of woman (21–22). This episode concludes the story even as the creation of man commences it. As I have said already, the ring composition suggests an interpretation of woman and man as equals. To establish this meaning, structure and content must mesh. They do. In both episodes Yahweh alone creates. For the last creation the Lord God "caused a deep sleep (*tardemah*) to fall upon the man." Man has no part in making woman; he is out of it. He exercises no control over her existence. He is neither participant nor spectator nor consultant at her birth. Like man, woman owes her life solely to God. For both of them the origin of life is a divine mystery. Another parallel of equality is creation out of raw materials: dust for man and a rib for woman. Yahweh chooses these fragile materials and in both cases processes them before human beings happen. As Yahweh shapes dust and then breathes into it to form man, so Yahweh takes out the rib and then builds it into woman.[36] To call woman "Adam's rib" is to misread the text which states carefully and clearly that the extracted bone required divine labor to become female, a datum scarcely designed to bolster the male ego. Moreover, to claim that the rib means inferiority or subordination is to assign the man qualities over the woman which are not in the narrative itself. Superiority, strength, aggressiveness, domi-nance, and power do not characterize man in Genesis 2. By contrast he is formed from dirt; his life hangs by a breath which he does not control; and he himself remains silent and passive while the Deity plans and interprets his existence.

The rib means solidarity and equality. *Adam* recognizes this meaning in a poem:[37]

> This at last is bone of my bones
>   and flesh of my flesh.
> She shall be called *ishshah* (woman)
>   because she was taken out of *ish* (man). (2:23)

The pun proclaims both the similarity and the differentiation of female and male. Before this episode the Yahwist has used only the generic term *adam*. No exclusively male reference has appeared. Only with the specific creation of woman *ishshah*) occurs the first specific term for man as male (*ish*). In other words, sexuality is simultaneous for woman and man. The sexes are interrelated and interdependent. Man as male does not precede woman as female but happens concurrently with her. Hence, the first act in Genesis 2 is the creation of androgyny (2:7) and the last is the creation of sexuality (2:23).[38] Male embodies female and female embodies male. The two are neither dichotomies nor duplicates. The birth of woman corresponds to the birth of man but does not copy it. In responding to the woman, man speaks for the first time and for the first time discovers himself as male. No longer a passive creature, *ish* comes alive in meeting *ishshah*.

Some read in(to) the poem a naming motif. The man names the woman and thereby has power and authority over her.[39] But again I suggest that we reread. Neither the verb nor the noun *name* is in the poem. We find instead the verb *kara*, to call: "she shall be called woman." Now in the Yahwist primeval history this verb does not function as a synonym or parallel or substitute for *name*. The typical formula for naming is the verb *to call* plus the explicit object *name*. This formula applies to Deity, people, places, and animals. For example, in Genesis 4 we read:

> Cain built a city and *called* the *name* of the city after the *name* of his son Enoch (v.17).
> And Adam knew his wife again, and she bore a son and *called* his *name* Seth (v. 25).
> To Seth also a son was born and he *called* his *name* Enoch (v.26a).
> At that time men began to *call* upon the *name* of the Lord (v. 26b).

Genesis 2:23 has the verb *call* but does not have the object *name*. Its absence signifies the absence of a naming motif in the poem. The presence of both the verb *call* and the noun *name* in the episode of the animals strengthens the point:

> So out of the ground the Lord God formed every beast of the field and every bird of the air and brought them to the man to see what he would *call* them; and whatever the man *called* every living creature, that was its *name*. The man gave *names* to all cattle, and to the birds of the air and to every beast of the field. (2:19–20)

In calling the animals by name, *adam* establishes supremacy over them and fails to find a fit helper. In calling woman, *adam* does not name her and does find in her a counterpart. Female and male are equal sexes. Neither has authority over the other.[40]

A further observation secures the argument: *Woman* itself is not a name. It is a common noun; it is not a proper noun. It designates gender; it does not specify person. *Adam* recognizes sexuality by the words *ishshah* and *ish*. This recognition is not an act of naming to assert the power of male over female. Quite the contrary. But the true skeptic is already asking: What about Genesis 3:20 where "the man called his wife's name Eve"? We must wait to consider that question. Meanwhile, the words of the ancient poem as well as their context proclaim sexuality originating in the unity of *adam*. From this one (androgynous) creature come two (female and male). The two return to their original unity as *ish* and *ishshah* become one flesh (2:24):[41] another instance of the ring composition.

Next the differences which spell harmony and equality yield to the differences of disobedience and disaster. The serpent speaks to the woman. Why to the woman and not to the man? The simplest answer is that we do not know. The Yahwist does not tell us any more than he explains why the tree of the knowledge of good and evil was in the garden. But the silence of the text stimulates speculations, many of which only confirm the patriarchal mentality which conceived them. Cassuto identifies serpent and woman, maintaining that the cunning of the serpent is "in reality" the cunning of the woman.[42] He impugns her further by declaring that "for the very reason that a woman's imagination surpasses a man's, it was the woman who was enticed first." Though more gentle in his assessment, von Rad avers that "in the history of Yahweh-religion it has always been the women who have shown an inclination for obscure astrological cults"(a claim which he does not document).[43] Consequently, he holds that the woman "confronts the obscure allurements and mysteries that beset our limited life more directly than the man does,'' and then he calls her a ''temptress.'' Paul Ricoeur says that woman ''represents the point of weakness,'' as the entire story ''gives evidence of a very masculine resentment.''[44] McKenzie links the ''moral weakness'' of the woman with her ''sexual attraction'' and holds that the latter ruined both the woman and the man.[45] But the narrative does not say any of these things. It does not sustain the judgment that woman is weaker or more cunning or more sexual than man. Both have the same Creator, who explicitly uses the word ''good'' to introduce the creation of woman (2:18). Both are equal in birth. There is complete rapport, physical, psychological, sociological, and theological, between them: bone of bone and flesh of flesh. If there be moral frailty in one, it is moral frailty in two. Further, they are equal in responsibility and in judgment, in shame and in guilt, in redemption and in grace. What the narrative says about the nature of woman it also says about the nature of man.

Why does the serpent speak to the woman and not to the man? Let a female speculate. If the serpent is ''more subtle'' than its fellow creatures, the woman is more appealing than her husband. Throughout the myth she is the more intelligent one, the more aggressive one, and the one with greater sensibilities.[46] Perhaps the woman elevates the animal world by conversing theologically with the serpent. At any rate, she understands the hermeneutical task. In quoting God she interprets the prohibition (''neither shall you touch it''). The woman is both theologian and translator. She contemplates the tree, taking into account all the possibilities. The tree is good for food; it satisfies the physical drives. It pleases the eyes; it is aesthetically and emotionally desirable. Above all, it is coveted as the source of wisdom (haskil). Thus the woman is fully aware when she acts, her vision encompassing the gamut of life. She takes the fruit and she eats. The initiative and the decision are hers alone. There is no consultation with her husband. She seeks neither his advice nor his permission. She acts independently. By contrast the man is a silent, passive, and bland recipient: ''She also gave some to her husband and he ate.'' The narrator makes no attempt to depict the husband as reluctant or hesitating. The man does not theologize; he does not contemplate; he does not envision the full possibilities of the occasion. His one act is belly-oriented, and it is an act of quiescence, not of initiative. The man is not dominant; he is not aggressive; he is not a decision-maker. Even though the prohibition not to eat of the tree appears before the female was specifically created, she knows that it applies to her. She has interpreted it, and now she struggles with the temptation to disobey. But not the man, to whom the prohibition came directly (2:6). He follows his wife without question or comment, thereby denying his own individuality. If the woman be intelligent, sensitive, and ingenious, the man is passive, brutish, and inept. These character portrayals are truly extraordinary in a culture dominated by men. I stress their contrast not to promote female chauvinism but to undercut patriarchal interpretations alien to the text.

The contrast between woman and man fades after their acts of disobedience. They are one in the new knowledge of their nakedness (3:7). They are one in hearing and in hiding. They flee from the sound of the Lord God in the Garden (3:8). First to the man come questions of responsibility (3:9,11), but the man fails to be responsible: "The woman whom Thou gavest to be with me, she gave me fruit of the tree, and I ate"(3:12). Here the man does not blame the woman; he does not say that the woman seduced him;[47] he blames the Deity. The verb which he uses for both the Deity and the woman is *ntn* (cf. 3:6). So far as I can determine, this verb neither means nor implies seduction in this context or in the lexicon. Again, if the Yahwist intended to make woman the temptress, he missed a choice opportunity. The woman's response supports the point. "The serpent beguiled me and I ate" (3:13). Only here occurs the strong verb *nsh'*, meaning to deceive, to seduce. God accepts this subject-verb combination when, immediately following the woman's accusations, Yahweh says to the serpent, "Because you have done this, cursed are you above all animals" (3:14).

Though the tempter (the serpent) is cursed,[48] the woman and the man are not. But they are judged, and the judgments are commentaries on the disastrous effects of their shared disobedience. They show how terrible human life has become as it stands between creation and grace. We misread if we assume that these judgments are mandates. They describe; they do not prescribe. They protest; they do not condone. Of special concern are the words telling the woman that her husband shall rule over her (3:16). This statement is not license for male supremacy, but rather it is condemnation of that very pattern.[49] Subjugation and supremacy are perversions of creation. Through disobedience the woman has become slave. Her initiative and her freedom vanish. The man is corrupted also, for he has become master, ruling over the one who is his God-given equal. The subordination of female to male signifies their shared sin.[50] This sin vitiates all relation-ships: between animals and human beings (3:15); mothers and chil-dren (3:16); husbands and wives (3:16); man and the soil (3:17, 18); man and his work (3:19). Whereas in creation man and woman know harmony and equality, in sin they know alienation and discord. Grace makes possible a new beginning.

A further observation about these judgments: They are culturally conditioned. Husband and work (childbearing) define the woman; wife and work (farming) define the man. A literal reading of the story limits both creatures and limits the story. To be faithful translators, we must recognize that women as well as men move beyond these cultur-ally defined roles, even as the intentionality and function of the myth move beyond its original setting. Whatever forms stereotyping takes in our own culture, they are judgments upon our common sin and disobedience. The suffering and oppression we women and men know now are marks of our fall, not of our creation.

It is at this place of sin and judgment that "the man calls his wife's name Eve" (3:20), thereby asserting his rule over her. The naming itself faults the man for corrupting a relationship of mutuality and equality. And so Yahweh evicts the primeval couple from the Garden, yet with signals of grace. Interestingly, the conclusion of the story does not specify the sexes in flight. Instead the narrator resumes use of the generic and androgynous term *adam*, with which the story began, and thereby completes an overall ring composition (3:22–24).

We approached this myth by asking if it presages a break with patriarchy. Our rereading has borne fruit. Remarkable is the extent to which partiarchal patterns fade; the extent to which the Yahwist stands over against his male dominated culture; the extent to which the vision of a transsexual Deity shaped an understanding of human sexuality.

Exegesis: Song of Songs

On this issue the Yahwist is not alone in Israel. Among his compan-ions are the female and the male who celebrate the joys of erotic love in the Song of Songs. This poetry contains many parallels to the Yahwist narrative. Perhaps the Paradise described in Genesis 2 and destroyed in Genesis 3 has been regained, expanded, and improved upon in the Song of Songs. At any rate, its words and images embody simultaneously several layers of meaning. The literal, the metaphoric, and the euphemistic intertwine in content and nuance.[51]

Canticles begins with the woman speaking.[52] She initiates love-making:

> Let him kiss me with the kisses of his mouth,
> for your love is sweeter than wine (1:2).

In this first poem (1:2–2:6) she calls herself keeper of vineyards (1:6). In the last poem (8:4–14) she returns to this motif (8:12), even as she concludes the unit by summoning her beloved (8:14). Thus the overall structure of the Song is a ring composition showing the prominence of the female. Within this design another *inclusio* emphasizes women. The daughters of Jerusalem commence and close the second poem (2:7 and 3:5).

As in Genesis 2–3, the ring composition of the Song of Songs encircles a garden.[53] Person and place blend in this imagery.

> Let my beloved come to his garden
> and eat its choicest fruit (4:16c).

The woman is the garden (4:10–15), and to the garden her lover comes (5:1, 6:2,11). Together they enjoy this place of sensuous delight. Many trees adorn their garden, trees pleasant to the sight and good for food:[54] the apple tree (2:3; 7:8; 8:5), the fig tree (2:13), the pomegranate (4:3, 13; 6:7), the cedar (5:15), the palm (7:8) and "all trees of frankincense" (4:14). Spices give pleasure as does the abundance of fruits, plants, and flowers: the meadow saffron (2:1), the lotus (2:1f, 16; 4:5; 5:13; 7:2), the mandrake (7:13), and others (2;12,.13; 4:13, 16; 6:11). Fountains of living water enhance further this site (4:12, 15), inviting comparisons with the subterranean stream watering the earth (Gen. 2:6) and with the rivers flowing out of Eden to water the garden (Gen. 2:10–14).

Animals inhabit two gardens. In the first they were formed, both beasts and birds, and received their names. As foils they participated in the creation of woman and provided a context for the total joy of *ish* and *ishshah*. In Canticles their names become explicit as does their contextual and metaphorical participation in the encounters of lovers. The woman describes her mate:

> My beloved is like a gazelle
>   or a young stag (2:9)
>   . . . . . .
>   his locks are wavy,
>   black as a raven (5:11).
> His eyes are like doves
>   beside springs of water (5:12).

The man also uses animal imagery to describe the woman:

> Behold, you are beautiful, my love
>   behold, you are beautiful!
> Your eyes are doves
>   behind your veil.
> Your hair is like a flock of goats,
>   moving down the slopes of Gilead.
> Your teeth are like a flock of shorn ewes
>   that have come up from the washing,
> Each having its twin,
>   and not one of them is bereaved (4:1–2)
>   . . . . . .
> Your two breasts are like two fawns,
>   twins of a gazelle,
>   that feed among the lilies (4:5).

The mare (1:9), the foxes (2:15), the turtledove (2:12), the lions and the leopards (4:8) also dwell in this garden where all nature extols the love of female and male.

The sensuality of Eden broadens and deepens in the Song. Love is sweet to the taste, like the fruit of the apple tree (2:3; cf. 4:16; 5:1, 13). Fragrant are the smells of the vineyards (2:13), of the perfumes of myrrh and frankincense (3:6), of the scent of Lebanon (4:11), and of beds of spices (5:13; 6:2). The embraces of lovers confirm the delights of touch (1:2, 2:3–6; 4:10, 11; cf. 5:1; 7:6–9; 8:1, 3). A glance of the eyes ravishes the heart (4:9; 6:13), as the sound of the beloved thrills it (5:4).

Work belongs both to the garden of Creation and to the garden of eroticism. Clearly man works in Eden and implicitly woman too. The Song alters this emphasis. The woman definitely works. She keeps vineyards (1:6; cf. 8:12), and she pastures flocks (1:8). Her lover may be a shepherd also (1:7), though the text does not secure this meaning.[55] By analogy he is a king (1:4, 12; 8:11, 12), but he neither rules nor dispenses wisdom. He provides luxury for the sake of love (3:9–11).[56] Together Genesis 2 and the Song of Songs affirm work in gardens of joy, and together they suggest fluidity in the occupational roles of woman and man. In Canticles nature and work are pleasures leading to love, as indeed they were before the primeval couple disobeyed and caused the ground to bring forth thorns and thistles and work to become pain and sweat (Gen. 2:15; 3:16, 18, 19).

Neither the primeval couple nor the historical couple bear names, but both are concerned with naming. When *adam* names the animals, it is an act of authority consonant with Creation. When he names the woman, it is an act of perversion preceding expulsion. In the erotic garden roles reverse, authority vanishes, and perversion is unknown. The woman names the man:

> For your love is better than wine,
> > your anointing oils are fragrant,
> Your *name* is oil poured out;
> > therefore the maidens love you (1:2b–3).

Her act is wholly fitting and good. Naming is ecstasy, nor exercise; it is love, not control. And that love marks a new creation.

Song of Songs extends beyond the confines of Eden to include other places, people, and professions. We move fron the countryside (2:14; 4:11; 6:11; 7:12) to the city with its squares, streets, and walls (2:9; 3:2, 3; 5:7). We hear of kings (1:9; 3:7; 4:4) and warriors (3:7; 6:4); queens, concubines, and maidens (6:8, 9); watchmen (3:3; 5:7) and merchants (3:6), brothers (1:6), sisters (8:8), mothers (6:9; 8:1, 2, 5). and companions male (1:7) and female (2:2, 7). Paradise expands to civilization. History, like nature, contributes to the encounter of the sexes.

Parental references merit special attention. Seven times the lovers speak of mother, but not once do they mention father.[57] The man calls his beloved the special child of the mother who bore her (6:9), even as the woman cites the travail of the mother who bore him (8:5). This concern with birth is also reminiscent of the theme of creation in Genesis 2. In yearning for closeness with her lover, the woman wishes he were a brother nursing at the breast of her mother (8:1). But these traditional images do not exhaust the meaning of mother. It is his mother who crowns Solomon on the day of his wedding (3:11). The female lover identifies her brothers as sons of her mother, not of her father (1:6). And most telling of all, the woman leads her lover to the "house of her mother" (3:4, 8:2). Neither the action nor the phrase bespeaks patriarchy.[58] This strong matriarchal coloring in the Song of Songs recalls the primeval man leaving his father and his mother to cleave to his wife (Gen. 2:24; cf. Gen. 24:28; Ruth 1:8).

Like Genesis 2, Canticles affirms mutuality of the sexes. There is no male dominance, no female subordination, and no stereotyping of either sex. The woman is independent, fully the equal of the man. Her interests, work, and words defy the connotations of "second sex." Unlike the first woman, this one is not a wife. Her love does not include procreation.[59] At times the man approaches her, and at other times she initiates their meetings. In one poem the man moves vigorously and quickly over the hills and mountains to stand at her window. He calls her to join him outside:

> Arise, my love, my fair one
>   and come away;
> for lo, the winter is past,
>   the rain is over and gone (2:10,11).

Next the woman actively seeks the man (3:1–4). Upon her bed she desires him. She rises to search in the streets and squares. Her movements are bold and open. She does not work in secret or in shame. She asks help of the night watchman: "Have you seen him whom my *nefesh* loves?" Finding him, she clasps him securely:

> I held him and would not let go
>   until I had brought him into
>   my mother's house,
>   and into the chamber of her that
>   conceived me (3:4).

This theme of alternating initiative for woman and man runs throughout the poetry.[60] Further, each lover exalts the physical beauty and charm of the other in language candid and covert. Their metaphorical speech reveals even as it conceals. They treat each other with tenderness and respect, for they are sexual lovers, not sexual objects. They neither exploit nor escape sex; they embrace and enjoy it.[61] Both are naked and they are not ashamed (cf. Gen. 2:25).

On occasion the woman expresses their relationship by the formula, "My beloved is mine and I am his" (2:16; 6:3). Once she says, "I am my beloved's and his desire is for me" (7:10). This word *desire* occurs only three times in the Old Testament: once in Canticles and twice in the Yahwist Epic (Gen. 3:16; 4:7). "Your desire shall be for your husband, and he shall rule over you" is the divine judgment upon the woman. As we have seen, its context is sin and perversion. *Desire* in the Song of Songs reverses this meaning of the male-female relationship. Here desire is joy, not judgment. Moreover, the possessive reference has switched from the wife's desire for her husband to the desire of the male lover for the female. Has one mark of sin in Eden been overcome here in another garden with the recovery of mutuality in love? Male dominance is totally alien to Canticles. Can it be that grace is present?

Let us stress that these lovers are not the primeval couple living before the advent of disobedience. Nor are they an eschatological couple, as Karl Barth would have us believe. [62] They live in the "terror of history" (Eliade) but their love knows not that terror. To be sure, the poetry hints of threats to their Paradise. If the first garden had its tree and its serpent, the second has its potential dangers, too. There is the sterile winter now past (2:11); the little foxes which spoil the vineyards (2:15); the anger of the brothers (1:6);[63] a knowledge of jealousy (8:6); and the anxiety of the woman seeking her beloved, finding him not (3:1–4; 5:6–8; 6:1), and suffering at the hands of the watchmen (5:7). In addition, death threatens eroticism even as it haunted creation (Gen 2:17; 3:3, 4, 19). But all these discordant notes blend into the total harmony of love. If death did not swallow the primeval couple, neither does it overpower the historical couple. "Love is strong as death" (8:6). The poetry speaks triumphantly to all terror when it affirms that not even the primeval waters of chaos can destroy love:

> Many waters cannot quench love, (*ahabah*)
> neither can floods drown it (8:7).

In many ways, then, Song of Songs is a midrash on Genesis 2–3.[64] By variations and reversals it creatively actualizes major motifs and themes of the primeval myth. Female and male are born to mutuality and love. They are naked without shame; they are equal without duplication. They live in gardens where nature joins in celebrating their oneness. Animals remind these couples of their shared superiority in creation as well as of their affinity and responsibility for lesser creatures. Fruits pleasing to the eye and to the tongue are theirs to enjoy. Living waters replenish their gardens. Both couples are involved in naming; both couples work. If the first pair pursues the traditional occupations for women and men, the second eschews stereotyping.

Neither couple fits the rhetoric of a male dominated culture. As equals they confront life and death. But the first couple lose their oneness through disobedience. Consequently, the woman's desire becomes the man's dominion. The second couple affirm their oneness through eroticism. Consequently, the man's desire becomes the woman's delight. Whatever else it may be, Canticles is a commentary on Genesis 2–3. Paradise Lost is Paradise Regained.

Yet the midrash is incomplete. Even though Song of Songs is the poetry of history, it speaks not at all of sin and disobedience. Life knows no prohibitions. And most strikingly, no Deity acts in that history. God is not explicitly acknowledged as either present or absent (though eroticism itself may be an act of worship in the context of grace). Some may conclude that these omissions make the setting of Canticles a more desirable paradise than Eden. But the silences portend the limits. If we cannot return to the primeval garden (Gen. 3:23–24), we cannot live solely in the garden of eroticism. Juxtaposing the two passages, we can appropriate them both for our present concern.

Conclusion: A Depatriarchalizing Principle

Suffice it to conclude that the Hebrew Scriptures and women's liberation do meet and that their encounter need not be hostile. Contrary to Kate Millett, the Biblical God is not on the side of patriarchy, and the myth of the Fall does not "blame all this world's discomfort on the female." Indeed, this myth negates patriarchy in crucial ways; it does not legitimate the oppression of women. It explores the meaning of human existence for female and male. It reveals the goodness yet frailty of both creatures; their intended equality under God and with each other; their solidarity in sin and in suffering; and their shared need of redemption. Thereby its symbols illuminate a present issue, even as they exercise a sobering check on it. In Yahwist theology neither male nor female chauvinism is warranted. Both are perversions of creation which signify life under judgment.

Song of Songs counterbalances this "undertone of melancholy" (von Rad) by showing woman and man in mutual harmony after the Fall. Love is the meaning of their life, and this love excludes oppression and exploitation. It knows the goodness of sex and hence it knows not sexism. Sexual love expands existence beyond the stereotypes of society. It draws unto itself the public and the private, the historical and the natural. It transforms all life even as life enhances it. Grace returns to female and male.[65]

Alongside Genesis 2–3 and the Song of Songs we place the themes of the nature of Yahweh, of the Exodus, and of corporate personality. In various ways they demonstrate a depatriarchalizing principle at work in the Hebrew Bible. Depatriarchalizing is not an operation which the exegete performs on the text. It is a hermeneutic operating within Scripture itself. We expose it; we do not impose it. Tradition history teaches that the meaning and function of Biblical materials is fluid. As Scripture moves through history, it is appropriated for new settings. Varied and diverse traditions appear, disappear, and reappear from occasion to occasion. We shall be unfaithful readers if we neglect Biblical passages which break with patriarchy or if we permit our interpretations to freeze in a patriarchal box of our own construction. For our day we need to perceive the depatriarchalizing principle, to recover it in those texts and themes where it is present,[66] and to accent it in our translations. Therein we shall be explorers who embrace both old and new in the pilgrimage of faith.

Notes

1. Kate Millett, *Sexual Politics* (Garden City, N.Y.: Doubleday & Company, 1970), pp. 51–54.

2. Mary Daly, "The Courage to See," *The Christian Century*, September 22, 1971, p. 1110. See also *The Church and the Second Sex* (New York: Harper & Row, 1968), pp. 32–42.

3. On the status of women in the male-dominated society of Israel, see Roland de Vaux, *Ancient Israel* (New York: McGraw-Hill Book Company, 1961), p. 39ff; J. Pedersen, *Israel* I (Oxford, 1959), pp. 60–81; 23–33; W.Eichrodt, *Theology of the Old Testament* I, (Philadelphia: The Westminster Press, 1961), pp. 80–82.

4. I Cor. 14:34–35; Col. 3:18; cf. Eph. 5:22–24.

5. On Paul see Krister Stendahl, *The Bible and the Role of Women* (Philadelphia: Fortress Press, 1966); Madeleine Boucher, "Some Unexplored Parallels to 1 Cor 11, 11–12 and Gal 3, 28: The NT on the Role of Women," *Catholic Biblical Quarterly,* January 1969, pp. 50–58. For efforts to exonerate Paul, see Robert C. Campbell, "Women's Liberation and the Apostle Paul," *Baptist Leader*, January 1972; Robin Scroggs, "Paul: Chauvinist or Liberationist?", *The Christian Century*, March 15, 1972, pp. 307–09; ibid, "Paul and the Eschatalogical Woman," *Journal of the American Academy of Religion*, Vol. XL, No. 3 (September 1972), pp. 283–303; G. B. Caird, "Paul and Women's Liberty," *Bulletin of the John Rylands Library*, Vol. 54, No. 2 (Spring 1972), pp. 268–81.

6. Happily, the paradigm in Josh. 24:14–15 resolves the predicament. It poses a choice between competing gods only if the people are unwilling to serve Yahweh.

7. Cf. Peggy Ann Way, "An Authority of Possibility for Women in the Church," in Sarah Bentley Doely, ed., *Women's Liberation and the Church*(New York: Association Press, 1970), pp. 78–82.

8. Eichrodt, *Theology*, I, pp. 121, 151ff; cf. Helmer Ringgren, *Israelite Religion* (Philadelphia: Fortress Press, 1966), p. 197ff.

9. E.g., Gen. 6:6; Ex. 32:14; I Sam. 15:11, 35; Jonah 3:10.

10. E.g., Num. 23:19; I Sam. 15:29.

11. Cf. Ludwig Köhler, *Hebrew Man* (New York: Abingdon Press, 1956), p. 58ff.

12. For much of this material I am indebted to an unpublished paper, "Yahweh's Relationship as Mother to Israel" (June 1972), by Ms. Toni Craven of Andover Newton Theological School. We have only begun to explore the topic.

13. Martin Noth, *Exodus* (Philadelphia: The Westminster Press, 1962), pp. 128–40. For a technical discussion of the murmuring theme, see George W. Coats, *Rebellion in the Wilderness* (New York: Abingdon Press, 1968), pp. 47–127, 249–54.

14. Gen. 21:19, 24:11, 13–20, 43–46; Exod. 2:16ff; I Sam. 9:11; I Kings 17:10.

15. Exod. 17·1–7; Num. 20:2–13; Neh. 9:15.

16. Prov. 31:14–15; Gen. 18:6; 27:9, 14; cf. II Sam. 13:7–10.

17. Exod. 16:4-36; Num. 11; Neh. 9:15; cf. Deut. 32:13-14; Hos. 11:4; Psalm 36:8; 81:10, 16.

18. Martin Noth comments tellingly on this passage in *Numbers* (Philadelphia: The Westminster Press, 1968), p. 86ff.

19. Prov. 31:21ff.

20. See James Muilenburg, "Isaiah 40–66," *The Interpreter's Bible*, V (New York: Abingdon Press, 1956), p. 473.

21. Muilenburg, op. cit., p. 765ff.

22. See the discussion on birth in de Vaux, op. cit., p. 42ff. Whether or not fathers were present at birth is debatable (cf. Jer. 20:15 and Gen. 50:23); certainly midwives were present (Gen. 35:17; 38:28; Exod. 1:15). While Samuel Terrien sees paternal imagery underlying Ps. 22:9–10, it is more likely that the metaphor is maternal (S. Terrien, *The Psalms and their Meaning for Today* (New York: Bobbs-Merrill, 1952), p. 154ff).

23. See James Muilenburg, "The History of the Religion of Israel," *The Interpreter's Bible*, I (New York: Abingdon Press, 1952), p. 301ff.

24. E.g., John L. McKenzie, *The Two-Edged Sword* (Garden City, N.Y.: Image Books, 1966), p. 116; Bishop C. Kilmer Myers, *United Church Herald*, January 1972, p. 14; Albert J. duBois, "Why I Am Against the Ordination of Women," *The Episcopalian*, July 1972, p.22.

25. For instance, the exodus theme is not a paradigm for "leaving home" and developing a community without models (so Mary Daly, "The Spiritual Revolution: Women's Liberation as Theological Reeducation," *Andover Newton Quarterly*, March 1972, p. 172ff.) The Exodus itself is a return home, with its models drawn from the traditions of the Fathers (e.g., Exod. 3:15–17; 6:2–8).

26. Cf. Hans Walter Wolff, "The Elohistic Fragments in the Pentateuch," *Interpretation*, Vol. XXVI, April 1972, p. 165: " . . . it is women whose actions are decisive for the formation of God's people."

27. H. Wheeler Robinson, "The Hebrew Conception. of Corporate Personality," in Paul Volz, Friedrich Stummer and Johannes Hempel, eds., *Werden und Wesen des Alten Testaments* (Berlin: Verlag von Alfred Töpelmann, 1936), pp. 49–62.

28. Cf. E. Jacob, *Theology of the Old Testament* (New York: Harper & Row, 1958), p. 172ff; S.H.Hooke, "Genesis," *Peake's Commentary on the Bible* (London: Thomas Nelson, 1962), p. 179.

29. E.g., Elizabeth Cady Stanton observed that Gen. 1:26–28 "dignifies woman as an important factor in the creation, equal in power and glory with man," while Gen. 2 "makes her a mere afterthought" (*The Woman's Bible*, Part I (New York: European Publishing Company, 1895), p. 20. See also Elsie Adams and Mary Louise Briscoe, *Up Against the Wall, Mother . . .* (Beverly Hills: Glencoe Press, 1971), p. 4, and Sheila D. Collins, "Toward a Feminist Theology," *The Christian Century*, August 2, 1972, p. 798.

30. Cf. Eugene H. Maly, "Genesis," *The Jerome Biblical Commentary* (Englewood Cliffs, N.J.: Prentice Hall, 1968), p. 12: "But woman's existence, psychologically and in the social order, is dependent on man."

31. See John L. McKenzie, "The Literary Characteristics of Gen. 2–3," *Theological Studies* 15 (1954): 559; John A. Bailey, "Initiation and the Primal Woman in Gilgamesh and Genesis 2–3," *Journal of Biblical Literature*, June 1970, p. 143. Bailey writes emphatically of the remarkable importance and position of the woman in Gen. 2–3, "all the more extraordinary when one realizes that this is the only account of the creation of woman as such in ancient Near Eastern literature." He hedges, however, in seeing the themes of helper and naming (Gen. 2:18–23) as indicative of a "certain subordination" of woman to man. These reservations are unnecessary; see below. Cf. also Claus Westermann, *Genesis, Biblischer Kommentar 1/4* (Neukirchen-Vluyn: Neukirchener Verlag, 1970), p. 312.

32. James Muilenburg, "From Criticism and Beyond," *Journal of Biblical Literature*, March 1969, p. 9ff; Mitchell Dahood, *Psalms* I, The Anchor Bible (New York: Doubleday & Company, 1966), *passim* and esp. p. 5.

33. I Chron. 4:4; 12:9; Neh. 3:19.

34. Psalms 121:2, 124:8; 146:5; 33:20; 115:9–11; Exod. 18:4; Deut. 33:7, 26, 29.

35. L. Koehler and W. Baumgartner, *Lexicon in Veteris Testamenti Libros* (Leiden: E. J. Brill, 1958), p. 591ff.

36. The verb *bnh* (to build) suggests considerable labor. It is used of towns, towers, altars, and fortifications, as well as of the primeval woman (Koehler-Baumgartner, p. 134). In Gen. 2:22 it may mean the fashioning of clay around the rib (Ruth Amiran, "Myths of the Creation of Man and the Jericho Statues," BASOR No. 167, October 1962, p. 24ff).

37. See Walter Brueggemann, "Of the Same Flesh and Bone (Gn 2, 23a)," *Catholic Biblical Quarterly*, October 1970, pp. 532–42.

38. In proposing as primary an androgynous interpretation of *adam*, I find virtually no support from (male) Biblical scholars. But my view stands as documented from the text, and I take refuge among a remnant of ancient (male) rabbis (see George Foot Moore, *Judaism*, I, (Cambridge: Harvard University Press, 1927), p. 453; also Joseph Campbell, *The Hero with a Thousand Faces* (New York: Meridian Books, World Publishing Company, 1970, pp. 152ff, 279ff).

39. See, e.g., G. von Rad, *Genesis* (Philadelphia: The Westminster Press, 1961), pp. 80–82; John H. Marks, "Genesis," *The Interpreter's One-Volume Commentary on the Bible* (New York: Abingdon Press, 1971), p. 5; John A. Bailey, op. cit., p. 143.

40. Cf. Westermann , op. cit., pp. 316ff.

41. Verse 24 probably mirrors a matriarchal society (so von Rad, *Genesis*, p. 83). If the myth were designed to support patriarchy, it is difficult to explain how this verse survived without proper alteration. Westermann contends, however, that an emphasis on matriarchy misunderstands the point of the verse, which is the total communion of woman and man (op. cit., p. 317).

42. U. Cassuto, *A Commentary on the Book of Genesis*, Part I (Jerusalem: The Magnes Press, n.d.), p. 142ff.

43. von Rad, op. cit., pp. 87–88.

44. Ricoeur departs from the traditional interpretation of the woman when he writes: "Eve n'est donc pas la femme en tant que "deuxième sexe"; toute femme et tout homme sont Adam; tout homme et toute femme sont Eve." But the fourth clause of his sentence obscures this complete identity of Adam and Eve: "toute femme peche "en" Adam, tout homme est seduit "en" Eve." By switching from an active to a passive verb, Ricoeur makes only the woman directly responsible for both sinning and seducing. (Paul Ricoeur, *Finitude et Culpabilité*, II. *La Symbolique du Mal* (Paris: Aubier, Editions Montaigne, 1960). Cf. Ricoeur, *The Symbolism of Evil* (Boston: Beacon Press, 1969), p. 255.)

45. McKenzie, "The Literary Characteristics of Gen 2–3," p. 570.

46. See Bailey, op. cit., p. 148.

47. So Westermann (op. cit., p. 340), *contra* Gunkel.

48. For a discussion of the serpent, see Ricoeur, *The Symbolism of Evil*, pp. 255–260.

49. Cf. Edwin M. Good, *Irony in the Old Testament* (Philadelphia: The Westminster Press, 1965), p. 84, note 4: "Is it not surprising that, in a culture where the subordination of woman to man was a virtually unquestioned social principle, the etiology of the subordination should be in the context of man's

primal sin? Perhaps woman's subordination was not unquestioned in Israel." Cf. also Henricus Renckens, *Israel's Concept of the Beginning* (New York: Herder and Herder, 1964), p. 217ff.

50. *Contra* Westermann, op. cit., p. 357.

51. I hold a natural (rather than an allegorical, typological, mythological, or cultic) interpretation of the Song of Songs as erotic love poetry. For various views, see Otto Eissfeldt, *The Old Testament* (New York: Harper & Row, 1965), pp. 483–91, and Ernst Sellin and Georg Fohrer, *Introduction to the Old Testament* (Nashville: Abingdon Press, 1968), pp. 299–303. A recent exposition of the cultic view, which revives the general theory of T.J. Meek, is Samuel Noah Kramer, "The Sacred Marriage and Solomon's Song of Songs," *The Sacred Marriage Rite* (Bloomington; Indiana University Press, 1969), pp. 85–106.

52. For structure I am dependent on the forthcoming article by J. Cheryl Exum, "A Literary and Structural Analysis of the Song of Songs," *Zeitschrift für die alttestamentliche Wissenschaft*. See also L. Krinetski, *Das Hohelied* (Düsseldorf, 1964).

53. In addition to the ring composition, Gen. 2–3 and the Song of Songs share other literary and rhetorical features: (1) Chiasmus: e.g., the order of serpent/woman/man, man/woman/serpent, serpent/woman/man (Genesis 3); face/voice, voice/face (Song 2:14) as well as the structure of Song 2:8–17. (2) Paronomasia: e.g., *adam* and *adamah* (Gen. 2:7); *ish* and *ishshah* (Gen. 2:23); *shemen* and *shmekka* (Song 1:3b); *tzei* and *hatzon* and *rei* and *haroim* (Song 1:8). For rhetorical devices in Canticles, see Exum, op. cit.

54. Cf. Gen. 2:9 and Song of Songs 2:3.

55. In Song of Songs 1:7 the verb *r'h* (to feed or to pasture) has no direct object, thereby producing ambiguous meanings. Some translators supply the object *flock* (or *sheep*) to make the man a shepherd (so RSV, NEB, JB, NJV). More likely, the verb is a *double entendre* for erotic play. In 2:16 and 6:3 the same verb occurs, again without objects in MT: the man pastures among the lilies. In 2:1,2 the woman is the lily.

56. See Albert Cook, *The Root of the Thing* (Bloomington: Indiana University Press, 1968), pp. 106, 125.

57. Cook, op. cit., p. 103.

58. Cf. de Vaux, op. cit., p. 20ff.

59. It is a moot question whether procreation is implied in the relationship of the primeval couple before their fall. Certainly it is not specified. Von Rad holds that "one flesh" (Gen. 2:24) signifies progeny (op. cit., p. 824). Gunkel maintains that the phrase means sexual intercourse (*Genesis*, HAT, Göttingen: Vandenhoeck und Ruprecht, 1902, p. 10). Westermann claims neither view is adequate; "one flesh" means the total communion of woman and man (op. cit., p. 317).

60. Cf. Cook, op. cit., pp. 131–46.

61. See Brevard S. Childs, *Biblical Theology in Crisis* (Philadelphia: The Westminster Press, 1970), pp. 191–93.

62. Karl Barth, *Church Dogmatics*, III/2, (Edinburgh: T. and T. Clark, 1960), pp. 291–300.

63. The meaning of the word anger (*nhr*) is uncertain; see Köhler-Baumgartner, op. cit., p. 609.

64. I use midrash here to designate a type of exegesis, not a literary genre. See Addison G. Wright, *Midrash* (New York: Alba House, 1967), pp. 43–45, 143, and Roger Le Deaut, "Apropos a Definition of Midrash," *Interpretation*, Vol. XXV, July 1971, pp. 259–82.

65. Cook, op. cit., p. 103ff.

66. The task of recovering the depatriarchalizing principle in Scripture has only begun. For another recent effort, see William L. Holladay, "Jeremiah and Women's Liberation," *Andover Newton Quarterly*, March 1972, pp. 213–23.

THE RESTORATION OF VASHTI
Mary Gendler

When I was a child, Purim was one of my favorite Jewish holidays. I loved to dress up as Queen Esther in a long, flowing gown, put a sparkling crown on my head, and feel brave and loyal at the thought that I might risk my life to save my people. As I grew older, this "acting out" felt less and less possible for me—at least, in this explicit way. The children dressed up in costumes, not the adults. Purim, at this level of identification anyway, seemed to have lost much of its intensive involvement for me.

I have only very recently come to see the deep significance of dressing up as the various characters in the Purim story. When we, as children—or adults—dress up as someone, we are, in a sense, identifying with them. The characters, in this way, serve as a kind of role model for us. It is at this level that I first began to have difficulty with the Purim story as I grew older. Queen Esther, although assuredly portrayed as a courageous woman in the story, felt less and less like someone with whom I wanted to identify totally.

Esther becomes queen as a replacement for Vashti, Ahasuarus's first wife. Vashti had been disposed of because of her refusal to display her beauty in front of Ahasuarus and other drunken princes of the land. Ahasuarus had prepared a great feast in order to consolidate his power and display his great wealth. Therefore, when the discussion turned to bragging about whose women were more beautiful, Ahasuarus was ready to display more property, this time his wife. However, unlike jewels and gold, people—even women—will not always allow themselves to be treated as objects. Vashti refused, and "therefore was the

King very wroth, and his anger burned in him" (Esther 1:12). He asks his ministers what he should do, and they advise him to get rid of Vashti, that she ". . . come no more before King Ahasuarus, and that the king give her royal estate unto another that is better than she." ("better" obviously meaning more obedient!) (Esther 1:19). They advise him to send out a decree to be published in all the kingdom that ". . . all the wives will give to their husbands honour, both to great and small . . . and that every man should bear rule in his own house" (Esther 1:20–22). The power struggle here is too obvious to necessitate elaboration.

Then the king decides that he wants another woman. He orders all of the beautiful virgins of the land to be brought before him. The one who pleases Ahasuarus will be chosen as queen; many of the others will remain as concubines. As we all know, it is Esther, cousin of Mordecai, who is chosen.

Esther is portrayed as beautiful and pious. On Mordecai's charge, she does not reveal that she is a Jewess, ". . . for Esther did the commandment of Mordecai, as when she was brought up by him" (Esther 2:20). When he first asks her to make supplication for her people during Haman's plotting, she is frightened and refuses, but later she acts more courageously and does, indeed, save the Jews.

What about Esther do I find objectionable? In most ways she sounds like an ideal woman—beautiful, pious, obedient, courageous. And it is just this which I find objectionable. Esther is certainly the prototype —and perhaps even a stereotype—of the ideal Jewish woman—an ideal which I find restrictive and repressive.

There are several layers on which this can be examined. On the most obvious level, the political or pseudohistorical, we can see that Ahasuarus, a typical Near Eastern autocratic king, holds absolute power of life and death over everyone in his kingdom, men and women alike. Open defiance like Vashti's is simply not tolerated from anyone. What is interesting in this tale, however, is the reasoning for punishing Vashti's refusal. The men seem to feel that their authority and power over women will be seriously undermined if Vashti is allowed to get away with her defiance. There is an interesting comparison with Mordecai here. When Mordecai refuses to bow down to Haman, Haman is furious because Mordecai's refusal undermines his authority and piques his vanity. He seeks to have not only Mordecai but all the Jews punished in retribution. So, as with Vashti, there is generalization to a broader group of people. But note that it is not

Vashti's "people" who are to be punished, but rather all females who are to be kept in line.

Esther succeeds in influencing the king. She does it in what I see as an idealized (as opposed to ideal) form of female behavior. *Esther's only power lies in making the king love her.* It had already been shown rather forcibly through Vashti's experience that the king did not love assertive women. Esther remains lovable by being somewhat bashful, modest, beautiful and, above all, by approaching him obliquely. Like a good Jewish mother, she first wines and dines him, and only then makes her request. And at the level of the story, she clearly has little choice. No one could approach the king directly, and it is certainly a tribute to Esther that she devises a plan—the banquets followed by her request—that leads to saving the Jews. It is, rather, the idealization of this kind of behavior for women which concerns me. On this score the stories which have grown up around Esther as well as around Vashti as reported by Louis Ginzberg in his *Legends of the Jews*, make fascinating and illuminating reading. These legends show the attitudes of the Rabbis toward the behavior of the two women.

In these *Legends* we learn, for example, that Vashti was really as cruel and arrogant and lascivious as her husband. For example, she used to force Jewish maidens to spin and weave on the Sabbath, even depriving them of all their clothes. Further, we are told that she recoiled from the king's order

> . . . not because it offended her moral sense. She was not a whit better than her husband. She fairly reveled in the opportunity his command gave her to indulge in carnal pleasures once again, for it was exactly a week since she had been delivered of a child. But God sent the angel Gabriel to her to disfigure her countenance. Suddenly signs of leprosy appeared on her forehead, and the marks of other diseases on her person. In this state it was impossible for her to show herself to the king. She made a virtue of necessity, and worded her refusal to appear before him arrogantly.

All of this, note, comes as an elaboration of the Biblical sentence, "But the queen Vashti refused to come at the king's commandment by the chamberlains . . ." (Esther 1:12). Further, in order to ensure that we really have no shred of sympathy left for Vashti, several sources credit her with responsibility for preventing the king from giving his consent to the rebuilding of the Temple.

These legends are very significant, for they reflect popular and rabbinic feeling. And it is very clear that in no way was Vashti's refusal to debase herself seen by succeeding Jews as noble or courageous. Quite the contrary. The Rabbis must have found themselves in somewhat of a bind initially. On the one hand, they couldn't possibly approve of the demand Ahasuarus makes on Vashti. On the other hand, to support her would be to invite female disobedience in other situations, an idea they apparently could not tolerate. They solve this by condemning Ahasuarus as foolish and by creating legends whereby Vashti is shown as getting exactly what she deserves. If, then, in addition to decrees on obedience (which the Rabbis said were foolish anyway) because everyone who read it exclaimed: "To be sure, a man is master in his own house!" you reinforce this by vixenizing a woman who shows characteristics you want to obliterate, you have a much better chance of ensuring that other women will not follow her example.

The parallels with Lilith here are too striking to be ignored. According to early myths, Lilith was Adam's first wife, created, like him, out of the dust of the earth. But, we learn in the *Legends* ". . . She remained with him only a short time, because she insisted upon enjoying full equality with her husband." Adam tries to force her to submission (portrayed in sexual terms in many accounts), and Lilith, in a rage, utters the magic name of God and disappears into thin air. God sends angels after her to try to get her to return, but Lilith refuses, preferring exile and the punishment of God (the destruction of one hundred of her children daily) to a submissive life with Adam. She is portrayed in the legends as a demoness, an unnatural woman who snatches babies, particularly uncircumcised males, from their cribs, and also as a seductive temptress who is responsible for male nocturnal emissions. She lives in eternal exile; the ultimate Bitch; the woman who said no!

So, as we see, it is pretty dangerous for a woman to refuse male authority. In Vashti's case she lost her royal position and most probably her life. Lilith lost a companion, children, a place in the Bible and, except in very negative ways and in obscure references, a legitimate place in mythology. How many people have even heard of Lilith? But assuredly we all know of Adam—and of Eve, Lilith's replacement created out of Adam's rib so that it would be clear once and for all who was the master! Vashti is vixenized; Lilith is demonized. The message is clear. Behave yourself, don't be assertive, don't be disobedient; or you will be a social outcast, you will lose home, children and happiness, your good name, and perhaps even your life.

And what of Esther? What is she like? In the *Legends* she is pictured as pious, graceful, charming, modest, pure in mind and soul, unassuming and undemanding. She makes no demands at the royal palace, despite her position, and she adheres faithfully to ritual law, despite the extreme difficulties of doing so.

In short, except for her momentary lapse when Mordecai asks her to petition the king, she is "perfect," a kind of ultimate Jewish Mother who risks her life in order to save her children (the People Israel). She accomplishes this miracle of salvation through her modesty, grace, lovability and quiet courage. Embodying all of the characteristics which we admire, she becomes a symbol or model for how women "ought to be."

The story of Esther can be read and appreciated on many different levels. On the pseudohistorical level it is a story of a close escape from annihilation, a holocaust averted through the defiance and piety of Mordecai and the courage and beauty of Esther. This is the level at which we generally celebrate Purim, an event certainly worthy of rejoicing. But, digging deeper, we can discover other layers of meaning.

Sociologically it is no secret that men were seen distinctly as the masters of their homes and of the society in general, not only at the period of history during which the story might have taken place, but throughout all of recorded Jewish history. Men were the leaders, the scholars, the rabbis, the authorities. Women tended the home and the babies. In this sense, Ahasuarus can be seen not only as an Ultimate Authority who holds vast power over everyone, but more generally as male, patriarchal authority in relation to females. As such, Vashti and Esther serve as models of how to deal with such authority. And the message comes through loud and clear: women who are bold, direct, aggressive and disobedient are not acceptable; the praiseworthy women are those who are unassuming, quietly persistent, and who gain their power through the love they inspire in men. These women live almost vicariously, subordinating their needs and desires to those of others. We have only to look at the stereotyped Jewish Mother to attest to the still-pervasive influence of the Esther-behavior-model.

All of this is in interesting contrast with Mordecai, who reacts with open defiance to Haman's arrogant demands; a reaction which we would expect to see from any red-blooded male. His direct challenge to authority, his refusal to debase himself as a person and as a Jew, is seen in all the succeeding commentaries as highly admirable. It is true that historically there is no comparison between the power held by Haman and that held by Ahasuarus, so at that level the comparison is unfair. What I am interested in here, however, is pointing up typical male and female models of behavior and, at that level, it is clear that society rewards men for being direct and aggressive while it condemns women, like Vashti, for equivalent behavior. For, in a sense, Mordecai and Vashti have behaved identically: both refuse to debase themselves by submitting to illegitimate demands. For this, Mordecai is praised and Vashti is condemned.

When viewed at the level of role models, we can again see how the story represents fairly accurate, if incomplete, sociological reality. If we go back to the Purim carnival which I mentioned at the beginning, we can see that my little male friends had quite a wide range of characters with whom to identify if they wished. For me there was only Esther. I never heard much about Vashti in Sunday school, and as far as I can remember no one ever appeared dressed up as Vashti at a carnival. This corresponds quite accurately with the kinds of options generally available within the society for boys and girls. Even today, most girls are trained to see their roles chiefly as wives and mothers. Little boys, on the other hand, have a much broader choice as to what they will do when they grow up, including the options of kings and prime ministers. Although there have been a few powerful queens throughout history, it is mainly true that most women have functioned as "the power behind the throne."

There is one more level which I want to explore here—the psychological. The Purim story read at this level offers us a beautiful array of many different psychological traits—all of which are, I would argue, aspects of all of us. Let's take a look at the various characters:

Ahasuarus: power, pride, arrogance.

Mordecai: dignity, piety, learning, courage, loyalty, tenacity.

Haman: ambition, hatred, destructive impulses, cunning.

Vashti: dignity, pride, independence, disobedience.

Esther: beauty, humility, courage, grace, loyalty, obedience.

Viewed at this level, Purim is an institutionalized, legitimate time for acting out these aspects of ourselves and of trying on new models for size. However, as I said earlier, Purim dress-up has become something just for the kids. Too bad. For if we would reclaim it, we could make contact with, and identify with, these various aspects of ourselves and we could sense how it feels to be that kind of a person.

The boys have a wide, well-rounded range of psychological qualities with which to identify. A male who combines the piety, learning and tenacity of Mordecdai with the personal power of Ahasuarus is mighty indeed.

But we females have fewer options. Since, in essence, Vashti has been removed or ignored as a source of identification, girls have had no way of identifying with and expressing anything besides the positive nonaggressive qualities embodied in Esther. For if, as the uniqueness of identification model seems to suggest, all girls are to be like Esther, this is equivalent to saying that females do not possess the other drives like power, ambition, hatred, independence, nay-saying, and aggressiveness.

If women would begin to identify also with Vashti, as I am proposing we do, we could discover our own sources of dignity, pride and independence. When and under what circumstances do we say no? How much will we let ourselves be pushed around? To what extent are we the property of our fathers, husbands, bosses, etc.? How much are we willing to sacrifice in order to control our own lives? What consequences will we suffer from openly expressing ourselves? Women, I suggest, have too long been deprived of role models for appropriate self-assertion.

I propose, then, that Vashti be reinstated on the throne along with her sister Esther, together to rule and guide the psyches and actions of women. Women, combining the attributes of these two remarkable females—beauty softened by grace; pride tempered by humility; independence checked by heartfelt loyalties; courage; dignity—such women will be much more whole and complete than are those who simply seek to emulate Esther. The Lilith, the Vashti in us is valuable. It is time that we recognize, cultivate, and embrace her!

AGGADIC APPROACHES TO BIBLICAL WOMEN
Linda Kuzmack

During the centuries that witnessed the creation and development of *aggadah,* an inseparable link was forged between the religious injunction to Israel to be a "a nation of priests and a holy people," and the pragmatic need for national survival. The social conditions of Palestinian society where Jews lived under the constant threat of persecution, nurtured the need for something that would both comfort and unify an oppressed people. *Aggadah* helped to fulfill this need.[1]

Aggadah is nonlegal Jewish literature which tries to complement the teachings of *halakhah.* It teaches the practical way of Jewish living through use of "views, opinions, and ethical maxims touching both on the life of the individual and that of the nation in all their phases."[2] *Aggadah* covers almost every aspect of life; nothing is too sacred or too mundane to be outside of its scope.

There are two general elements in aggadic literature:

1) Folk stories and legends which center around the lives of famous historical persons or historical episodes. The Bible is the center of these stories.

2) A "conscious effort on the part of the sages to make the entire Bible . . . a source of inspiration for the people. This effort expressed itself in commenting upon the Bible and its interpretation."[3]

Appealing to the masses with its informal, captivating format, *aggadah* was an ideal tool for the Rabbis to use in order to bring hope and a sense of national/religious purpose to the people.

The same needs that forced the development of *aggadah* as a whole also influenced the creation of those *aggadot* relating to women. Each individual had his or her part to play in fulfilling communal goals: women's roles were spelled out in the *aggadah* so that they, like the men, could see how they were to help in the perpetuation of *Am Yisrael*. Because of this communal purpose, when the Rabbis looked at the stories of Biblical women and commented upon them through the *aggadah*, they were not only dealing with what they thought the Bible was saying about that particular woman, but were also saying —however allegorically or indirectly—what they thought the characteristics or actions of that woman meant in relation to all Jewish women, particularly the women of their own time. The centrality of the Bible as the source *par excellence* for *aggadot* in general, meant that stories of Biblical women were seen by the Rabbis as the ultimate examples—whether positive or negative—for Jewish women throughout history.

Sarah, for example, was seen as the ultimate role-model for virtuous Jewish women. When Rebeka practiced her *mitzvot* in the same way, she also was glorified by the Rabbis through comparison with Sarah:

> . . . as long as Sarah lived, a cloud hung over her tent; when she died, that cloud disappeared; but when Rebekah came, it returned. As long as Sarah lived, her doors were wide open; at her death that liberality ceased; but when Rebekah came, that openhandedness returned. As long as Sarah lived, there was a blessing on her dough, and the lamp used to burn from the evening of the Sabbath until the evening of the following Sabbath; when she died, these ceased, but when Rebekah came, they returned. And so when he [Isaac] saw her following in his mother's footsteps, separating her *hallah* in cleanness and handling her dough in cleanness, straightway, "And Isaac brought her into the tent." (Gen. R. 60:16)

If the patterns of Sarah's and Rebeka's lives were, on the whole, glorified to provide a positive model for Jewish women, other lives, such as Delilah's, were used to demonstrate sin through illicit sexual temptations.

> She enfeebled his [Samson's] strength, she enfeebled ¡his action, she enfeebled his determination. (Num. R. 9:24)

When "Dinah the daughter of Leah . . . went out" (Gen. 34:1) she set in train a succession of events that were to involve her family in deception and war. The Rabbis use this story as a means of condemning women who spend excessive time outside their homes. Their condemnation extends to any behavior in women which is outside of the accepted societal norm.

Few women, however, were seen as all good or all bad. Sarah eavesdrops. It is said that Rachel was not buried with Jacob because she bribed Leah to obtain her son's mandrakes, which the barren Rachel believed would cause fertility (Gen. R. 72:3).

In addition, not all Rabbis viewed women in the same ways. The different approaches may well have been a reflection of experiences in their own lives, as well as of their theological positions.

The diversity of views on women's characters expressed in these midrashim does not carry over to views on women's roles in Jewish society. The mainstream of Rabbinic tradition views women's role as that of wife and mother, and the *aggadah* reflects that approach. Leah, for example, is no longer disliked precisely because she bears many children. (Gen. R. 71:1). R. Ammi taught: "Who secures the woman's position in her home? Her children." (Gen. R. 71:5). This theme runs throughout the *aggadah*.

A corollary to this theme is the view that barrenness is the worst thing that can happen to a woman. Rachel "said unto Jacob: give me children, or else I am dead." (Gen. 30:1). R. Samuel said that we learn from Rachel that the childless are among four who are as dead: the leper, the blind, the childless one, the impoverished one. (Gen. R. 71:6).

The urgent need for children and the desperation of those who are barren runs consistently throughout the *aggadot* as it does throughout the Bible. Indeed, the need for children is seen as so great that even those women who are known for other reasons—such as Deborah—are usually also commented upon in their status as wives and mothers. Deborah is called a "mother in Israel" (Judg. 5:7), though we do not hear of her children; one commentator interprets this passage to mean that she rescued the "mother-cities" in Israel (M.T.Ps. 3:3). One can infer that it was important to the Rabbis to depict important women as mothers to glorify that role.

It is said that Deborah was too proud: her spirit of prophecy went from her after boasting that she was a "mother in Israel," and it had to be revived by urging her to "arise" and utter a song of prophecy (Pes. 66b).

Although independent action appears to be condemned except in strictly limited circumstances, independence in personal prayer appears to be generally approved by the Rabbis. It is intriguing that women's personal prayers seem to command such respect; particularly in light of the fact that within Jewish society, in communal, public prayer, women were separated from the men and were relegated to an inferior position. In the *aggadah*, the prayers of Hannah and Esther, for example, receive some of the most strikingly favorable commentary.

It seems apparent that the Rabbis not only saw women most favorably when they acted in the roles of wives and mothers, but attempted within the *aggadah* to place women within wife-mother-sexual being roles whenever Biblical women appeared to step "too freely" outside of these boundaries. A word of caution, however, may be necessary: the singleness of purpose that the Rabbis exercised in viewing women primarily as wives and mothers must not be seen as negative—or necessarily even confining—within the societal structure of the times. In a society where the greatest good was seen as fulfillment of God-commanded *mitzvot,* in order to preserve the covenant between God and His people, the greatest good was felt to be preservation of the nation so that it might continue to act "as a nation of priests and a holy people" in compliance with the divine command. The family was seen as the key to the physical and spiritual survival of such a nation; therefore, the role of wife and mother, preserver of the family, assumed tremendous importance.[4] At the same time, however, one must question whether this goal necessitated the many severely critical views of independent women found in aggadic literature.

There are various possible explanations of why the *aggadah* overwhelmingly presented women in relation to men, with relatively little freedom to act on their own initiative.

Alternative 1

The first theory suggests that the choice was automatic, the result of absorption of a thousand years of human tradition—the Rabbis really could not conceive of any other alternatives for women. Many children were seen in the Biblical era as the basis for a man's (and, therefore, a woman's) status, as well as for survival of the extended family and nation.

In Talmudic times, the massive loss of population due to wars, forced migration, and persecution might well have reinforced an already existent assumption: that childbirth was the key to survival, and motherhood therefore the natural role for women.

Theologically, the Rabbis believed that "he shall rule over her" was a divine dictum, a part of the revelation from Mt. Sinai that continues to be ever-present in Jewish history. To a society that considered its covenant with God to be totally binding, this, like other parts of the covenant, could not be ignored. The result was that the husband in the rabbinic era remained the absolute head of the family, with extensive control over his wife.

Another major component of "he shall rule over her" was the attitude that male supremacy—as well as the pains of childbirth—were a direct result of Eve's sin: she not only rebelled against God's command, she also enticed Adam into the same sin. Thus, she released the *yetzer hara* (evil inclination) which was waiting to come into the world.

This evil inclination had many attributes, one of which was illicit sexual temptation. Because it had been released by a woman, it was natural for the Rabbis to see women as sexual tempters. The mass of *aggadah* on Biblical women—as well as the stories of Rabbis who heroically resisted their temptation—testify to the rabbinic view. Once such a major evil had been brought into the world by women, it was natural to assign lesser "sins" to women, such as eavesdropping, gossiping, pride, etc. All of these sins, or weaknesses, gave support to the view that the man should "rule over her." This would at least partially explain why the Rabbis were less than elated when women such as Deborah acted on their own initiative and did not defer to male opinion.

The Jewish communal construct, however, had other, more positive aspects. Precisely because they bore the children, and were their primary educators in their early years, mothers were seen as the key to continuation of generations that would maintain Judaism. As a result, it was typical to glorify the role of mother. In addition, since it was the wife who supported and comforted her husband so that he could study Torah and find more meaningful ways to enrich the covenant between God and Israel, it was equally logical to glorify the role of wife. The personal experiences of Rabbis with happy marriages reinforce this attitude. R. Jose said: "I have never called my wife 'my wife', only 'my home' " (Shabbat 118b).

A further extension of this tendency to glorify the wife and mother, would be to extoll "womanly" virtues, particularly those which seemed to result from these roles. An example of this is the story of Abbà Hilkiah, who explained that the rain came when his wife prayed because she was home, and able to care for the poor and needy better than he.

Alternative 2

The second alternative presents a different view: that the Rabbis deliberately chose to make an already existent role the only role for Jewish women, because they felt that the physical and spiritual survival of the Jewish people was being threatened to the point of extinction. The Rabbis felt that the threat of obliteration by war and persecution on the one hand, and assimilation by the temptations of Exilic society on the other, demanded conscious focus on the family as the key to survival.

Because the Rabbis felt the necessity to preserve the family, they would use *aggadah* for this purpose in their sermons and lectures. While all of this would imply that the Rabbis did not automatically assume that women's role was in the home, but that they consciously supported the role of wife and mother, it would not necessarily assume the denigration of any other roles. Other facts, however, point to their deliberate suppression of other options for women.

By the rabbinic era there were no women communal leaders. Salome Alexandra was the last ruling queen of a briefly independent Palestine. Beruriah was the only woman whose legal discussions are quoted in the Talmud. These, however, are "one of a kind" women in unusual societies—isolated instances in an era that lasted centuries, from the last days of Palestine independence through generations of Exile until the medieval period.

We know, too, that in the Biblical era there were women prophetesses (Huldah),tribal leaders, judges (Deborah) a ruling queen (Athaliah), powerful queen consorts (Esther), and a variety of other women who acted with decision outside the home sphere (Jael).

What is striking, however, is that so many of the *aggadot* on these women tend to denigrate them wherever possible, or link them with husbands who might be mentioned only slightly in the Biblical text.

> Haughtiness does not befit women. There were two haughty women, and their names are hateful, one being called a hornet (Deborah) and another a weasel (Huldah). Of the hornet it is written, "And she sent and called Barak," instead of going to him. Of the weasel it is written, "Say to the man,"instead of "say to the king." (Meg. 14b)

Of Huldah the prophetess it is also written that Jeremiah allowed her to prophesy (Megillah 14b). It is thus implied that she was not worthy to receive the word of God directly, without her relative's permission. Her husband, Shallum, has his role built up in the Midrash far more than seems consistent with the text. Aggadot on him outweigh in number those relating to Huldah.

In speaking of Deborah, Ginzberg sums up much of the traditional attitudes toward these independent women: "Prophetess that she was, she was yet subject to the frailties of her sex."[5] Even Beruriah, held up as a shining example of the learned woman, was subject to a story that she had been seduced and committed suicide (AZ 18b).

There are few women in the Bible about whom some Rabbi does not find something unfavorable to say, even if she is as great and noble as Sarah. This should be understood as part of the theological construct deriving from the story of Eve. If the second hypothesis is to be accepted, however, this tendency should also be understood as an effort (conscious or unconscious) to make certain that "he shall rule over her," and that some weaknesses should be found to justify that rule. Positively approved independent women would threaten that position.

It seems that whereas the Biblical text may not criticize the actions of independent women, much in the aggadah tends to do just that. This trend is so significant that it cannot be dismissed lightly. It outweighs the possible biases of two or three Rabbis who may simply dislike women.

The uniformity of rabbinic opinion on women's roles is most striking, precisely because the Rabbis expressed such divergent views on the character of women as a result of their varying backgrounds, the varieties of their personal relationships with their wives and families, and their approach to theological issues.

Given all these factors, why would they all accept uniformly one specific role for women, with minimal allowance for individual initiative and independence from men? If one accepts the second alternative, the major reason had to be the communal good, which the Rabbis placed above all other goals: preservation of *Am Yisrael*, which was threatened by outside forces of persecution and assimilation. Given their theological position, that the mission of Israel as God's Chosen People was of supreme importance, and given the social reality of threat to that mission by the possible extinction of the Jewish nation, the Rabbis would act unhesitatingly to protect the divine mission at all costs. In regard to women, therefore, they felt that these circumstances necessitated emphasizing woman's role in the family which was seen as the bastion against Gentile attack.

Alternative 3

The third alternative is that the reason for emphasizing the domestic role lies somewhere between assimilation of traditional concepts and deliberate selection of material.

There do seem to be views on women which were part of the Rabbis' inherited conditioning, and which they probably did not question: that the "natural" roles for most women, at least, were that of wife and mother. These roles would also be approved specifically as a way of furthering the survival of the Jewish nation. Not least, the wifely role would be prized by men who loved their wives and enjoyed the care, attention, and support a happy marriage brought them.

Theologically, the "sin" of Eve, with its implications for other women had long been a facet of Jewish tradition. At the same time, however, the Pharisees and their rabbinic disciples considerably extended ancient beliefs and transformed them into a more sophisticated system. That most of this took place during eras of persecution and exile, with the resultant threat to the survival of the Jewish nation, cannot be ignored.

In speaking about the causes for various codifications of Jewish law, Isadore Twersky cites Isa. 29:14 "and the wisdom of their wise men shall perish" which was quoted by both Maimonides and Joseph Karo as their reasons for writing their codes. Twersky comments:

> The correlation of political adversity and intellectual decline becomes a constant theme and appears almost as a stereotype justification for halakhic abridgements or codifications. Difficult times necessitate the composition of books which would facilitate the study and perpetuate the practice of *halakhah*.[6]

If eras of persecution consciously resulted in codification of the Law, it seems reasonable that they would also result in the development of aggadah to unify Israel. In the case of aggadah on women, this would mean that interpretation of relevant Biblical passages would tend to glorify the role of wife and mother and play down other roles—even where those roles were approved in the Bible. As evidenced by the aggadah, this is precisely what occurred.

In dealing with independent women such as prophetesses and rulers, the aggadic practice did seem to glorify them on the one hand, but was very careful to disparage them on the other. These independent roles were supported when these women protected Israel in an "acceptable" way, but denigrated when their role was seen as too aggressive.

In general, then, the roles delineated for women in the aggadot were the result of a mixture of "inherited" traditional beliefs about women, and careful amplification of these roles to fit what was felt to be the particular needs of rabbinic society.

Notes

1. Salo Baron, A Social and Religious History of the Jews (New York: Columbia University Press, 1937–), Vol. I, p. 107.

2. Meyer Waxman, A History of Jewish Literature, Vol. I (New York: Yoseloff, 1960), p. 75.

3. Ibid., p. 76.

4. Baron, History of the Jews, Vol. 1, p. 124.

5. Louis Ginzberg, The Legends of the Jews 7 vols., (Philadelphia: Jewish Publication Society, 1968), Vol. IV, p. 36.

6. Isadore Twersky, "The Shulhan Arukh: Enduring Code of Jewish Law," Judaism 16 (2)(1967), p. 142, n. 5.

WOMEN AS SOURCES OF TORAH IN THE RABBINIC TRADITION [1]
Anne Goldfeld

Talmudic thinking can be regarded as an open ended system in which no question is ultimately solved and very few definitive decisions are ever reached. Underlying all Talmudic thought is the conviction that the give and take of dialogue, and the process of inquiry, together, point the way to deeper and more profound understanding of Jewish law. Unfortunately, in relation to the status of women in the *halakhah*, this open approach has been all but abandoned. The culture's rigid definitions of women and qualities of femininity center almost exclusively on the female's sociobiological functions of wife and mother. In creating the woman's role, the culture seems consciously to have sifted out opinions with a certain bias from the numerous other opinions found within the Talmud. Consequently, the traditional view of the woman's role is often significantly more limited than is suggested by the texts themselves. For in the pages of the Talmud, women appear who not only seem to have broken out of the female stereotype but who also may be considered sources of Torah. This paper attempts, first, to prove that certain women in the Talmudic period could be, and were, sources of Torah, and, second, to explore rabbinic attitudes to such women. By way of background, however, it is necessary first to investigate rabbinic attitudes towards women and study and to define what exactly is meant by "sources of Torah."

In many instances in the Talmud, the sages make clear their attitudes concerning women and study. In the tractate Kiddushin, for example, they expound the following three points: women have no obligation to teach others; women have no obligation to teach themselves; and others have no obligation to teach women.[2] When set in the context of a society that believed the intellect to be an instrument of sanctification, and study to be one of the most sanctified of acts, these statements reveal a good deal, for women, being not obligated to study and, at times, prohibited from so doing, were thus deprived of participation in one of the most hallowed expressions of faith.

In supplementation of the above, Kiddushin 34a exempts women from all positive *mitzvot* limited to time—including the obligations to wear phylacteries and to pray three times daily.[3] Women were also freed from the obligation to make pilgrimages and to dwell in a *sukkah*, and because women were not obligated to perform certain rituals, the culture did not permit them to act as representatives of the community by leading a religious service.

The three positive *mitzvot* that fell to women and that are generally considered the woman's realm are *niddah* (the laws of family purity), *hallah* (the separation of dough to prepare loaves of bread), and the lighting of the Sabbath candles. Women were obligated to know the laws pertaining to such duties. Centered on the family and the home, these *mitzvot* illustrate the different modes of experience that men and women participated in and for which they were educated.

That women were not obligated to pray is significant. Both as a movement towards God and a movement away from the narrowness of human self-interest, prayer stands at the center of spiritual living. Again, however, the male population seemed to have a monopoly on spiritual interests; for the quality of, and opportunity for, spiritual enrichment offered to men was not offered to women. Groomed to participate in a wholly different facet of life, women in this context were perhaps understandably considered "temperamentally light-headed" (Kiddushin 80b), as well as trivial, ignorant beings wasting their husbands' time. Women, of course, could not make a dent in such opinions because that most significant of endeavors, sacred study, was closed to them. Whatever merit women earned had to come in a different way.

In the Talmud, in Berakhot, Rav and Rabbi Hiya engage in discussion. Rav asked Rabbi Hiya: "What is the merit of the woman in the Torah?" Rabbi Hiya answered: "Their merit arises from the fact that they take their children to their places of study and that they receive their husbands when they return home."[4] Thus, by preparing children for their education and by helping to further their husbands' studies, women contributed to, and functioned in, the community. Through such actions they acquired spiritual merit and, no doubt, women who conformed to their roles gained respect as well. Within the family, the woman may have had a revered and noble task to fulfill, or, as the apologists will tell us: "separate but equal." The crux of rabbinic Judaism, however, clearly remained centered on communal prayer and study, pursuits almost exclusively reserved for men.

Throughout Jewish history, certain women did, of course, break out of the traditional mold and assume responsibilities associated with males; for example, the prophetesses Deborah and Huldah. Rabbinic reaction to these Biblical women offers information about the rabbis' own views towards women who departed from the accepted model. The etymological coincidence that in Hebrew *Devorah* is the word for bee and *Huldah* the word for weasel moved the rabbis to comment:

> R. Nahman said: haughtiness does not befit women. There were two haughty women, and their names are hateful, one being called hornet and the other a weasel. Of the hornet, it is written, "And she sent and called Barak" instead of going to him. Of the weasel it is written "Say to the man" instead of "Say to the king."[5]

Louis Ginzberg, quoting a rabbinic source, says:

> Eminence is not for women; two eminent women are mentioned in the Bible, Deborah and Huldah, and both proved to be of a proud disposition . . . This unpleasant feature of their character is indicated by their ugly names.[6]

The images of self-confidence projected by Deborah and Huldah apparently challenged rabbinic conceptions of womanhood. For the rabbis did not rest easy with a proud or eminent woman.

Huldah's success raised problems for the rabbis in yet another way, for in seeking out her prophecy, Josiah bypassed the great male prophet, Jeremiah, an action disturbing in its implication that the woman Huldah could prophesy better than the man Jeremiah. To come to terms with this fact, the rabbis assumed that Josiah went to Huldah, not for her brilliance or talent, but precisely because she was a woman. They speculated that Josiah, desiring as compassionate a prophecy as possible, felt it could best be given to him by a woman.[7] The story highlights two rabbinic attitudes: first, women by nature are alleged to be more compassionate than men (again the stereotype of a receptive and family-centered female); and second, a woman's character is composed first and foremost of "feminine" characteristics as defined by the rabbis. In other words, a woman, even as exceptional a one as Huldah, must be seen through a screen of female qualities. The rabbinic commentaries see Huldah primarily as the "compassionate woman" and their interpretation filters Huldah's talent through her femininity.

Despite their emphasis on Huldah's feminine qualities, the rabbis nonetheless recognized her intellectual capacities, as evidenced by their extensive commentary on the following passage, 2 Kings 22:14, in which Huldah is introduced.

> So Hilkiyahu the priest and Ahikam and Akhbor and Shafan and Asaya went to Huldah the prophetess, the wife of Shallum the son of Tikva the son of Harhas, keeper of the wardrobe; now she dwelt in Jerusalem in the mishneh (in the second quarter) and they spoke to her.

The rabbinic exegesis of this verse is formulated by the medieval commentators, Rashi and the Ralbag (Rabbi Levi ben Gershon). The word in the verse, *mishneh*, has a double meaning. In the Tanakh it is used to designate the "second quarter of the city" or some geographical location:

> "Bamishneh (in the second quarter):" In the house of Ulpana there is a gate in the courtyard whose name is the Huldah Gate as mentioned in the Tractate Midot. And there are those who explain that the "mishneh" was outside the wall between two walls and it is the "mishneh of the city."[8]

The word *bamishneh* was also associated with the root "to teach." Rashi, on the verse in 2 Kings comments:

> "Bamishneh:" She taught the oral law to the elders of the generation and that is the *mishneh*.
> She taught from the beginning to the end of Deuteronomy (*Mishneh Torah*). And all of the extra words in the Torah, she exegeted in public. And she revealed the punishments and the exiles that would be multiplied for those who transgress the secrets and the hints of the Torah.

The Ralbag cites Targum Jonathan[9] on this verse: "And she sat in Jerusalem in the *mishneh*: Targum Jonathan translates 'in the *mishneh*' as 'in the house of study.' "This information, therefore, draws a slightly different picture of Huldah, that of a brilliant source of Torah, a teacher, an explicator of verse, and a prophetess.

In the light of this emphasis, still other commentaries further clarify her portrait, for they try to come to terms with Huldah's prophetic role itself. In answer, they suggest that the righteousness of Shallum, Huldah's husband, was rewarded through his wife's powers of prophecy.[10] Huldah was thus made into a prophetess, not on her own merit, but on her husband's. Her exegetical and pedagogical abilities took second place in her success to her dependence on a man, her husband. However great and brilliant a human being she might have been, Huldah's reflection in rabbinic literature took its colors from the female stereotype which the culture had mapped out.

In working toward a definition of the term "source of Torah," several elements must be considered, many of them functions associated with a rabbi of the Talmudic period: exegesis, the performance of rituals, and teaching, as well as the possession of the "power of Torah," the embodiment of revelation in action, and leadership of the spiritual community. In fulfilling these functions, as Jacob Neusner puts it, "the rabbis believed that they themselves were projections of heavenly values onto earth."[11] "The rabbis thus conceived that on earth they studied Torah just as God, the angels, and Moses our Rabbi did in heaven."[12] The rabbis emerge as sources as of Torah on earth.

With these basic rabbinic attitudes towards women and study providing a common ground, we may now consider exceptions to the rule: women who can be considered sources of Torah. Beruriah and the wife of Abba Hilkiah serve as ready examples.

Beruriah, who lived in the second century C.E. in Palestine, gained fame "as the only woman in Talmudic literature whose views on halakhic matters are seriously reckoned with by the scholars of her time."[13] As the daughter of Hanina ben Teradyon, an illustrious rabbi martyred in the Bar Kokhba War of 135, and the wife of Meir, a renowned rabbi of the period, her highly unusual, superb education can be accounted for.

The units of tradition concerning Beruriah can be divided into those which deal only with her and those in which both Beruriah and Meir are present. This analysis begins with the materials in which only Beruriah appears.

As an attestation to Beruriah's great learning, Pesahim 62b states:

R. Simlai came before R. Johanan [and] requested him, "Let the master teach me the Book of Genealogies." Said he to him, "Whence are you?" He replied, "From Lod." "And where is your dwelling?" "In Nehardea." Said he to him, "We do not discuss it either with the Lodians or with the Nehardeans, and how much more so with you, who are from Lod and live in Nehardea." But he urged him and he consented. "Let us learn it in three months," he proposed. Thereupon he took a clod and threw it at him, saying, "If Beruriah, wife of R. Meir [and] daughter of R. Hanina ben Teradyon, who studied three hundred laws from three hundred teachers in one day could nevertheless not do her duty in three years, yet you propose [to do it] in three months!"[14]

This pericope makes three important statements about Beruriah: her brilliance as a student "who studied three hundred laws from three hundred teachers in one day;" her example of intense scholarly application; and her unfulfilled duty in learning the Book of Genealogies.

Since R. Simlai was a first generation Amora and lived in the second half of the third century C.E. [15], the composition of this unit must date from at least a full hundred years after Beruriah's death, at which time we can assume that stories still circulated about her brilliance and ability. R. Simlai, himself, considered to be a renowned authority on *aggadah* (Ber. 32a–b), was a respected and prominent member of Judah II's entourage. Significantly, therefore, Beruriah, a woman, is held up as an example to an esteemed male rabbi, for the rabbinic impression of Beruriah recorded in this passage is of a remarkable, astute, and dedicated scholar with considerable motivation to learn.

The observation that Beruriah "did not fulfill her obligation" in study also carries some weight, for, from the materials examined previously (Kiddushin 29b), she clearly should not have had any such obligation. Understandably, Rashi himself found difficulty with the nature of Beruriah's obligation and had to interpret "*lo yatztah yide hovatah*" by departing from normal usage. Usually, this expression carries legal connotations: for example, if someone did not say the Shema at the proper time, one would say, "*lo yatzah yide hovo*," he has not fulfilled his obligation. This expression would apply to any *mitzvah* that was not properly fulfilled. Rashi, however, could not bring himself to interpret the expression in its legal idiom (because this would presuppose that Beruriah had a legal obligation to study), and, instead, asserted that Beruriah felt a duty towards a self-imposed but unfulfilled task.

To interpret this passage as it would generally be understood (in the legal sense) raises certain questions. If it presupposes that Beruriah did have an obligation, what was the nature of that obligation? Could second-century women take on obligations to study, as could any ordinary man? Or, perhaps, were second-century women permitted to occupy positions that would presuppose an obligation to study?

Beruriah was also an acknowledged teacher, as Eruvin 53b–54a states:

> Beruriah once discovered a student who was learning in an undertone. Rebuking him, she exclaimed, "Is it not written, 'ordered in all things and sure?' If it [the Torah] is 'ordered' in your 248 limbs it will be 'sure,' otherwise it will not be 'sure.' "[16]

Beruriah here shows herself as a Biblical exegete with a keen understanding of the text. Taking a verse out of its literal context, she teaches from it and applies it to a living situation. Not only is one impressed by Beruriah's exegetical ability but one realizes her very real interest in her students. Warmth and understanding mingle with rebuke, and reveal the personality of a master-rebbe seriously concerned with a student's spiritual and educational welfare.

The setting of this pericope and of the one following, among other units in Eruvin dealing with education, reveals that the redactors of the Talmud seemed to recognize Beruriah's teaching abilities. Further, by way of inference, this pericope hints that Beruriah felt a personal obligation to teach, despite the fact that as a woman she was exempt from such an obligation (Kiddushin 29a). In Eruvin 53b Beruriah again appears taken up with the moral welfare of an individual:

> R. Jose the Galilean was once on a journey when he met Beruriah. "By what road," he asked her, "do we go to Lydda?" "Foolish Galilean," she replied, "did not the sages say thus: 'Engage not in much talk with women?' You should have asked: 'By which to Lydda?' "[17]

In refusing to exchange idle words with R. Jose, Beruriah lives the words of Torah, and her actions conform to rabbinic teachings. Again showing herself as a teaching figure, Beruriah seems concerned with instructing R. Jose and demonstrating to him his violation of a rabbinic precept.

One can also interpret Beruriah's encounter with R. Jose to mean something a bit different from the above. For the verse which she quotes to him, "Engage not in much talk with women," implies that time spent talking with women (those frivolous creatures, prone to gossip) is time wasted. However, certainly R. Jose would not have wasted his time in discussion with scholarly Beruriah. Thus, it has been suggested by Robert Gordis[18] (and, I believe, rightly so), that this passage makes sense only on the assumption that Beruriah is speaking ironically. In this way Beruriah expresses her opposition to the rabbinic dictum against much talk with women. One might conjecture that she strongly felt the disabilities of her position and resented the restrictions placed on her sex. Beyond this, the verse which Beruriah quotes to R. Jose is by Jose b. Johanan,[19] one of the first pairs of the earliest Tannaim. Significantly, in quoting R. Jose b. Johanan's tradition, Beruriah proves that she knew Talmud as well as Bible.

In Berakhot 10a, Beruriah again stands up favorably in comparison to a man—a position she repeatedly occupies, a position never marked by comparison with other women. Qualities such as her intellectual ability, dedication to learning, and commitment to teaching, overshadow many of the stereotypes associated with women and were recognized by the rabbis for their superior merit. By their very mode of redacting materials concerning Beruriah (placing her in these comparative positions), the rabbis seem to acknowledge that her actions embody Torah. Perhaps they sense a rabbinic kinship, for, in acting out paradigmatic examples, Beruriah acts as a rabbi to these men. Thus, in Berakhot 10a:

> A certain Min (sectarian) said to Beruriah: "It is written 'Sing, O barren thou didst not bear' (Isa. 54:1). Because she did not bear is she to sing?" She replied to him: "You fool! Look at the end of the verse where it is written, 'For the children of the desolate shall be more than the children of the married wife, saith the Lord.' But what then is the meaning of 'a barren that didst not bear?' Sing, O community of Israel, who resemblest a barren woman, for not having born children like you for Gehenna."

Beruriah's interpretive skills and sharp wit are favorably cited in this pericope, as she shows the man his shallowness and lack of exegetical perception. By retracing the steps of her own insightful interpretation, Beruriah once more demonstrates both her own pedagogy and her constant concern with educating individuals. Furthermore, the principle upon which Beruriah's interpretation rests, "Look at the end of the verse," became an exegetical rule current among later sages of the Talmud.[20] The sages, therefore, must have looked with favor upon her skills and methodology.

The following three pericopae, in which both Beruriah and Meir appear, offer important biographical facts and characteristics of Beruriah through the details of their relationship. Berakhot 10a states:

> There were once some highwaymen in the neighborhood of R. Meir who caused him a great deal of trouble. R. Meir accordingly prayed that they should die. His wife Beruriah said to him; How do you make out [that such a prayer should be permitted]? Because it is written: 'Let *hattaim* (sins) cease?' Is it written *'hotim'* (sinners)? It is written *hattaim* (sins)'! Further, look at the end of the verse 'and let the wicked men be no more.' Since the sins will cease, there will be no more wicked men! Rather pray for them that they should repent, and there will be no more wicked." He did pray for them, and they repented.

In this comparative situation with a male, Beruriah again emerges favorably. Yet, the element of mutual respect sets this encounter strongly apart from those recorded with other males in previous quotations.

By her more astute exegesis, Beruriah gives the lie to Meir's actions in the situation: she teaches him by a careful examination of her line of reasoning and shows him his error. In one sense, Beruriah adapts her manner to Meir. While in previous passages, when she found men at fault, she reacted harshly, here she neither calls Meir a fool nor treats him with condescension. Instead, Beruriah patiently teaches him and treats him with the utmost respect, as Meir does her. Apparently holding her abilities in high regard, Meir listened to her interpretation and changed his course of action.

Himself a rabbi of some renown, Meir has been termed "one of the leaders of the post Bar Kokhba generation. Essentially a halakhist, he played a decisive role in the development of the Mishnah,"[21] and was granted the epithet "holy" because he not only preached standards of purity but also carried them out. Seen in this light, the high opinions of Meir in the rabbinical world only enhance the already impressive image of Beruriah drawn in this pericope.

Another passage in which Beruriah appears with Meir is taken from the late aggadic work, Midrash on Proverbs 31:1.[22]

> When two of their sons died on Sabbath, Beruriah did not inform Meir of their children's death upon his return from the academy in order not to grieve him on the Sabbath! Only after the *havdalah* prayer did she broach the matter, saying "Some time ago a certain man came and left

something in my trust, now he has called for it. Shall I return it to him or not?'' Naturally Meir replied in the affirmative, whereupon Beruriah showed him their dead children. When Meir began to weep, she asked: ''Did you not tell me that we must give back what is given on trust? 'The Lord gave, and the Lord hath taken away.'''[23]

This pericope strikingly highlights, among other things, Beruriah's profound belief in God and his ways: ''The Lord gave and the Lord hath taken away.'' All of her talents and abilities, exegetical and interpretive, are directed towards justifying God's action to Meir. Even after her two sons die, she refuses to break the Sabbath spirit and inform Meir of the tragedy, but, rather, waits until Meir has performed *havdalah*. Through her dedication to observance, therefore, Beruriah embodies Torah. Furthermore, the passage interestingly reverses the expected male-female roles. While Meir weeps, Beruriah plays the part of the strong, righteous ''masculine figure'' by expounding a verse from Scripture and bringing it in touch with the reality of their immediate situation.

In a comment of Rashi to a passage in Avodah Zarah directly following the story of the martyrdom of Beruriah's father, Hanina ben Teradyon, still different attitudes towards Beruriah come to the fore. Her sister had been placed in a brothel and Beruriah said to her husband, R. Meir, ''I am ashamed to have my sister placed in a brothel'' (Avodah Zarah 18b). The passage then goes on to detail R. Meir's rescue of the girl and its ramifications in his life. The Romans ran after him and ''He then arose and ran away and came to Babylon. Some say it was because of that incident that he ran to Babylon; others say because of the incident about Beruriah'' (Avodah Zarah 18b). In explanation of Rabbi Meir's flight to Babylon, Rashi relates the following legend of unknown origin:

> Once Beruriah scoffed at the rabbinical saying, ''Women are light-minded'' (Kiddushin 80b), and her husband warned her that her own end might yet testify to the truth of the words. To put her virtue to the test, he charged one of his disciples to endeavor to seduce her. After repeated efforts she yielded, and then shame drove her to commit suicide. R. Meir, tortured by remorse, fled from his home.

Rashi's comment indicates that, at some point, attitudes toward Beruriah began to change. Opinion turned sufficiently against the woman as a source of Torah allegedly to cause Beruriah to kill herself and to cause Meir to run away to Babylon. The supposition that Beruriah was enticed by one of Meir's students is shocking in the face of every impression we have thus far gleaned of her. Beruriah never appears light-minded and her emotional strength is certainly well attested to. But even Beruriah could not escape her sex and, however successful or learned, she would still be looked on as a "female trespasser." In a certain light, Beruriah can be regarded as an early feminist, for she seemed to resent the society's systematic definition of women and the low opinion of their mental faculties held by certain rabbis. Both her sarcastic remark to R. Jose, "Engage not in much talk with women" (Eruvin 53b), warning him not to waste his time speaking with her, and her ridicule of the rabbinical saying, "women are light-minded" (Avodah Zarah 18b), point in this direction.

Responding to her derision of the sages' attitudes towards women, Meir warns Beruriah that she herself (like all women) is flawed with feminine weakness and that "her own end might yet testify to the truth of the words." The implication is that her "feminist attitudes" play a part in her bad end, and such an interpretation would be one way of accounting for the otherwise unexplained negative elements in the later tradition's attitude towards her.

Yet, despite Beruriah's potentially subversive influence, the rabbis did recognize her as a source of Torah. The documents bear witness to her able exegesis and skillful interpretations, to her piety and observance of the law. The Tosefta records Beruriah as settling questions of Jewish law.[24] By including her scholarly accomplishments in the Talmud, the rabbis recognized that women can, indeed, have a productive place in the world of scholarship.

In many ways, Beruriah does not essentially differ from the male rabbis around her, a fact that the redactors carefully note. Yet, according to the tradition which generated Rashi's comment, Beruriah's downfall derives from her feminine weakness. If Beruriah, perhaps the most brilliant and moral woman of Talmudic Judaism, could fall, how much more easily could ordinary women. If, therefore, we commend the rabbis for painting such an admirable portrait of a woman, we must not forget to keep an eye fixed on how the later commentators were able to manipulate that portrait for their own ends.

Abba Hilkiah's wife is another woman who may be considered a source of Torah in rabbinic literature. Her name appears only once, in Taanit 23a–23b. Of an aggadic and historical nature, the unit describes how two scholars have come to Abba Hilkiah,[25] the grandson of Hone the circle-drawer, to ask him to pray for rain. So he and his wife "went up to the roof; he stood in one corner and she in another; at first the clouds appeared over the corner where his wife stood."[26] When questioned by the scholars why the clouds first appeared in the corner where his wife stood and only then in his corner, he replied,

> Because a wife stays at home and gives bread to the poor which they can at once enjoy, whilst I give them money which they cannot at once enjoy. Or perhaps it may have to do with certain robbers in our neighborhood; I prayed that they might die, but she prayed that they might repent (and they did repent).[27]

Abba Hilkiah's wife's attempts at making rain draw more response than do those of the righteous Abba Hilkiah. An interesting situation, in the light of Jacob Neusner's documentation that to the rabbis "There was clearly some relationship between mastery of Torah and ability to make rain."[28] The text may suppose her a greater master of Torah and more righteous than he. Perhaps because her mastery of Torah surpassed that of Abba Hilkiah and she arrived at a new insight into the situation, she was rewarded with a superior ability to make rain. For the text implies that the wife knew and understood the verse about sinners upon which her actions are based. Abba Hilkiah, on the other hand, lacking a thorough understanding of the verse, did not act correctly.

The striking resemblance to the Beruriah and Meir pericope (Ber. 10a), where Meir also prayed, as Abba Hilkiah did, for the robbers' death is significant. For the sentence

> "I prayed that they might die, but she prayed that they might repent (and they did)"

is not consistently found in all extant versions of this tractate. Henry Malter has suggested that the line was added with Berakhot 10a in mind,[29] thus indicating that the redactors found a kinship between Abba Hilkiah's wife and Beruriah. There certainly are similarities between the two women. Both are depicted with their husbands, who were well respected in their various circles. Both pericopae are marked by the mutual respect of the couples, and in each of the units the women outshine the men.

Although Beruriah and Abba Hilkiah's wife do resemble one

another, that ought not obscure the differences between them. In Berakhot 10a, Beruriah, in her usual pedantic manner, advised Meir to change his prayers and he did, but she received no known reward for her insightful act. Abba Hilkiah's wife also found her husband's prayers wrong but because she was not interested in teaching her husband the "right way," we have no record of her train of thought. By contrast with Beruriah, Abba Hilkiah's wife does not advise her husband to change his prayers, but, rather, she herself prays for the robbers to repent. Her initiative brings its own reward.

Abba Hilkiah gives another reason to explain his wife's successful rainmaking.

> Because a wife stays at home and gives bread to the poor which they can enjoy at once, whilst I give them money which they cannot at once enjoy.

This statement implies that, as a reward for their greater involvement and sensitivity to the poor, women's prayers are more effective than are those of men.

Abba Hilkiah's wife, as a source of Torah, shows herself different from Beruriah. Involved in ritual, and a mistress of "white magic" in her ability to make rain, she is a very positively drawn portrait of a woman. The differences between the actions of Abba Hilkiah's wife and of Beruriah exemplify the different functions which they fulfill as sources of Torah: Beruriah a teacher and exegete and Abba Hilkiah's wife a charismatic and independent rainmaker.

From these two examples of female sources of Torah in the Talmudic period, therefore, we can see that women could fulfill the functions of both scholar and ritualist, if only in the most unusual situations. As colorful and rare as are Beruriah and Abba Hilkiah's wife, they in no way change the status of Jewish women. They *do*, however, attest to the capability of the tradition to recognize and respect such women.

Notes

1. An earlier version of this article was originally written for a course on "Judaism in Late Antiquity" given by Professor Jacob Neusner at Brown University in the Spring of 1973. The author would like to express her deep

gratitude to Professor Neusner for his searching criticism and encouragement. She would also like to thank the editors of *Judaism*, David Bellin, Lawrence Moser and Baruch Bokser for their helpful comments.

2. *The Babylonian Talmud*: Tractate Kiddushin, translated by H. Freedman, edited by I. Epstein (London: The Soncino Press, 1966) 29b.

3. Ibid., 34a.

4. B. Berakhot 17.

5. B. Megillah, 14b.

6. Louis Ginzberg, *Legends of the Jews* (Philadelphia: Jewish Publication Society, 1912), Vol. 6, p. 377.

7. Ibid., Also, see Rashi on 2 Kings 22:14.

8. Rashi, commenting on 2 Kings 22:14.

9. This source is of debatable date, but surely no later than the seventh century, though drawing on sources that are much earlier. (*Encyclopedia Judaica,* [Jerusalem: Keter Publishing House, 1972], Vol. 4, p. 846).

10. Ginzberg, Vol. 4, p. 216.

11. Jacob Neusner, *There We Sat Down* (Nashville: Abingdon Press, 1972), p. 74.

12. Ibid., p. 78.

13. *Encyclopedia Judaica*, Vol. 4, p. 701.

14. B. Pesahim 62b.

15. *Encyclopedia Judaica*, Vol. 14, p. 1574.

16. B. Eruvin, 53b-54a.

17. Ibid.

18. Robert Gordis, "Valeria Beruriah," *Universal Jewish Encyclopedia* (New York: The Universal Jewish Encyclopedia, Inc., 1940), Vol. 2, p. 243.

19. With respect to the dating of this unit, the conversation between R. Jose and Beruriah raises no problems since R. Jose the Galilean was a second-generation Tanna (90–130 C.E.) whose lifetime easily coincides with Beruriah's.

20. *The Jewish Encyclopedia* (New York: Funk and Wagnalls Co., 1902), Vol. 3, p. 109.

21. *Encyclopedia Judaica,* Vol. 12, p. 1240.

22. Ibid., p. 1512. (The Midrash on Proverbs was composed in the years 640–900 C.E.)

23. Ibid., Vol. 4, p. 701.

24. In Tosefta, Kelim, Baba Metzia 1:6, Beruriah is acknowledged as settling a question of Jewish law and is taken seriously by one of her scholarly contemporaries. "Beruriah says: 'A door bolt may be removed and dragged along from one door and hung on another on the Shabbat.' When these words were said before R. Judah (alt. Joshua), he commented, 'Nicely has Beruriah said.' " Interestingly enough, Mishnah Kelim 11:4 is extremely similar to this passage from the Tosefta, except that Beruriah's name is not present. If there is a relationship between the two quotations we must ask why the Mishnah credits Beruriah's decision to someone else. Does the Mishnah delete her name because she is a woman?

25. Abba Hilkiah is referred to in one other place in the Talmud. "And worketh righteousness as Abba Hilkiah." (B. Makkot 24a).

26. B. Taanit, 23b.

27. Ibid.

28. Neusner, *There We Sat Down*, p. 83.

29. Henry Malter, *The Treatise Taanit of the Babylonian Talmud* (New York: The American Academy for Jewish Research, 1930), p. 101.

MOTHERS AND DAUGHTERS IN AMERICAN JEWISH LITERATURE: THE ROTTED CORD

Sonya Michel

In Erica Jong's recent novel, *Fear of Flying* (1973), the heroine, Isadora Wing, describes her vexed relationship with her mother:

> I never know who is who. She is me and I am she and we are all together. The umbilical cord which connects us has never been cut so it has sickened and rotted and turned black. The very intensity of our need has made us denounce each other. We want to eat each other up. We want to strangle each other with love. We want to run screaming from each other in panic before either of these things can happen.[1]

Jong uses the rotted cord to symbolize the tension between a second-generation Jewish mother and her daughter, evoking the dual themes of intergenerational conflict and the desire for reconciliation between mothers and daughters.

Intergenerational conflict is, of course, a familiar theme in studies of the American national character, found among the native-born, and even more often among immigrant members of the population. Reflections of this conflict within the American-Jewish community occur so frequently in its fiction that it seems to be an inevitable by-product of assimilation. Although the most celebrated of all intergenerational rivalries is that between the Jewish mother and her son, conflict occurs between mothers and daughters as well, in both immigrant and succeeding generations. The counter-theme, the desire for reconciliation, has received less attention, although it appears in both fiction written by Jewish women and memoirs of Jewish mothers and daughters.

What generates the two themes, causing intergenerational conflict and making reconciliation between mothers and daughters so problematic, is the difference between two sets of assumptions about women: those East European Jews brought with them, and those they found waiting in America. In the Old Country, women were found at the emotional center of family life, and often had important economic functions outside the home as well. Although jealousy and disharmony were not uncommon, mothers usually served as role models for their daughters. In her memoir, *The Promised Land* (1912), Mary Antin recalls:

> A girl's real schoolroom was her mother's kitchen. There she learned to bake and cook and manage, to knit, sew and embroider; also to spin and weave, in country places. And while her hands were busy, her mother instructed her in the laws regulating a pious Jewish household and in the conduct proper for a Jewish wife, for, of course, every girl hoped to be a wife. A girl was born for no other purpose.[2]

As long as *shtetl* culture remained homogenous and relatively stable, this pattern held; but even before immigration it had begun to break down, as first the Enlightenment and then migration to the cities exposed Jewish women to new ideas and social customs, and offered them new job opportunities in budding East European industries. The conflict between these Jewish daughters and their traditional parents foreshadowed what would take place when East European Jews arrived in America.

Because of their social and economic roles, East European Jewish women had developed strong personalities and sharp business skills, relying on traits which, by American standards, were considered dominating and aggressive—in a word, unfeminine. Jewish women did not readily fit the ideal of "the lady" which held sway in American culture when they arrived. The lady, of course, enjoyed at least middle-class status, and depended on her husband for support. Most Jewish women, at least when they first arrived, either held jobs or earned money at home. Many were dubious of—or oblivious to—the ways of the lady, and clung to their own customs. But others, the younger matrons, and most of the immigrants' daughters, embraced the code of genteel womanhood as part of the magical formula for becoming "real Americans."

One of the most important lessons Jewish children learned in public school was what American women were really like. Their teachers and the mothers of their native-born classmates impressed them deeply, and when they returned to the ghetto, Jewish girls often found their immigrant mothers wanting. In her memoir, *My Mother and I* (1917), Elizabeth Stern wrote that she had thought her mother the best of all the women in the ghetto, but

> all my standards fell before the vision of the strange mother I saw at the party given by my classmate. I could not believe that the woman who opened the door . . . was my friend's mother. A woman in *white*! Why, mothers dressed in brown and black, I always knew. And this mother sang to us. She romped through the two-step with us, and judged the forfeits. This strange mother opened a new window in me in the possibility of women's lives. To my eyes my mother's life appeared all at once as something to be pitied—to be questioned.[3]

Even the young women who never attended school but went straight to work in the sweatshops were exposed to the ideal of the lady. These workers envied the lives of the women who would wear the waists and millinery they sewed, and from their low wages they saved what they could to buy similar finery. But for older immigrant women, looking like a lady had a low priority. Their main concerns were keeping their families minimally fed and clothed and holding the landlord at bay. They also had religious compunctions about changing some of their customs—for example, discarding their *sheitels*, and appearing in their own hair.

Differences in customs often became issues of contention between mothers and daughters. Rose Cohen, a labor activist who recorded her early experiences in *Out of the Shadow* (1918), recalls trying to convince her mother to take off her wig; not only because it made her look old and old-fashioned, but also because Rose was afraid her father would leave her mother, as a number of men did who found their wives' appearances embarrassing.

Yet the women who went along with their daughters did not necessarily close the generation gap; their transformations were inevitably superficial and incomplete, and the results were unsatisfactory both to their daughters and themselves. In one of Anzia Yezierska's short stories, "The Fat of the Land" (1920), Fanny complains about her mother: "'I dress her in the most stylish Paris models, but Delancey Street sticks out from every inch of her. Whenever she opens her ~uth, I'm done for. . . . I, with all my style and pep, can't get a man my equal because a girl is always judged by her mother.'"⁴ In Thyra Winslow's novella, "A Cycle of Manhattan" (1923), Mrs. Rosenheimer participates more actively in her own transformation than Fanny's mother does. Striving to dissolve the gap not only between herself and her daughters, but also between herself and other "ladies," she readily discards her wig and has her hair done stylishly, accompanies her daughters on shopping trips, follows their advice on fashion and deportment, and attempts to diet and change her way of speaking. But as her husband becomes more successful and the family moves to more exclusive neighborhoods, Mrs. Rosenheimer feels increasingly isolated and ill at ease, never sure of being accepted by more assimilated and native-born women.

Fiction also portrays some of the women who resisted change, with various consequences. In Charles Angoff's novel, *Journey to the Dawn* (1951), for instance, Alte Bobbe, a matriarchal figure, refuses to capitulate to American mores; yet she retains the respect of her children and grandchildren. But in Meyer Levin's *The Old Bunch* (1937), the unassimilated Mrs. Greenstein comes into continual conflict with her daughter Estelle. She fears that her daughter will marry a goy, and is appalled by Estelle's open displays of sexuality. Estelle gets her hair bobbed, despite her mother's objections and finally, to escape her mother's interference, she moves out altogether. Mrs. Greenstein, who has never learned English and fears even answering the telephone, retreats further and further from reality and eventually loses her senses.

First-generation women could not, then, serve as role models for their daughters, either because they refused to assimilate, or because they were gingerly stepping for the first time into cultural waters where their daughters were rapidly learning to swim. These mothers could not teach their daughters to dress and behave like ladies, or even how to cook and keep house under American conditions.

Although their daughters may have felt the loss of maternal guidance, they rarely expressed it—at least not in fiction. More often they displayed unshakable self-confidence in their ability to learn the new ways on their own, and struggled to assert their independence.

Immigrant mothers may have admitted defeat in the sphere of fashion and etiquette, but they, along with their husbands, attempted to retain control over their daughters on one issue: marriage. Mothers felt that it was not only their right—but also their duty—to select mates for their daughters who, of course, wanted to choose their own—on the basis of love. (Jewish mothers tended to regard with jaundiced eye the haphazard, *laissez faire* customs of courtship decreed by romantic love.) Jewish mothers wanted to ensure not only that their daughters married, but that they married men who promised to be adequate breadwinners.

Although arranged marriages were an iron-bound tradition in the old country, even early immigrant fiction satirizes overzealous mothers who hover over unmarried daughters, shepherding them from one "marriage arena" to another, masterminding "chance" meetings with eligible young men, scrimping to buy them attractive clothing, conducting extensive investigations of prospects, and pooh-poohing the mere mention of the word "romance." The sympathies of the modern-minded authors of these stories lay with embarrassed Jewish daughters. For example, in Daniel Fuch's novel, *Homage to Blenholt* (1936), Rita Balkan reflects, "The older generation was terrible when it came to girls and getting married. They had no romance, they were from the old country where a person went off to a matchmaker in a dirty wig and ordered one husband, fat and juicy. All her mother thought about was getting her married off."[5]

There is a curious reversal to the pattern of practical mother versus romantic daughter in Abraham Cahan's novel, *The Rise of David Levinsky* (1917). Dora Margolis, who came from Eastern Europe as a young matron, has struggled since her arrival to become Americanized. She has schooled herself on the fine points of American dress and manners and learned English from her children's readers. Married to a dull and boorish man, she endures years of an unhappy marriage, looking to her daughter Lucy to fulfill her own unsatisfied romantic yearnings. Lucy, however, seems to be a throwback to the old country; she does not consider love to be as important as financial security. She disappoints her mother by marrying a considerably older man whom she does not love, but who has a substantial fortune.

While Dora's romantic desires were unusual in fictional mothers of her generation, she did share their hope that their daughters would have whatever it was they had been denied. For example, although many of them had worked as a matter of course during their married lives, they understood that American middle-class women did not work outside the home, and they expected their daughters to marry men who would support them. In Sholem Asch's novel, *The Mother* (1930), Sarah Rifkah, the archetypical self-sacrificing mainstay of her family, wails when her husband the Talmudic scholar goes off for the first time to toil in a sweatshop. But when her daughter Dvoryele continues to work after marrying a penniless sculptor, Sarah Rifkah is critical; she had hoped that her daughter's life would be easier than her own had been.

Dvoryele is one of the few second-generation female characters to follow almost exactly in her mother's footsteps. While Haskel chisels away at his marble, Dvoryele cleans up the studio, standing over the sink as her mother stood over the washtub while her father chanted the psalms. But Dvoryele's sacrifices do not earn her the vicarious honor her mother enjoyed; the status of the sculptor in America was not equal to that of the Talmudic scholar within the Jewish community.

Many immigrant mothers realized that a life of sacrifice had few rewards in American society and encouraged their daughters to live for themselves, particularly stressing the importance of education which they themselves had been denied by *shtetl* tradition. Elizabeth Stern recalls that her mother provided her with a great deal of support, both emotional and financial. When Elizabeth was a child, her mother scraped together a few pennies for music lessons, telling her, "'In America, to be a gentlewoman I hear, you must know how to play the piano. So you go take lessons.'"[6] (Here, notably, the mother, not the daughter, invokes the ideal of the lady.) When Elizabeth was in high school, her mother relieved her of household chores so that she could study; and when her father refused to send her to a liberal arts college, (which he felt was frivolous and bound to alienate his daughter from Jewish tradition), her mother somehow managed to put her through.

But there were also mothers like Mrs. Smolinsky, in Yezierska's *Bread Givers* (1925), who, when her daughter Sara asks, " 'But won't you be proud of me when I work myself up for a school teacher in America?' " replies, " 'I'd be happier to see you get married. What's a school teacher? Old maids—all of them. It's good enough for *Goyim*, but not for you.' "[7] And there were daughters who looked ahead to marriage as their only career, and who, like one of Winslow's Rosenheimer girls, took a few "harmless courses for something to do" while they were waiting.[8]

Because of the rapid changes Jewish culture was undergoing and the deep differences between generations, the theme of reconciliation is a minor one in the literature of this period. Nevertheless, Stern, Antin, and Yezierska, among others, do express it, sympathizing with hard-working immigrant mothers and showing respect for their strength and forbearance. Stern, for example, understood that although she and her mother disagreed on methods of child rearing and housekeeping, and could never be comfortable in each others' homes, still, her mother's character and devotion were admirable, and she was grateful for the sacrifices her mother had made for her education. Women writing during this period shared a sense of realism, tempering praise for their mothers with a strong desire to find different roles for themselves. The sentimentalized encomiums to "My Yiddishe Momme," which came later, were usually written by men who did not really understand the situation of immigrant women.

The differences between the two generations had psychological implications for both mothers and daughters. Mothers felt the anguish of rejection; while their daughters often suffered from identity crises related to their mothers, whose behavior and personality traits they felt compelled (by American standards) to reject, but which they had not avoided internalizing. Psychiatrist Alexander Grinstein, described the identity problems common to a small group of his patients who were all second-generation women:

> Their own crudeness and inappropriateness in their dress, the excrescence of harshness in their behavior toward their children, loudness in their manner, the lack of accepted values—all speak for an identification with some of their mothers' striking characteristics. Their sense of identity is thus seriously disturbed and they are constantly dissatisfied with themselves in the role that they are playing. . . . It is as though one can see the middle European ghetto community living within the "modern personality" of these women, like Williamsburg in the middle of New York.[9]

Grinstein's identification of the elements of the conflict of these women seems accurate; but the language of his description and analysis reveals, quite inadvertently, something far more profound: the reason there is a conflict in the first place. By characterizing immigrant women as "primitive," and their daughters as "crude," "harsh," "loud," "inappropriately" dressed, and lacking "accepted values," Grinstein is imposing conventional American standards on Jewish women and their daughters. He assumes that the "normal" female will be ladylike—quiet, cultured, refined, and well-dressed, when in fact East European women were revered for being strong, practical, and nonmaterialistic, qualities Grinstein considers "primitive." Because this same set of standards held sway in American culture at the time second-generation women were maturing, they felt compelled to reject the example set by their mothers in order to become assimilated. The ideal of the lady, bearing the imprimatur of the cultural hegemony, caused Jewish women to dismiss values and traits that were theirs by tradition, engendering self-hatred among women of the first generation, and conflict among those of the second and the third.

Second-generation women are, of course, the "Jewish mothers" of literary fame, reviled chiefly by their sons, but recently by their daughters as well—those very same third-generation women whom culture has stereotyped as "Jewish-American princesses." These mothers and daughters differed over many of the same questions which had created rifts in the generations which preceded them, although the issues take slightly different form in the fiction of writers steeped in post-Freudian influence.

To some male authors, the generational clash is responsible for the sexual ambivalence of the Jewish princess. Because the liberated ideas of her peers conflict with the somewhat prudish values of her parents, the Jewish princess denies her desires by withholding her favors until she has been granted some commitment from her partner—either marriage or in more recent schemes, at least a "relationship." In Philip Roth's *Goodbye, Columbus* (1959), this conflict turns Brenda Patimkin neurotic. On the outside, she appears to be perfectly well-adjusted sexually, even passionate. But guilt and shame fester within. So this seemingly liberated Jewish princess goes off to Radcliffe, leaving her diaphragm in a bureau drawer where her mother, predictably a snoop, discovers it and brings the roof down on Brenda and her lover.

Herman Wouk, Myron Kaufmann and Norman Mailer have also created sexually ambivalent female characters of this generation, attributing their dilemmas to parents—particularly mothers—whom they cast as moral heavies. But this assignment of blame may be the result of an overabundance of psychoanalytic zeal. In the forties and fifties, Jewish parents were not raising their daughters in a social vacuum, but in a cultural milieu in which the sexual double standard had by no means dissolved. Peer influences were probably just as important as parental ones, as Alix Kates Shulman's novel, *Memoirs of an Ex-Prom Queen* (1972), dramatically illustrates.

Fiction also suggests that not all second-generation mothers conveyed stringent sexual attitudes. In Violet Weingarten's *Mrs. Beneker* (1967), one of the few novels written from the point of view of a "Jewish mother" herself, the title character reveals great sympathy when her son's girlfriend becomes pregnant, even helping the girl obtain an abortion. But Mrs. Beneker's efforts to communicate compassion to the young people are blocked by their prejudice, apparently generated out of their fear of her disapproval. If Mrs. Beneker is at all representative of second-generation mothers, then perhaps they are not as sexually repressive (or repressed) as the stereotype makes them out to be.

Many third-generation female Jewish authors are less concerned with questions of sexuality than with those of identity. In their novels, the Jewish mother who single-mindedly propels her daughter toward the marriage canopy comes in for severe castigation. While the daughters of immigrants criticized the *style* of their mothers' interference in courtship, contemporary daughters quarrel with the notion that they have to marry at all. Represented by the heroines of such novels as Gail Parent's *Sheila Levine is Dead and Living in New York* (1972), Louise Blecher Rose's *The Launching of Barbara Fabrikant* (1974), and Susan Lukas's *Fat Emily* (1974), this generation of young women seems to be claiming that parental expectations—again, particularly those of mothers—hamper their freedom to define themselves in new ways.

One reason third-generation female characters are so eager to find alternatives to the domestic role is that they have been witness to—and in some cases, indirect victims of—their mothers' frustrations and dissatisfaction. Roth's Brenda, for example, feels that her mother is jealous because she is living out some of the fantasies her mother, who married a plumbing contractor and was quickly relegated to suburban life, has never been able to realize herself. Jong's Isadora Wing seems to understand that it was partly her mother's role—and not some innate character flaw—which prompted her to attempt to rechannel her own frustrated ambitions and energy into her daughter's life. Although Isadora never knows whether her drive to succeed stems from her own gifts and creativity, or from her mother's command, "Above all, never be *ordinary*,"[10] at the same time she realizes that her mother has never been able to express her own individuality to the full. "There is nothing fiercer than a failed artist,"[11] the poet Isadora reflects.

Jong treats the mother-daughter relationship in a seriocomic vein; in Susan Fromberg Schaeffer's *Falling* (1973), a striking and and complex novel, the mother-daughter ties become pathological. Schaeffer's depiction of the links between three generations of Jewish women seems to illustrate how one generation maps (in the Laingian sense) its psychological patterns onto another, inducing family members to personify traits and play out roles not of their own choosing. The grandmother, Belle, is a second-generation woman who, although spoiled and infantilized by her own parents, becomes a powerful figure vis-à-vis her own offspring. Her entrance into the household of her daughter Sarah has profound effects on both Sarah and her daughter Elizabeth. Belle imposes her values and opinions on Sarah, and both women terrorize Elizabeth in nightmarish scenes which Elizabeth recalls during the painful aftermath of a suicide attempt.

But even Elizabeth recovers, earning a Ph.D. and beginning a teaching career as part of her healing process. At the novel's end, the night before her wedding, Elizabeth has a dream about her mother which suggests understanding—if not complete acceptance—of her mother's behavior. In the dream, Sarah, who cannot swim, plunges bravely into the ocean to rescue Elizabeth's drowning brother. After witnessing this act, Elizabeth asks her mother to help *her* swim:"'You hold me, and I'll kick.'''[12]

This final image of mother and daughter is one of the most explicit expressions of the theme of reconciliation in American-Jewish literature. Elizabeth is able to ask for help because she has achieved a degree of independence and autonomy through her own efforts. Her struggle for identity culminates in a synthesis of two roles ordinarily defined as opposites: she is a professional and she is about to become a wife. While not totally atavistic, she draws on the tradition of Jewish women who often had dual roles, to resolve —for herself, at least—one of the major issues of female identity.

The theme of reconciliation reminds us that conflict between mothers and daughters, or between generations, is not inevitable—or at any rate—not irreparable. Even in native-born families, intergenerational conflict appears as the result of continuous redefinition and reevaluation of female roles. In Jewish families, fiction suggests, immigration and assimilation may have created even greater tension. But as the values which American culture once condemned in Jewish women come to be respected, the rotted cord may fall away—to be replaced by a bond which can nurture in both directions.

Notes

1. Erica Jong, *Fear of Flying* (New York: Holt, Rinehart and Winston, 1973), p. 163.

2. Mary Antin, *The Promised Land* (Boston: Houghton Mifflin, 1912; rpt. 1969), p. 34.

3. Elizabeth Stern, *My Mother and I* (New York: Macmillan, 1917). p. 110.

4. Anzia Yezierska, "The Fat of the Land," in *Hungry Hearts* (Boston & New York: Houghton Mifflin, 1920), p. 208.

5. Daniel Fuchs, *Homage to Blenholt* (New York: 1936; rpt. New York: Basic Books, 1961), p. 128.

6. Leah Morton (pseud. for Elizabeth Stern), *I am a Woman—and a Jew* (New York: J. H. Sears, 1926), p. 41.

7. Yezierska, *Bread Givers* (New York: Doubleday, 1925; rpt. New York: Braziller, 1975), p. 172.

8. Thyra Samter Winslow, "A Cycle of Manhattan" in *Picture Frames* (New York: A.A. Knopf, 1923), rpt. in *A Treasury of American Jewish Stories*, Harold U. Ribalow, ed. (New York: Yoseloff, 1958), p. 388.

9. Alexander Grinstein, "Profile of a Doll," in *The Psychodynamics of American Jewish Life*, Norman Kiell, ed. (New York: Twayne, 1967), p. 86.

10. Jong, p. 162.

11. Jong, p. 164.

12. Susan Fromberg Schaeffer, *Falling* (New York: Macmillan, 1973), p. 307.

A SELECTED BIBLIOGRAPHY

GENERAL WORKS

Ezrat Nashim. *Study Guide on the Jewish Women*. Available from The Jewish Feminist Organization, 16 East 85 Street, New York, N.Y. 10028.

Jung, Leo, ed. *The Jewish Library*. Vol. 3. *Woman*. London: Soncino, 1970. Essays on Jewish women in literature, history and religion.

Koltun, Liz, ed. The Jewish Woman; An Anthology. *Response* magazine No. 18, Summer 1973.

Preisand, Sally. *Judaism and the New Woman*. New York: Behrman House, 1975.

Siegel, Richard et al. *The Jewish Catalog,* Philadelphia: Jewish Publication Society, 1973. Manual of Jewish practice, including sections on weddings, *mikveh,* women, etc.

Sisters of Exile; Sources on the Jewish Woman. New York: Habonim, 1973. Women in Jewish history and different Jewish communities today, largely drawn from women's writings.

Zuckoff, Aviva Cantor, comp. *Bibliography on the Jewish Woman*. 3rd ed. Fall 1974. Available from the Jewish Feminist Organization.

AMERICA

BOOKS

Baum, Charlotte; Hyman, Paula; and Michel, Sonya. *The Jewish Woman in America*. New York: Dial Press, 1976.

Drinnon, Richard. *Rebel in Paradise: A Biography of Emma Goldman*. Chicago: University of Chicago Press. 1961. Life of anarchist and feminist.

Fineman, Irving. *Woman of Valor–Life of Henrietta Szold*. New York; Simon & Schuster, 1961.

Glanz, Rudolf. *The Jewish Woman in America: Two Female Generations 1820–1929*. 2 volumes. New York: Ktav. Vol. I, *The Eastern European Jewish Woman*, 1975. Vol. II, *The German Jewish Woman*, 1976.

Jacob, H. E. *The World of Emma Lazarus*. New York: Schocken Books, 1949.

Kramer, Sydelle and Masur, Jenny. *Jewish Grandmothers*. Boston: Beacon, 1976.

Lebeson, Anita. *Recall to Life; The Jewish Woman in America*. New York: Yoseloff, 1970.

Schneiderman, Rose and Goldthwaite, Lucy. *All for One*. New York: Paul S. Eriksson. Life of labor leader involved in Triangle Fire.

Schwartz, Gwen and Wyden, Barbara. *The Jewish Wife*. New York: Peter Wyden, 1969. New York: Paperback Library, 1970.

Suhl, Yuri. *Ernestine Rose and the Battle for Human Rights*. New York: Reynal, 1959.

Wald, Lillian, *The House on Henry Street*. New York: Holt, 1915

ARTICLES

Bluestone, Naomi. "Exodus From Eden: One Woman's Experience." *Judaism* XXIII(1), Winter 1974.

Gellis, Audrey. "The View From the Back of the Shul." *Ms.* July 1974.

Gold, Doris B. "Jewish Women's Groups: Separate—But Equal?" *Congress Bi-Weekly*, Feb. 6, 1970.

Gold, Doris B. "Women and Voluntarism." In Gornick, Vivian, ed. *Woman in Sexist Society*. New York: Basic Books, 1971.

Hapgood, Hutchins. "The Old and New Woman," in Hapgood, *The Spirit of the Ghetto*. New York: Funk and Wagnalls, 1902.

Levine, Jacqueline. "The Changing Role of Women in the Jewish Community." *Response*, 18. Summer 1973.

Sheedy, Charlotte Baum. "What Made Yetta Work? The Economic Role of the Eastern European Jewish Woman in the Family." *Response*, 18. Summer 1973.

Whelton, Clark. "The Triangle Fire."*Village Voice*, Mar 25, 1971.

Yezierska, Anzia. "1,000 Pages of Research." *Commentary*, July 1963. Writer of period of great immigration tells of growing old in New York.

ISRAEL

BOOKS

Ben-Zvi, Rachel Yanait. *Coming Home*. New York: Herzl Press, 1964. Autobiography of pioneer of Second Aliya period.

Cohen, Geula. *Woman of Violence*. New York: Holt, 1966. Autobiography of her years in the Stern Group.

Katznelson-Rubashow, Rachel. *The Ploughwoman—Records of Pioneer Women of Palestine*. 1932. Reprint. New York: Herzl Press, 1975. Personal accounts, testimonies.

Lindheim, Irma L. *Parallel Quest*. New York: Yoseloff, 1962. Autobiography of woman from assimilated German-Jewish family who becomes a Zionist and settles on kibbutz.

Maimon, Ada. *Women Build a Land*. New York: Herzl, 1962. History of working women's movement in Palestine from early 1900's.

Meir, Golda. *My Life*. New York: Putman, 1975.

ARTICLES

Aloni, Shulamit. "Israel's Women Need Women's Lib." *Israel Magazine,* April 1970.

Aloni, Shulamit. "The Status of the Woman in Israel." *Judaism,* Spring 1973.

Ben-Yosef, Avraham C. "The Woman on the Kibbutz." *Israel Horizons,* February 1957.

Bondy, Ruth. "Granddaughter Wants Conservative Femininity." *Hadassah,* May 1972.

Elizur, Judith Neulander. "Women in Israel." *Judaism,* Spring 1973.

Fallaci, Oriana. "Interview with Golda Meir." *Ms.,* April 1973.

Kahanoff, Jacqueline. "Grandmother Was a Militant Feminist." *Hadassah,* May 1972.

Keller, Suzanne. "The Family in the Kibbutz: What Lessons For Us?" in Curtis, Michael and Chertoff, Mordecai, eds. *Israel: Social Structure and Change*. New Brunswick, N.J.: Transaction Books, 1973.

Kahanoff, Jacqueline. "Independence." *Features of Israel*.

Meir, Golda. "My First Days in Kibbutz Merhavia." *Midstream,* May 1970.

Yuval, Annabelle. "The Israeli Woman." *Judaism,* Spring 1973.

HISTORY

Arendt, Hannah. *Rachel Varnhagen* (rev. ed.) New York; Harcourt, 1974.

Schenirer, Sarah "Mother of the Beth Jacob Schools." In Davidowicz, Lucy, ed. *The Golden Tradition*. New York: Holt, 1967.

Gluckl of Hameln. *Life of Gluckl of Hameln, Written by Herself*. London: East and West Library, 1962.

Noble, Shlomo. "The Jewish Woman In Medieval Martyrology." In Berlin, Charles, ed. *Studies in Jewish Bibliography, History and Literature in Honor of I. Edward Kiev*. New York: Ktav, 1971.

Rakowski, Puah. "A Mind of My Own." In Davidowicz, Lucy, ed. *The Golden Tradition*. New York: Holt, 1967.

HOLOCAUST AND RESISTANCE
BOOKS

Birenbaum, Halina. *Hope is the Last to Die*. New York: Twayne, 1971. paperback. Motherhood and sisterhood in ghettos and camps.

Langfus, Anna. *The Whole Land Brimstone*. New York: Pantheon, 1962.

Masters, Anthony. *The Summer that Bled; the Biography of Hannah Senesh*. New York: St. Martin's Press, 1972.

Moskin, Marietta D. *I Am Rosemarie*. New York: John Day, 1972. Fictionalized autobiography of survivor of Holocaust and concentration camps.

Senesh, Hannah. *Her Life and Diary*. New York: Schocken Books, 1972.

Suhl, Yuri. *They Fought Back*. New York, 1967. Reprint. New York: Schocken, 1975. Biographical accounts include Zofia Yamaika, Mala Zimetbaum, Rosa Robota, Nuita Teitelboim.

Syrkin, Marie. *Blessed is the Match*. Philadelphia: JPS, 1947, Accounts of Resistance—Hannah Senesh, Zivia Lubetkin and others.

ARTICLES

Benkler, Rafi. "Haviva Reik." *Israel Horizons,* April 1964. The other (forgotten) woman parachutist, from HaShomer Hatzair.

Birman, Tzippora. "From the Bialystok Ghetto." *Jewish Spectator,* September 1971.

Grossman, Chaika. "Revolt in the Bialystok Ghetto." In Barkai, Meyer, ed. *The Fighting Ghettos*. New York: Tower Books, 1972.

Klibanski, Bronya. "Bialystok Underground," *Jewish Spectator,* November 1969.

Korczak, Ruzka. "Flames Out of Ashes." *Israel Horizons,* April 1967.

Melamed, Aliza. "From the Diary of a Young Fighter." *Israel Horizons,* April 1967.

"Diary of Justina (Gusta Davidson) of the Cracow Resistance." In Nirenstein, Albert. *A Tower from the Enemy*. New York: Orion, 1959.

Rozycka, Eugenia. "Looking Through My Window."*Yad Vashem Bulletin* No. 22. Book review of testimony of Orthodox woman and her form of resistance.

WOMEN IN JEWISH RELIGION, LAW AND TEXTS
BOOKS

Epstein, Louis M. The Jewish Marriage Contract. New York, 1927. Reprint. New York: Arno, 1973.

Falk, Ze'ev. *Jewish Matrimonial Law in the Middle Ages*. New York: Oxford University Press, 1966.

Feldman, David M. *Birth Control in Jewish Law*. New York, 1968. Reprint. New York: Schocken, 1974.

Moses ben Maimon (Maimonides). *The Book of Woman*. New Haven: Yale University Press. 1972/

Patai, Raphael. *The Hebrew Goddess*. New York: Ktav, 1968.

Schneid, Hayyim, ed. *Marriage*. Philadelphia: JPS, 1973.

ARTICLES

Adler, Rachel. "The Jew Who Wasn't There: Halacha and the Jewish Woman." *Davka*, Summer 1971.

Blumenthal, Aaron H. "Aliyah for Women." *Proceedings of the Rabbinical Assembly* XIX. 1955.

Davidowicz, Lucy S. "On Being Woman in Shul." *Commentary* 45(6), July 1968.

Feldman, David M. Testimony on abortion law reform in New York State. In Schulder, Diane and Kennedy, Florynce. *Abortion Rap* New York: McGraw-Hill, 1971.

Gendler, Mary. "Male and Female Created He Them. *Jewish Heritage*, Winter 1971/72.

Gershfield, Edward M. The Jewish Law of Divorce (pamphlet). National Council of Jewish Women. 1 West 47th St., New York, N.Y. 10036.

Greenberg Simon. "And He Writes Her a Bill of Divorcement." *Conservative Judaism*, Spring 1970.

Hauptman, Judith. "Images of Women in the Talmud." in Reuther, Rosemary, ed. *Religion and Sexism*. New York: Simon and Schuster, 1974.

Hauptman, Judith. "Women's Liberation in the Talmudic Period: an Assessment." *Conservative Judaism*, Summer 1972.

Rivlin, Lily. "Lilith; the First Woman." *Ms.*, December 1972.

Weisbart, Gladys. "Experiencing the Shekhinah." *Reconstructionist*, April 14, 1967.

Weiss-Rosmarin, Trude. "The Seventh Commandment." *Jewish Spectator*, October 1971.

Weiss-Rosmarin, Trude. "The Unfreedom of Jewish Woman." *Jewish Spectator*, October 1970.

Weissman, Deborah. "Toward a Feminist Critique of Judaism." *Congress Bi-Weekly*, November 24, 1972.

LIFE CYCLE AND NEW RITUALS

Blau, Zena Smith. "In Defense of the Jewish Mother." Reprinted in *Sisters of Exile*. New York: Habonim, 1973.

Charry, Ellen and Dana Charry. "Brit Kedusha: A Home Ceremony Celebrating the Birth of a Daughter."In Swidler, Arlene, ed. *Sister celebrations.* Philadelphia: Fortress Press, 1974.

Gendler, Mary. "Sarah's Seed—a New Ritual for Women." *Response* 24, Winter 1974-75.

Golub, Mark S. and Norman Cohen. "Kiddush Peter Rehem." *CCAR Journal,* Winter 1973.

Greenberg, Blu. "Abortion." *Judaism,* Spring 1976.

Schacter, Zalman. "Modern Covenants Need a Modern *Ketubah.*" *Sh'ma.* October 18, 1971.

JEWISH WOMEN'S MOVEMENT

Baron, Sheryl. "National Liberation and the Jewish Woman." *Davka,* Summer 1971.

Dworkin, Susan. "A Song for Women, in Five Questions." *Moment,* May/June 1975.

Furstenberg, Rochelle. "Women's Lib and Halakhah: Orthodox Women Demand Rights." *Jerusalem Post:* June 12, 1972, p. 11.

Greenberg, Blu and Greenberg, Yitzhak. "Equality in Judaism." *Hadassah,* December 1973.

Segal, Sheila. "Feminists for Judaism." *Midstream,* August/September 1975.

CHILDRENS BOOKS

Armstrong, William H. *Hadassah: Esther, the Orphan Queen.* Garden City, N.Y.: Doubleday, 1972.

Asimov, Isaac. *The Story of Ruth.* Garden City. N.Y.: Doubleday, 1972.

Blue, Rose. *Grandma Didn't Wave Back.* New York: Franklin Watts, 1972.

Blume, Judy. *Are You Listening God? It's Me, Margaret.* Englewood Cliffs, N.J.: Bradbury, 1970.

Burstein, Chaya. *Rivka Bangs the Teakettle,* New York: Harcourt, 1970.

Cone, Molly. *Hurry Henrietta.* Boston: Houghton Mifflin, 1966.

Cone, Molly. *Dance Around the Fire.* Boston: Houghton Mifflin, 1974.

Frank, Anne. *Diary of a Young Girl.* Garden City, N.Y.: Doubleday, 1967.

Goldberg, Leah. *Little Queen of Sheba.* New York: UAHC, 1959.

Hautzig, Esther. *The Endless Steppe: Growing Up in Siberia.* New York: Thomas Y. Crowell, 1968.

Kerr, Judith. *When Hitler Stole Pink Rabbit.* New York: Coward-McCann, 1972.

Merriam, Eve. *Emma Lazarus: The Voice of Liberty.* Philadelphia: JPS, 1959.

Morris Terry. *Shalom Golda.* New York: Hawthorn Books, 1971.

Omer, Devorah. *The Gideonites: The Story of the Nili Spies in the Middle East.* New York: Sabra, 1968.

Slobodkin, Florence. *Sarah Somebody.* New York: Vanguard, 1969.

Stadtler, Bea. *The Adventures of Gluckel of Hameln.* New York: United Synagogue Commission on Jewish Education, 1967.

Stadtler, Bea. *The Story of Dona Gracia Mendes.* New York: United Synagogue Commission on Jewish Education, 1969.

Taylor, Sydney. *All-of-a-Kind Family.* Chicago: Follett, 1951.

Taylor, Sydney. *More All-of-a-Kind Family.* Chicago: Follett, 1954.

Taylor, Sydney. *All-of-a-Kind Family Uptown.* Chicago: Follett, 1972

Taylor, Sidney. *All-of-a-Kind Family Downtown.* Chicago: Follett, 1972.

Vineberg, Ethel. *Grandmother Came from Dworitz: A Jewish Story.* Montreal: Tundra, 1969.

NOTES ON CONTRIBUTORS

Martha Ackelsberg, a founder of Ezrat Nashim, teaches government at Smith College.

Rachel Adler is a Jewish feminist writer and teacher. Together with Aron Hirt-Manheimer, she is collecting material for an anthology on the Jewish woman.

Arlene Agus founded the first Jewish women's *kolel* (Talmudic institute) in 1973, and works as Community Relations Director for the Greater New York Conference on Soviet Jewry. She is a member of Ezrat Nashim and Yosher, the Jewish Ethics Committee.

Pauline Bart, a sociologist, teaches at the Abraham Lincoln Medical School. Her current interest is the interface between sex-role and health-care issues, such as sexism and abortion, gynecological and obstetrical care and psychotherapy.

Rabbi Saul Berman is Chairman of the Department of Judaic Studies, Stern College for Women, Yeshiva University.

Carol Christ is Assistant Professor of Religion at Columbia University. She has recently completed a manuscript titled "Elie Wiesel's Stories: Still the Dialogue," and is working on a book on women's poetry and fiction called *Women's Spiritual Quest*.

Carol N. Clapsaddle and her husband have lived since 1971 in Jerusalem, where she is one of two women partners in a new company which produces Jewish educational toys. She has been attending a women's *minyan* and writes when possible. Her book reviews have appeared in the Jerusalem *Post* and her article, "Disraeli through *Coningsby*," in *The Jewish Quarterly*.

Steven Martin Cohen, Assistant Professor of Sociology at Queens College, C.U.N.Y., is an editor and publisher of *Response* Magazine.

Susan Dessel is the Executive Director of the North American Jewish Students' Appeal.

Susan Dworkin is a writer, speechwriter, playwright, and contributing editor of *Moment* Magazine.

Laura Geller will be ordained as a rabbi by Hebrew Union College in May 1976. She plans to work with Hillel foundations.

Mary Gendler lives on a farm in Andover, Mass., with her husband and two daughters. She divides her time between doing family therapy and other counseling, homesteading, and involvement in the Jewish feminist movement.

Anne Goldfeld is currently a student at the University of California at Berkeley.

Blu Greenberg teaches Religion at The College of Mt. St. Vincent, N.Y., and is on the faculty of the Institute for Women Today, a non-denominational religious feminist organization. Married to Irving Greenberg and the mother of five children, she is a doctoral student in Jewish History at Yeshiva University and is currently editing a book on Jewish women.

Paula Hyman is Assistant Professor of Jewish History at Columbia University. She is a member of Ezrat Nashim and co-author, with Charlotte Baum and Sonya Michel of *The Jewish Woman in America* (New York: Dial Press, 1976).

Rachel Janait was a leading figure in the Women's Labor Movement, the general labor movement, and in agricultural education in Palestine. She is the widow of the second President of Israel, Yitzhak Ben Zvi.

Marion Kaplan is completing her doctoral dissertation on the Judischer Frauenbund at Columbia University. She teaches history at the City University of New York.

Cherie Koller-Fox, a doctoral candidate in Education at Harvard University, pioneered the concept of the open classroom in Jewish education.

Elizabeth Koltun, a member of Ezrat Nashim and the New York Havurah, edited *The Jewish Woman; An Anthology (Response* Magazine, No. 18, Summer 1973) and contributed to *The Jewish Catalog*. She has taught courses on the Jewish woman at the high school and college level.

Linda Kuzmack is studying for her Ph.D. in Jewish History at George Washington University. She writes and teaches about the history and changing roles of Jewish women.

Daniel I. Leifer is the Hillel rabbi at the University of Chicago, a graduate of the Jewish Theological Seminary Rabbinical School, and the president of the International Association of Hillel Professionals.

Myra Leifer has a Ph.D. in Human Development from the University of Chicago. She does individual, group, and family therapy, and is a member of a neighborhood counseling center.

Sonya Michel, a long-time activist in the women's movement, has also done feminist studies in her graduate work at San Francisco State and Indiana University, where she is currently enrolled in a doctoral program. She is a co-author, with Charlotte Baum and Paula Hyman, of *The Jewish Woman in America.*

Michael Pelavin, an attorney in Flint, Michigan, is President of the Flint Jewish Community Council and past Chairman of the UJA Young Leadership Council.

Judith Plaskow has a Ph.D. in religious studies from Yale University. She is a member of Ezrat Nashim and the New York Havurah.

Esther Ticktin is a psychotherapist in Washington, D.C., and a member of the Fabrengen community. She is married and the mother of three daughters.

Phyllis Trible is Professor of Old Testament at Andover Newton Theological School.

Deborah Weissman lives and teaches in Jerusalem. This article is part of her Master's dissertation in Sociology.

Aviva Cantor Zuckoff, a Socialist-Zionist and Socialist-Feminist, is a founding member of the editorial board of *Lilith* Magazine, a Jewish feminist quarterly.